THE CANISIUS COLLEGE LIBRARY
BUFFALO, N. Y.

HARVARD ECONOMIC STUDIES

I. The English Patents of Monopoly. By William H. Price. 8vo.
II. The Lodging House Problem in Boston. By Albert B. Wolfe. 8vo.
III. The Stannaries: A Study of the English Tin Miner. By George R. Lewis. 8vo.
IV. Railroad Reorganization. By Stuart Daggett. 8vo.
V. Wool-Growing and the Tariff. By Chester W. Wright. 8vo.
VI. Public Ownership of Telephones on the Continent of Europe. By Arthur N. Holcombe. 8vo.
VII. The History of the British Post Office. By J. C. Hemmeon. 8vo.
VIII. The Cotton Manufacturing Industry of the United States. By M. T. Copeland. 8vo.
IX. The History of the Grain Trade in France. By Abbott Payson Usher. 8vo.
X. Corporate Promotions and Reorganizations. By A. S. Dewing. 8vo.
XI. The Anthracite Coal Combination in the United States. By Eliot Jones. 8vo.
XII. Some Aspects of the Tariff Question. By F. W. Taussig. 8vo.
XIII. The Evolution of the English Corn Market from the Twelfth to the Eighteenth Century. By N. S. B. Gras. 8vo.
XIV. Social Adaptation: A Study in the Development of the Doctrine of Adaptation as a Theory of Social Progress. By L. M. Bristol. 8vo.
XV. The Financial History of Boston, from May 1, 1822, to January 31, 1909. By C. P. Huse. 8vo.
XVI. Essays in the Earlier History of American Corporations. By J. S. Davis. 8vo. 2 volumes.
XVII. The State Tax Commission. By H. L. Lutz. 8vo.
XVIII. The Early English Customs System. By N. S. B. Gras. 8vo.
XIX. Trade and Navigation between Spain and the Indies in the time of the Hapsburgs. By C. H. Haring. 8vo.
XX. The Italian Emigration of Our Times. By R. F. Foerster. 8vo.
XXI. The Mesta: A Study in Spanish Economic History, 1273–1836. By Julius Klein. 8vo.
XXII. Argentine International Trade under Inconvertible Paper Money: 1880–1900. By J. H. Williams. 8vo.
XXIII. The Organization of the Boot and Shoe Industry in Massachusetts before 1875. By Blanche E. Hazard. 8vo.
XXIV. Economic Motives. By Zenas C. Dickinson. 8vo.
XXV. Monetary Theory before Adam Smith. By Arthur E. Monroe. 8vo.
XXVI. Canada's Balance of International Indebtedness 1900–1913. By Jacob Viner. 8vo.
XXVII. The History of the United States Post Office to the Year 1829. By W. E. Rich. 8vo.
XXVIII. The Theory of International Prices. By James W. Angell. 8vo.
XXIX. Forests and Sea Power. By Robert G. Albion. 8vo.

HARVARD UNIVERSITY PRESS
CAMBRIDGE, MASS., U.S.A.

HARVARD ECONOMIC STUDIES

PUBLISHED UNDER THE DIRECTION OF
THE DEPARTMENT OF ECONOMICS

VOL. XXX

LONDON : HUMPHREY MILFORD
OXFORD UNIVERSITY PRESS

BANKING THEORIES
IN THE UNITED STATES
BEFORE 1860

BY

HARRY E. MILLER, Ph.D.
ASSISTANT PROFESSOR OF ECONOMICS IN BROWN UNIVERSITY

CAMBRIDGE

HARVARD UNIVERSITY PRESS

1927

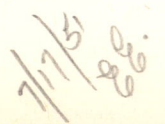

COPYRIGHT, 1927
BY THE PRESIDENT AND FELLOWS OF
HARVARD COLLEGE

PRINTED AT THE HARVARD UNIVERSITY PRESS
CAMBRIDGE, MASS., U.S.A.

TO THE MEMORY OF

MY FATHER

IN GRATEFUL AND AFFECTIONATE
REMEMBRANCE

PREFACE

This study of the earlier development of banking theories in the United States has grown out of a doctoral thesis presented at Harvard University in 1923, and is now published through the generous interest of the Department of Economics of that University.

In pursuing his research the author has become indebted to Professor Davis R. Dewey, of the Massachusetts Institute of Technology, and to Professor Edwin R. A. Seligman, of Columbia University, for having graciously accorded him the privilege of examining at leisure the collections of early American tracts contained in their private libraries. To these scholars I gladly acknowledge a deep sense of gratitude. I would also express appreciation to Professor Henry B. Gardner, my senior colleague and the head of the Department of Economics at Brown University, for having read the manuscript and offered helpful criticism. And, finally, I would make such acknowledgment as the printed page permits to Professor Allyn A. Young of Harvard University. A profound scholar, inspiring teacher, and generous friend, his interest has done much to point the way and to minimize its difficulties.

Harry E. Miller

Brown University
Providence, Rhode Island
  September, 1926

CONTENTS

INTRODUCTION 3
    General characteristics of the period. — Relativity of its banking theories and practices.

PART I

THE UTILITY OF BANKS AS A SOURCE OF MEDIA OF PAYMENT

I. THE FUNCTIONS OF BANKING 11
    Tendency to make banking synonymous with note issue. — Banking operations classified as deposit, discount and issue. — Is note issue essential? — Banks considered as agencies in the distribution of loanable funds. — Banks as clearing houses for the cancellation of debts and credits. — Summary.

II. EARLY MINOR ARGUMENTS CONCERNING THE MERITS OF BANKS 19
    The desirability of banks a moot question. — Minor advantages ascribed to banks. — Arguments of their early critics.

III. BANKS INCREASE THE COUNTRY'S CAPITAL 26
    Inflationist notions in the colonies. — Their revival with the appearance of modern commercial banks. — Their general refutation after the first few decades. — The doctrine that bank-note inflation lowers the interest rate. — Douglass's doctrine of appreciation and interest.

IV. BANKS PROVIDE AN INEXPENSIVE SUBSTITUTE FOR METALLIC CURRENCY 39
    Smith's statement of the doctrine. — Minor corrections at the hands of American writers. — Critics of this alleged benefit of banking. — Conclusion.

V. BANKS DRIVE SPECIE OUT OF THE COUNTRY 48
    Colonial treatment of the doctrine. — Its influence at the end of the eighteenth century. — The views of later writers.

VI. BANKS CAUSE PRICE FLUCTUATIONS 55
    Introductory. — The charge that banks cause price fluctuations. — The doctrine that convertibility prevents overissue. — Criticism of this thesis. — Theory that the manner in which notes are placed in circulation prevents overissue. — And that the amount of notes in circulation is a *result* of conditions of trade. — A just adjudication of the dispute. — Colwell's well-considered views. — Summary.

VII. BANKS PROVIDE AN ELASTIC CURRENCY 70
    The elasticity of bank currency, except in its mischievous aspects, generally ignored. — But a few writers did give attention to it.

PART II

THE UTILITY OF BANKS AS AGENCIES IN THE DISTRIBUTION OF LOANABLE FUNDS

VIII. BANKS SERVE AS INTERMEDIARIES BETWEEN BORROWERS AND LENDERS 79

> The thesis that banks are mere intermediaries in their lending operations the prevailing one. — Their alleged benefits as such. — Basis of the dogma that banks cannot lend more than they receive from depositors and shareholders. — The error into which the quantity theorists fell here. — Some inklings of a deeper insight. — The persistence of this issue even to the present day.

IX. BANKS DIRECT CAPITAL INTO UNDESIRABLE CHANNELS . 92

> Banks of no assistance to farmers. — Their loans encourage speculation primarily. — Possibilities of discrimination in making loans.

X. SUMMARY OF VIEWS ON THE NATURE AND UTILITY OF BANKS. 98

> The dual rôle of commercial banking. — The utility of banks as source of a form of currency. — The utility of banks as distributors of loanable funds.

PART III

BANK NOTES AND BANK DEPOSITS

XI. THE NATURE OF BANK DEPOSITS 109

> Early recognition that deposits constitute part of the currency. — Failure generally to realize that deposits may be created by the banks. — A few instances in which this was understood. — Conclusion.

XII. PRINCIPLES OF NOTE ISSUE — CONVERTIBILITY 125

> The need of convertibility little understood in the colonies. — Convertibility was generally assumed in the later period. — Belated land-bank projects. — Other advocates of an inconvertible currency. — The banking principle as basis for such a proposal. — Stephen Colwell's notable statement of the thesis.

XIII. PRINCIPLES OF NOTE ISSUE (*continued*) 139

> The currency principle. — The question of small notes. — Bond-secured issue. — The safety-fund system.

XIV. PRINCIPLES OF NOTE ISSUE (*continued*) 152

> Legal reserve requirements. — Suffolk Bank System. — Taxing banks for regulative purposes. — Banking structure.

PART IV

BANKING POLICY AND THE BUSINESS CYCLE

XV. Banking Policy 171
   The importance of short loans. — The relative merits of different types of commercial paper. — The discount rate.

XVI. Theories of the Causes of Crises and Cycles . . 187
   Agnostic theories. — Emphasis placed upon the influence of the credit system. — Attention to the psychology of business men. — Periodicity of commercial crises. — Critics of the theory that banks cause the business cycle. — Theory of the self-generating cycle. — Influence of maladjustments of production.

XVII. Suggestions for Moderating the Cycle 208
   Loan policy. — Surplus reserves at New York. — Abolition of the payment of interest at New York. — The call-loan evil at New York.

Bibliography 223
   The English background. — The colonial background. — The period 1780–1860: (*a*) Secondary sources, (*b*) Primary sources. — Periodicals.

BANKING THEORIES IN THE UNITED STATES

INTRODUCTION

Characteristics of the Period — Relativity of Its Banking Theories and Practices

The theories of banking that prevailed in the United States before 1820 were, in general, wretchedly primitive. Colonial discussions had dealt largely with paper money emitted by the government, or by the land banks that we have learned to associate with the period. Such tracts as considered paper money redeemable in specie referred almost invariably to post notes. Accordingly, what progress was made in the theory of banking had little bearing upon more than the most elementary principles of commercial banking of the modern type.

Not until about 1820 does the knowledge of banking principles in this country seem to have reached a degree of development comparable to that found in the *Wealth of Nations.* Smith's doctrine that the use of paper money effects an economy by releasing metallic money for export was, apparently, scarcely known much before 1810. A decade later, exports of metallic money were still being explained in terms of Smith's vague overflow of the "channels of circulation," in apparent obliviousness of the work, at the beginning of the century, of Boyd and Thornton and later English writers in substituting an explanation in terms of the definite and clear-cut mechanism of rising prices, diminishing exports, and increasing imports.[1] The notion that a certain fixed quantity of currency is necessary to circulate the annual product of each country's industry underlay the views of almost all the writers. Those who, in common with Douglass and others of the preceding

---

[1] Precursors of Smith, notably Hume and Harris, had explained the distribution of the precious metals in terms of the quantity theory, but Smith had not adopted their ideas. Thornton and the other immediate predecessors of Ricardo had brought the doctrine anew to the general attention. See Hollander, "Development of the Theory of Money from Smith to Ricardo," *Quarterly Journal of Economics,* xxv, 429–470.

century, showed that they understood the quantity theory, still retained with it this crude idea of a given volume of media of payment that would "fill the channels of circulation."

Throughout most of the period, indeed, the problems that were discussed were more like those which had concerned Smith than the new ones to which the contemporary discussion in England had advanced. Quotations from English works were still preponderantly from the early master.[1] The noteworthy debates aroused by the British Restriction Period were not without their influence in America, especially in the latter decades; but, with few exceptions (in particular, Colwell's *Ways and Means of Payment*), its more subtle aspects found little counterpart here. The American theory remained, on the whole, less sophisticated than the English.

Not that there was lack of progress. About 1820 the consideration of banking became more philosophical. Hitherto nearly all the writings had been distinctly occasional, called forth from hurried pens by some special question of the day. First we have the controversy in Philadelphia precipitated in 1785–1786 with respect to the Bank of North America; then Hamilton's *Report on a National Bank* and the arguments centering around the Bank of the United States; next, the problems of suspended specie payments, beginning in 1814. To be sure, it was in just such an atmosphere that the English writers had contributed so markedly to the progress of banking principles. But our problem was different: we were too new at the business of banking to develop sound theories at first hand; our experience had been too

---

[1] As late as 1837 the scholarly Senator Rives of Virginia declared Smith to be the best authority upon currency problems, and asserted that "the general principles he has laid down on the subjects of banking and currency continue still to be appealed to by the enlightened writers who have followed him, as affording the soundest exposition of those subjects, whatever modifications of subordinate points may have been made by subsequent inquirers." William Cabell Rives, Speech in the Senate on the Currency of the United States (January 10, 1837), pp. 6, 7.

Not all the unlearned writers were as candid as one pamphleteer of 1826, who pleaded that any error in his argument be attributed "to the head and not to the heart," since his knowledge of the subject of banking, like that of a purchaser "sight unseen," was "more from the outside of books than a correct knowledge of their content."

completely with banking in a pathological state. Cliffe Leslie has justly remarked that the greatest scientific progress is made when economic disorders raise vexing questions as to their causes.[1] But first there must be some notion of the differences between normal and abnormal states. Before we could discuss intelligently the ills of our banking system, we had to have some conception of how a properly adjusted system functions. This our own experience had not yet given us, and the quickest way to acquire it was by digesting what the English already knew.

For some reason little was done in this direction much before the turn of the quarter-century. But now there appeared among the "voluminous essays, . . . 'thick as autumnal leaves,'" which the currency question evoked, a significant number of works that centered less completely around the specific conditions that prompted them, and savored far more of the abstract treatment of universal problems, approached from a detached point of view. First there were Raymond's books, then Cooper's, Cardozo's Phillips's, and Lord's. Raguet, McVickar, and Gallatin were beginning to write. As we turn into the eighteen-thirties the list of such writers lengthens. Men had taken the time to acquaint themselves with what had been said in England, and with the work of such writers as Say. With them the crude fallacies of Hamilton and the childish dawdlings of lesser writers disappear.

The American discussion remained throughout, we have said, relatively unsophisticated. Its concepts were simpler than those of the English discussion; it ran in terms that the lay mind could more readily grasp. But it was none the less significant. In the analysis of the nature of bank deposits, of the dogma that the issue of notes against real commercial paper is self-regulative, of the nature of the business cycle, American writers seem to have reached sound conclusions before their English cousins did.

That we should find inconsistencies in the writings of these early students of banking problems need not surprise us. Rather would their absence in such a formative period be strange. Problems abounded, the existence of which was not realized.

[1] T. E. C. Leslie, "Political Economy in the United States," *Fortnightly Review* (1880), xxxiv (old series), 491.

The full significance of their views was often hidden from the writers themselves. Not merely did they frequently change their opinions — the notions they held at any one time often embodied clashing principles. Raguet furnishes a classic example; he was at once one of the most suggestive and one of the most inconsistent of the men with whom we are concerned. A leading contradiction, which was the rule rather than the exception (and it was shared by English writers), was that involved in asserting that banks can but distribute the purchasing power that they receive from stockholders and depositors, while recognizing at the same time that by expanding their loans banks can raise prices.[1] Again, after many writers observe the similarity between notes and deposits as components of the currency, must we regard their persistent reasoning in terms of notes alone, when discussing prices and like problems, simply as a shorthand manner of expression, or as an illustration of the way in which man's brain works in water-tight compartments?

The work of several of the writers was marred by what seems like studied combativeness. Raymond and H. C. Carey showed this disposition in highest degree. One cannot escape the feeling that they often opposed generally received views merely because of the pressure of their pugnacious non-conformist instincts. The general effect is much like that of the bitter personalities that characterize the colonial tracts.

The relativity of economic theory to its institutional setting is too familiar a matter to call for more than casual notice here. Needless to say, illustrations of it abound in our study. The chief differences between the characteristics of the American and the English discussions were due to the different questions which banking, as practised in each country, raised. American theory in general did not dig so far below the surface because it was still largely concerned with the relative utility and disutility of banking. In England the advantages of fairly orderly banking had been too long enjoyed to make this a matter of much more than academic interest. To turn to other examples, the thesis that

---

[1] See Chapter VIII.

bank notes can never be overissued so long as they remain convertible on demand scarcely took root in this country because the poor homing power of our notes forbade. Again, the English discussion differed from our own because of the peculiar significance of Bank of England notes as cash reserves of the other banks. The question of a national bank, which occupied so much attention in this country, raised essentially different issues. And, finally, in England criticism of a central bank led to detailed discussion of bank policies in their relation to the price level, whereas in America, with its decentralized banking, lack of a suitable mechanism for putting the more refined notions into effect made the legal safeguarding of note issue a more practical problem.

Reversing the relationship, the influence which the developing principles of banking exerted upon banking practice is no less obvious. As the crass doctrines of the early inflationists began to be abandoned, legislation became more intelligent. With the growing realization of the essential part played by specie reserves, a sounder policy was adopted, whether voluntarily or by legal compulsion. Better understanding of the nature of deposits called a halt to the practice of limiting the volume of notes by that of deposits. And legal reserve minima began to be related to deposits as well as to notes.

There are few men who stand out as meriting attention by reason of definite original contributions. With the exception of an occasional Raguet or Colwell, most of those who contributed to the discussion are significant chiefly as reflecting the general state of banking theory at the time. Our study is decidedly one of doctrines and not of men. The questions asked are, "What was known about this matter or that?" rather than what a certain writer thought.[1] And with respect to the former type of inquiry a study of the period is fruitful. There was, almost to the end, much criticism, richly merited, of the practices of individual bankers as such. Fraud and artifice constituted a large chapter in the history of our early banking; and when they were lacking,

[1] It is pleasing, withal, to find interspersed among the gamut of merchants and bankers, physicians and statesmen, a goodly number of writers who were scholars of no mean distinction.

gross ignorance all too frequently took their place.[1] Niles and Gouge and Raguet complained vehemently and often of these evils. But there was also a growing perception of faults in the system itself — faults which, quite apart from the delinquencies of the individual banker, were certain to work mischief. There was a better analysis of the nature of banking. The new doctrines stressed the fluctuations in the value of the monetary standard and bore fruit in discussions of the business cycle. On the one hand, they assumed the form of opposition to all banks of issue; on the other, they took a more promising turn — a groping toward sounder principles of banking.

[1] The president and directors of the People's Bank of Roxbury, Massachusetts, which was accused within three years of its founding in 1833 of practices inviting forfeiture of charter, pleaded in attenuation of their blame that they were "not themselves capitalists, nor men of previous experience in banking; and acquired their first knowledge of its rules and principles in this comparatively humble institution."

PART I

THE UTILITY OF BANKS AS A SOURCE OF MEDIA OF PAYMENT

CHAPTER I

THE FUNCTIONS OF BANKING

Tendency to make banking synonymous with note issue. — Banking operations classified as deposit, discount and issue. — Is note issue essential? — Banks considered as agencies in the distribution of loanable funds. — Banks as clearing houses for the cancellation of debts and credits. — Summary.

THE colonists saw in a bank little more than the source of a form of currency. They complained frequently of a scarcity of circulating medium, and urged the issue of paper money to supply the want that an unfavorable balance of trade was alleged to have occasioned with respect to metallic money. With the exception of some reference to the service rendered by banks as safe depositories for the precious metals and other valuables, virtually the whole discussion of banks turned upon the matter of securing an adequate currency. Indeed, so completely did the issue of notes express the prevailing conception of the operations of a bank, that the institution of private banks and the emission of bills of credit by the provincial governments were debated as practically equivalent alternatives.[1] The friends of a paper currency disagreed among themselves simply as to which was the more expedient way of accomplishing the common purpose, and the demand for the establishment of a bank largely disappeared

[1] Adolph O. Eliason concludes, in his study of the early development of commercial banking in America, that the failure to establish commercial banks during the colonial period was owing to the conditions of trade and industry. "There were no manufactures requiring extensive capital and banking facilities; the financial aid necessary to carry on the operations under the agricultural and domestic systems was supplied by individuals in the Colonies; the retail trade and the coasting and shipping industries were conducted on English capital; the banking for the merchants was done in England; and colonial merchants, with the aid of their own capital, and their banking connections in England, were able to give to individuals and small traders, the limited banking services and accommodations which they required." (*Rise of Commercial Banking in the United States*, p. 49.) It seems a fair question whether some of the conditions which Eliason enumerates to explain the absence of commercial banks were not quite as largely caused by that lack.

whenever the province issued a considerable quantity of its bills of credit.[1]

The tendency to identify banking operations with the issue of notes for circulation persisted in theory long after the development of modern commercial banking belied it in practice.[2] As late as 1839, Daniel Webster made note issue the distinctive feature of a bank. "What is that, then," he asked, "without which any institution is not a bank, and with which it is a bank? It is a power to issue promissory notes with a view to their circulation as money." [3]

And those who did not so completely confuse banking with the issue of circulating notes frequently made the latter the principal function of a bank. Here American practice bore them out. It is a commonplace of our banking history that many early banks were established in remote parts of the country for the sole purpose of issuing notes — notes which, being put into circulation through travelling agents and like resorts, would seldom be returned for redemption because of the inaccessibility of the issuer's location.

One must guard, however, against attaching too much significance to the apparent overemphasis of note issue. While some, like Webster, made the exercise of that power the *sine qua non* of banking, not a few of those who seemed to share this position had reference simply to the facts of American practice, and would have answered in the negative a direct question whether

[1] "A colonial bank was not at all like that of modern days, — a convenient institution for receiving deposits, making discounts, and negotiating drafts, — it was, as Francis A. Walker tersely defined it, 'simply a batch of paper money,' whether organized by private individuals or by public authorities." Dewey, *Financial History of the United States*, p. 24. Cp. Walker, *Money in its Relation to Trade and Industry* (1879), p. 267.

[2] In discussing the Bank of North America, Pelatiah Webster refers to the use of demand deposits subject to check as so convenient that "it is almost universally adopted by people who keep their cash in our present banks." Essay on Credit (1786), in *Political Essays*, p. 434.

[3] *Works*, vi, 127. For further examples, see *An Enquiry into the . . . Tendency of Public Measures* (1794), p. 77; Putnam, *Tracts on Political Economy* (1834), pp. 9, 10; etc. It was apparently in the belief that the two were synonymous that the first constitution of Iowa (1846) prohibited any person or corporation "from exercising the privilege of banking, or creating paper to circulate as money."

THE FUNCTIONS OF BANKING 13

or not a bank need necessarily issue notes. Such, for example, was obviously the case with Gallatin, who referred to American practice and not to general principles when he said of banking that it "always implies the right and practice of issuing paper money as a substitute for a specie currency." [1] For we shall have occasion to note elsewhere that Gallatin urged that banking by unincorporated institutions be allowed, *so long as they issued no notes.*

With growing appreciation of the fact that the important functions of banking were not to be comprehended in that of note issue alone, came an effort to derive a satisfactory classification of these functions. That of deposit, discount, and note issue, since made familiar through its adoption by Dunbar, is the one most frequently met.[2] Usually the classification was not of the operations of banks, but of types of banks themselves. These were resolved into banks of deposit, banks of discount, and banks of issue, with the explanation that American banks united the characteristics of all three.[3] Raguet adopted this classification in 1821, as did Phillips, Hare, and a great many other writers.[4]

[1] *Writings*, ii, 514; iii, 369. Cp., also, Vethake, *Principles of Political Economy* (1838), pp. 153, 154, 209. Critics have at times failed to give this fact its due. Chaddock (*The Safety Fund System*) accordingly seems to have become involved in the inconsistency of remarking in one place (p. 261) upon the identification of banking with note issue, and stating elsewhere (p. 371) that, while prohibition of note issue by private banks had seemed just, like action with respect to private banking of deposit and discount had from the first been regarded as an unwarranted interference.

[2] A curiously early statement of it is to be found in "Money the Sinews of Trade" (1731), Davis's *Reprints*, ii, 435.

[3] The minor operations, especially that of dealing in exchange, received their due notice, of course.

[4] Raguet, *The Examiner and Journal of Political Economy*, ii, 338; Phillips, *Manual of Political Economy* (1828), p. 249; Vethake, *Principles of Political Economy* (1838), p. 153; Robert Hare, *Suggestions Respecting the Reformation of the Banking System* (1837), p. 9.

Daniel Raymond offered a slightly different classification, dividing the function of discounting into those of serving as offices of discount and as loan offices; the basis of the distinction being, apparently, whether the bank advanced money in the discount of paper representing an actual transaction, already completed, or advanced it in some other way. *Elements of Political Economy* (1823), p. 126. Other variations may be found in Thomas Paine, *Decline and Fall of English Finance* (1796), p. 24, and Publicola, *Letters to Gallatin* (1815), p. 28.

These writers did not all agree in the interpretation they gave to the three operations which they assigned to banking; but this matter must be left for consideration elsewhere.

Not only did other functions than note issue receive attention, but the desirability of permitting banks to exercise the very power that many still regarded as synonymous with banking came to be questioned. The prominent part which the circulation of banks played in their early history, just as it led some to identify note issue with banking, led others to ascribe to this function all the evils of banking. It was inevitable, then, that some of those who recognized that banks could exist without the power of issuing notes should urge that they be deprived of that privilege. Such were the suggestions of Appleton, for example, and of Raymond, Gouge, Hare, Vethake, as of many others; accompanied, usually, by the proposal that the government should reserve for itself the privilege of issuing paper money.[1]

Meanwhile another line of analysis, upon a different and, perhaps, more significant plane, was being developed. This studied banks not with respect to their more obvious types of activity, but with respect to their underlying influence upon the distribution of credit. Robert Hare was apparently the first to break out the new path. Credit, he tritely remarked, enables those who can employ the means of production most advantageously, to gain possession of them. But individuals with loanable funds are not always in a position to know who merits their confidence. "Hence, to give a more general efficiency to the credit of individuals, banking institutions are established; which, by the notoriety of their wealth and punctuality, obtain universal credit: and by their extensive means of information, are enabled duly to estimate the degree of confidence to which traders may be entitled."[2] Banks, then, furnish credit that is generally accepted, on the one hand, and determine who merits credit, on the other.

[1] Appleton, *Examination of the Banking System of Massachusetts* (1831), p. 7; Raymond, *Elements of Political Economy* (1823), p. 129; Gouge, *Paper Money* (1833), p. 119; Hare, *Suggestions Respecting the Reformation of the Banking System* (1837), pp. 9, 10; Vethake, *Principles of Political Economy* (1838), p. 209.

[2] Hare, *A Brief View of the Policy and Resources of the United States* (1810), p. 60.

This promising approach to the problem of ascertaining the fundamental part that banks play in our economic organization received but little attention for a time. We meet with it again in Thomas Cooper's *Lectures on the Elements of Political Economy* (1826). The supply of gold and silver, Cooper explained, is inadequate for effecting all the payments of modern commerce. This leads to the use of promises to pay, which is further commended by the inconvenience of making large payments in coin. But it is only the notes of a well-known promisor that can circulate widely. It is the province of banks to supply such acceptable notes by exchanging their own credit for that of their customers.[1]

It was upon the furnishing of a widely accepted credit that Cooper laid emphasis. The other aspect of the matter — determining who shall receive credit — was stressed by a writer in the *North American Review* of the following year. Banks remedy the defect that individuals, in a position to extend credit to those who need it, are unable to ascertain who is worthy of their trust. "They assume the responsibility of the debtor; they relieve the creditor of his anxiety and doubt;[2] they enable him to divide into small pieces, and transfer some of his risk to those with whom he deals."[3] John Rae made the same point. A business man may be unable to convince the many with whom he wishes to deal that he is capable of discharging the transactions in question, and even if he could do so, the credit he would receive would frequently fail to satisfy his needs. He is far more likely to be able to persuade one person, his banker, that his stocks and establishment afford ample security for the accommodation he seeks. The banker lends him money when he wants to buy, and receives money from him when he has effected sales. The banker serves, then, as "the general lender, and receiver of the society," a "dealer in credits."[4]

[1] Cooper, *Lectures on the Elements of Political Economy* (1826), pp. 37, 38.

[2] In discounting, "the bank insures the parties to the note discounted; and the community, which is the loser if the bank fails, virtually insures the bank." J. C. Calhoun, in a speech in the Senate, October 3, 1837.

[3] Jonathan Porter, "Review of Cardozo's Notes on Political Economy," *North American Review* (1827), xxiv, 183.

[4] Rae, *New Principles of Political Economy* (1834). (Mixter's *Reprint*, p. 298, under title, "The Sociological Theory of Capital.")

We turn now to a third interpretation of the functions of banks, and one that, again, concerns itself with matters more significant than the attempt to classify their operations.[1]

The colonial writers, in common with early English writers, often conceived of banks as places where payments could be effected by the transfer of book credits that had originated through the deposit of money, or of other valuables. The influence of the early continental banks, such as those of Hamburg and Amsterdam, is, of course, obvious. "Banks emitting Bills of Credit, as they are at this time used in Hamburgh, Amsterdam, London, and Venice," said Benjamin Franklin, are "the general Cashiers of all Gentlemen, Merchants and great Traders in and about those cities."[2] Despite the allusion to so modern a bank as that of London, there seems to be little to warrant the belief that deposits were regarded as an extension of credit by the banks, and little analogy can be drawn with the activities of modern banks as clearing centers in the mechanism of making payments through the cancellation of debits and credits, represented by checks.

Indeed, this aspect of banking operations was virtually neglected[3] until close to the Civil War, when Stephen Colwell devoted to it the most important volume of the period.[4] Banks, he believed, had been incorrectly viewed as being primarily institutions with the privilege of issuing and lending notes for circulation as currency. They are, rather, the chief agencies in the process of making payments by the offsetting of debts with credits. Ninety-five per cent of all payments in this country and Great Britain, Colwell asserted, were already being made by

---

[1] The conception of banks as agents in the distribution of credit raised one of the most vexing problems of the period — do banks, except to the extent that they have capital of their own to lend, serve merely as intermediaries between borrowers and lenders, advancing to the one the surplus funds they gather from the other; or do they, in addition, *create* something? Suffice here to say, that, while the former view was the one more generally held, the latter was not without its adherents.

[2] Franklin, "A Modest Inquiry into the Nature and Necessity of a Paper Currency" (1729). In A. M. Davis, *Colonial Currency Reprints*, ii, 347.

[3] For a minor exception, see Gallatin, Letter to Maison (1836), in Gallatin's *Writings*, ii, 515.

[4] Colwell, *Ways and Means of Payment* (1859).

such cancellation, instead of by the less convenient resort to transfer of metallic money. (He did not regard bank notes as money.) Two equal funds arise, the one of credits, or credit securities, the other of debts.[1] Banks intervene for two purposes; their own promissory notes, or book credits, substituted for the notes of their customers, are of more generally recognized credit, and better fitted to serve as means of payment;[2] and, secondly, the fund of credits becomes very active and efficient as a medium of payment only when concentrated in banks. "As the debts of men of business find their way into the banks, so do their credits; and the functions of the banks, stripped of their many complications, consist chiefly in balancing and thus extinguishing the debts and credits of their customers."[3] The banks are "substantially bookkeepers for their customers" in the process of cancellation that constitutes the credit system.[4]

The colonial conception of banks, then, as little more than the source of a form of media of payment, still had its adherents, but they were becoming relatively few. The mechanical operations of banking were commonly classified as those of deposit, discount, and note issue; and while that of note issue was regarded by many as virtually synonymous with banking, others, whose number increased as the years progressed, urged that it be denied to banks completely.

Meanwhile the significance of banks as agencies in the distribution of credit, whereby the nation's capital was more effectively utilized, was being emphasized. From this point of view the functions of banks were described as those of assuming for prospective lenders the responsibility of determining who merits loans, and of providing borrowers with a form of credit that is universally accepted.

Finally, we find one writer who regarded banks primarily as clearing centers, capping that modern system of payments in which debts offset credits. This view gave attention once more to the relation of bankers to the media of payment rather than

[1] Colwell, p. 4.
[2] Ibid., p. 444.
[3] Ibid., pp. 5, 194.
[4] Ibid., p. 9.

to their part in the distribution of credit, but it did so with emphasis no longer upon note issue, but instead upon the clearing of checks in the utilization of that deposit currency which was becoming increasingly important.

In the lengthy discussion that occurred concerning the economic influence of banking in the exercise of the functions ascribed to it and concerning the ultimate social value of the institution, we shall find that, consciously or otherwise, banks were commonly regarded in their dual aspect, already suggested: first, as the source of an important form of media of payment; secondly, as agents in the distribution of loanable funds. In fact, this conception of the functions of banking underlay all those that were explicitly advanced, and it was, perhaps, correspondingly more important.

CHAPTER II

EARLY MINOR ARGUMENTS CONCERNING THE MERITS OF BANKS

The desirability of banks a moot question. — Minor advantages ascribed to banks. — Arguments of their early critics.

WHEN the first few banks of the eighteenth century had been established, writes J. B. Felt, in his *Historical Account of the Massachusetts Currency*, the "fewness of these monied compeers and rivals for the golden fleece, drew upon them much attention, and made their chief officers to be highly honored, and especially on gala occasions."[1] Their popularity was not of long duration. The desirability of banks was, in fact, by no means accepted as the matter of course that it has become today. Nor need this surprise us, in view of the evils that attached to banking in the early decades of our national history — evils from which the escape was far from clear.[2]

On the other hand, the early antipathy to banking cannot be dismissed as entirely a matter of reaction against the abuses of its practice; to some extent, at least, it was based upon failure to understand the nature and significance of banking aside from its perversions.

"Think of the locusts of Egypt: — These were to the people precisely what banks are to our farmers," wrote one who saw in banks nothing more than "miserable institutions, a million of which would not add a cent to the wealth of the nation."[3] The "Bank of the United States," wrote another, "never raised a single bushel of wheat, nor even a single head of cabbage, nor a single pumpkin, potato, or turnip, during its whole existence, nor

---

[1] J. B. Felt, *Historical Account of the Massachusetts Currency* (1839), p. 211.

[2] Most interesting contemporary accounts of the evils attending American banking in the first part of the century are found in Gouge, *A Short History of Paper Money and Banking in the United States* (1833), *Niles' Register* (1811–49), and the writings of Condy Raguet.

[3] Jesse Atwater, *Considerations on the Approaching Dissolution of the U. S. Bank* (1810), pp. 8, 9.

never will." [1] And Thomas Jefferson, who seems to have profited little from a reading of Hume and Smith, favored "banks of *discount* for cash" and banks of deposit, but was irreconcilably opposed to banks with the privilege of note issue.[2] "I sincerely believe, with you," he wrote to John Taylor in 1816, "'that banking establishments are more dangerous than standing armies.'" [3] His fellow patriot, John Adams, condemned the institution with characteristic vigor. "Our whole banking system," he wrote in 1811, "I ever abhorred, I continue to abhorr [sic] and I shall die abhorring." For "every bank of discount, every bank by which interest is to be paid or profit of any kind made by the deponent, is downright corruption. It is taxing the public for the benefit and profit of individuals; it is worse than old tenor, continental currency, or any other paper money." [4] Every dollar of a bank bill that is issued beyond the quantity of gold and silver in the vaults," Adams maintained, "represents nothing, and is therefore a cheat upon somebody." [5]

The dislike of banks that Jackson's hard-money school had nurtured during the period of the "bank war" was fanned to fever heat by the suspension of 1837. An anti-bank convention was held in Harrisburg, Pennsylvania, on July fourth of that year, and the Loco Foco party held indignation meetings in several cities.[6] As late as 1853 the secretary of the treasury expressed the hope that the increase in supply of the precious metals in this country (following upon the California discoveries) would continue a few years longer, so that we might yet find it possible to abolish banks and return to a purely metallic currency.[7] This animosity toward banks found reflection in their

[1] "Country Clown," cited in Matthew Carey's *Letters to Seybert* (1810), p. 56.
[2] *Writings*, ix, 417.
[3] *Ibid.*, x, 31.
[4] John Adams, Letter to Benjamin Rush (August 28, 1811), *Works* (C. F. Adams edition), ix, 638.
[5] Letter to F. A. Vanderkemp (February 16, 1809), *ibid.*, ix, 610. See also, Letter to John Taylor (March 12, 1819), *ibid.*, x, 375.
[6] See *Niles' Register* (1837), vol. lii, for an account of these.
[7] James Guthrie, *Finance Reports* (1853), p. 10. Cp. Message of the Governor of Michigan (January 2, 1843), in United States House of Representatives, 29th Congress, First Session, Document 226, p. 1215.

prohibition by the constitutions which some of the states adopted during these decades.[1]

With the very desirability of banks so moot a question, no small part of the literature on banking was concerned with the economic influence of the institution and its relative merits and demerits. To this problem we now turn.

In the colonial period, we have already observed, the conception of a bank was quite different from that of our own time, and this must be borne in mind in interpreting the bearing of the colonial views concerning the utility of banks upon those of the period in which our primary interest lies. For the most part, the colonists meant by a bank little more than an emission of paper money, with infrequent provision for convertibility on demand; and less continuity can be established between their general conclusions as to the desirability of banks and the views of the later writers, than between the lines of reasoning by which each arrived at the conclusions.

The first important discussion of the merits of banks of the modern type occurred in Pennsylvania soon after the Revolution, when the repeal of the charter of the Bank of North America was being considered. In 1785 a bill [2] was introduced to repeal the charter which the state had granted three years before, and a spirited controversy followed. Mathew Carey has, fortunately, preserved for us a record of the debate in the General Assembly,[3] to which we have to add several pamphlets that were called forth by the issue.

The advantages ascribed to banks in this early discussion were chiefly that they (1) make for punctuality in payments;

---

[1] The original constitutions of both Iowa (1846–1857) and Texas (1845), for example, contained such clauses. Not until 1904 did Texas grant any state charters to banks, although a loophole was found in the constitution for the practice of private banking.

Sumner states that in 1852 banking was illegal in nine of the states and in the District of Columbia. (*History of Banking in the United States*, p. 415.)

[2] The bill was enacted in September of that year. In 1787 the bank, which had continued in business in the meantime, was given a new charter.

[3] Carey, *Debates and Proceedings of the General Assembly* (1786).

(2) offer the government a potential source of loans in times of war, or in other emergencies; (3) supply places where valuables may be deposited for safety; (4) furnish a convenient and inexpensive currency; (5) gather surplus funds lying idle in their owners' possession and give them employment by lending them to men in need of borrowed capital. The last two of these arguments — that banks provide an inexpensive currency, and that they give activity to what would otherwise be idle surpluses of capital — have a long and important development, which must be traced at length elsewhere.

The importance of habits of punctuality in meeting one's obligations was frequently emphasized by writers who urged it as one of the merits of banks that they foster such habits. Gallatin refers to it, adding that punctual fulfillment of engagements was not common in the several sections of the country until banking developed in them.[1] And that banks, through loans, give the government valuable aid, especially during wars, was a frequent and obvious observation. Hamilton made considerable of it in his report of 1790,[2] and the influence that it had at the time of the passage of the National Bank Act, during the Civil War, is, of course, well known.

The value of banks as places of safe deposit for money and other valuables was frequently urged in the colonial period, and concerns us but little. The colonists also made much of the convenience of bank notes as currency, because of their lightness and of the ease with which they are counted. A few urged also the con-

[1] Gallatin, "Suggestions on the Banks and Currency" (1841), *Writings*, iii, 370. A writer in the *Southern Quarterly Review* of 1854 (xxvi, 223) remarked that by inducing punctuality in business affairs, banks economize the use of money, enabling each dollar to serve in twenty payments in the same interval in which it could otherwise effect but one or two.

[2] Banks help the government, said Hamilton, by large direct loans, rendered possible by the concentration of the loanable funds in a single place and under unified control. They also aid in the collection of taxes, by "the increasing of the quantity of circulating medium, and the quickening of circulation," thereby making it easier for the citizen to acquire the money that he needs for the payment of taxes. Also by loans to individuals for the payment of taxes. Report on a National Bank, *American State Papers, Finance*, i, 68. See also Hamilton's *Works*, ii, 443.

venience as a medium of payment of bank deposits, representing credit for money actually brought to the bank.[1]

No less primitive arguments furnished the bulk of the weapons of opponents of banks in the early years. On both sides much more attention was given to superficial assertions derived from naïve prejudices than to arguments based upon thoughtful analysis of the part banks play in our economic life. Gouverneur Morris summarized conveniently the objections offered in 1785.[2] The danger of permitting so powerful a monied interest, coupled with chauvinistic fear of its control by foreign capitalists — both rendered familiar by the debates later occasioned by the two Banks of the United States — were already playing a part in this discussion of our earliest bank.[3]

Along with the fear of foreign domination of so important an institution, was sometimes found the Mercantilistic notion that the holding of our stock abroad was in itself undesirable because of the loss of specie which the payment of dividends would represent.[4] Robert Morris, who took a leading part in the Pennsylvania Assembly in championing the cause of his favorite, the Bank of North America, replied most effectively to this. "Pennsylvania," he aptly said, "so long as her citizens can derive a better income from the capitals of Europeans vested in our bank stock, than those Europeans derive from the dividends, ought to hold out encouragement for an increase of such stockholders, rather than pursue measures for diminishing their shares."[5] Mathew Carey still dealt, not without impatience, with a similar objection during the parallel controversy that attended the question of rechartering the first Bank of the United States.[6]

[1] Cp. Pelatiah Webster, Essay on Credit (1786), in *Essays*, p. 443, on the advantages of payment by checks drawn upon deposit credits.
[2] Gouverneur Morris, Address on the Bank of North America (1785), Sparks's *Life of Morris*, iii, 440, 441.
[3] *Ibid.*, iii, 440. See also, *An Inquiry into the* ... *Tendency of Certain Public Measures* (1794), p. 47; and Newman, *Elements of Political Economy* (1835), p. 115.
[4] Sparks, *op. cit.*, p. 440.
[5] Carey, *Debates and Proceedings, etc.* (1786), p. 56.
[6] ... "the merest sciolist in political economy well knows that the employment of foreign capital is eminently beneficial." Carey, *Desultory Reflections* (1810), p. 21.

Banks were also said to share with Hamilton's funding system (with which critics frequently associated them) the evil of tending to increase inequalities in the distribution of wealth.[1] This they were thought to do not only by virtue of the advantages, somewhat mystical, which their owners were thought to enjoy, but also through favoritism in making their loans. As late as 1833, Thomas Cooper, president of South Carolina College, regarded it a very serious defect of banks, that they "tend mainly to create a money aristocracy." He explained that banking "affords its facilities never to the poor, but as much as possible to the rich. The poor deal in small and insignificant sums, not worth the attention of a great banking house. Hence these institutions tend to make the rich richer, and the poor poorer and more dependent."[2]

These considerations were political rather than economic. Their significance lies not so much in their influence on theory as in the evidence they give of the state of knowledge of the time with respect to banking. Moreover, similar arguments played no small part at a later date in determining practical policies. Jackson's opposition to the second Bank of the United States placed the bank question in politics, and for a while the monetary system of the country could scarcely be discussed on its merits. Curiously enough, with Jefferson and Jackson bitterly opposing the banking system in the introduction of which Hamilton had played so prominent a rôle, it was the political forefathers of William Jennings Bryan who were the "sound-money" men of our earlier days. The opposition was at first to a national bank only, and was accompanied by approval of state banks. The

---

Cp. Hamilton, Report on a National Bank (1790), *American State Papers, Finance*, i, 69; and Report of Virginia Committee on Banks (1816), *Niles' Register*, ix, (Sup.) 156. See Jackson's Veto Message (1832), in Richardson's *Messages of the Presidents*, ii, 579–581.

[1] Morris, Address on the Bank of North America (1785), Sparks's *Life*, iii, 441; *Enquiry into the . . . Tendency of Certain Public Measures* (1794), p. 47; George Logan, *Letters to the United States Yeomanry* (1793), p. 8; "The Paper System," *Niles' Register* (1818), xiv, 242.

[2] Cooper, *Manual of Political Economy* (1833), p. 88.

ensuing debacle made opposition to all banks the badge of a Democrat; support, that of a Whig. Prejudice, rather than judgment, prevailed; triumph, rather than truth, was the object; and in such circumstances the quasi economic arguments that we have noted could not but bulk large.

CHAPTER III

BANKS INCREASE THE COUNTRY'S CAPITAL

Inflationist notions in the colonies. — Their revival with the appearance of modern commercial banks. — Their general confutation after the first few decades. — The doctrine that bank-note inflation lowers the interest rate. — Douglass's doctrine of appreciation and interest.

No such mild considerations as those dealt with in the preceding chapter occupied the attention of colonial writers. To them the all-important advantage to be derived from banks was nothing less than a direct enrichment of the community through an increase in the amount of media of payment. They saw, for the most part, no essential distinction between the founding of a bank for the issue of paper money, and emission by the government itself; and, barring administrative considerations, they intended their analysis of the economic influence of the one to apply equally to the other.

The colonial arguments for an increase in the volume of currency ranged all the way from the naïve inflationist view that a larger currency would be in itself an enrichment of the community, or that it would make the colony wealthier by increasing values, to the more reasonable opinion that the lack of an adequate currency retarded trade. Plenty of money, wrote the Reverend John Woodbridge in 1682, "multiplies Trading; Increaseth Manufacture, and Provisions; for domestic use, and foreign Returns; abateth Interest." [1] No less sanguine was the Reverend John Wise, who wrote that an abundance of bills of credit, whether public or private, "will beget and bring forth whatsoever you shall please to fancy. For do but Fancy or wish a Noble Fort in any of your Frontiers; set the Bills to work and up it goes in a Trice." The growth of Harvard, waging successful

---

[1] "Severals Relating to the Fund" (1682), A. M. Davis, *Reprints*, i, 113. Woodbridge had been inspired by William Potter, the author of an early English pamphlet called *The Key to Wealth*. (See *Reprints*, i, 3.)

wars against the Indians, commercial and agricultural development — "all is to be attributed to our Bills of Credit." [1]

The dominant theory among the colonists, however, was not that increase in the quantity of media of payment was in itself an addition to wealth, or that it need always lead to such; but that, in the absence of a certain adequate supply of currency, the issue of paper money would greatly stimulate industry and trade. "There is a certain proportionate Quantity of Money," wrote Benjamin Franklin in 1729, in a passage typical of the time, "requisite to carry on the Trade of a Country freely and currently; More than which would be of no Advantage in Trade, and Less, if much less, exceedingly detrimental to it." [2] There were few, however, to question that this necessary quantity was lacking; and complaint of the scarcity of currency was made by nearly ever writer.[3] A number of them pointed to the frequent resort to "truck trade," or barter, as indicating this lack.[4] The customary explanation of the want of media of payment was that the unfavorable balance of trade with England caused the metallic money of the colonies to flow to the mother country.[5]

---

[1] "A Word of Comfort," etc. (1721), *Reprints*, ii, 172–178.

[2] "Modest Inquiry into the Nature and Necessity of a Paper Currency" (1729), *Reprints*, ii, 336. In his *Autobiography* (Weld edition, p. 113) Franklin informs us that, upon the enactment of an inflation bill soon after the appearance of his "Modest Inquiry" (which was published anonymously), his friends in the Pennsylvania legislature "thought fit to reward me by employing me in printing the money; a very profitable job and a great help to me. This was another advantage gained by my being able to write."

[3] The preamble of the Massachusetts act of 1690, authorizing the first emission of bills of credit by any colony, reads, "Considering the present Poverty, and (through Scarcity of Money) the want of an Adequat Measure of Commerce . . ." (*Reprints*, ii, 307.)

Some of these preambles of colonial currency legislation make interesting reading. In authorizing its public land bank of 1715, Rhode Island explained in a two-page opening sentence that, "Whereas it hath pleased God to suffer the French and Indians, our late Enemies, to maintain a long, bloody, and expensive War," the colony was sore distressed for want of circulating medium, and "Trade is sensibly Decayed." The "decay" of trade was a perennial complaint.

[4] "Distressed State of . . . Boston Once More Considered" (1720), *Reprints*, ii, 74, for example.

[5] Governor Pownall, upon whom the lessons of the colonial issues were not entirely lost, wrote in 1774 that in "colonies, the essence of whose nature requires a progressive increase of settlements and trade, and yet, who from the balance of

Many urged that this should be remedied by bounties encouraging home industry, sumptuary laws reducing the use of imported commodities, and like practices made familiar to us by the English Mercantilists.

Yet the notion that want of specie currency rendered the issue of a paper substitute necessary did not long go unchallenged. As early as 1714, one writer, while demanding that colonial bills of credit be issued to supply the want of a circulating medium, recognized that a land bank, such as that projected at Boston in that year, would "make Money Vile and Contemptible," and argued that, "that which really makes the Value of Money, among other things, is its Rarity: So that upon the whole, the Remedy proposed by these Projectors, will be much worse than the Disease."[1] In 1719 another pamphleteer urged reduction of the quantity of bills of credit in order to raise their value, and criticized the cry that there was scarcity of circulating medium, claiming that the real trouble was the driving out of silver by the operation of Gresham's Law, as a result of the depreciation of the vast amount of bills of credit issued.[2] In 1734 Governor Belcher warned: "Of late, it is most certainly apparent that emissions of bills of what sort soever, have sunk the value of all bills that were extant before, more or less in proportion to the sums that have been emitted."[3]

The staunchest friend of a sound currency, however, and the ablest of all the writers of the colonial period, was Dr. William Douglass, whose works gained him the distinction of favorable mention in the *Wealth of Nations*, and whose *Discourse* heads McCulloch's *Select Tracts on Paper Currency and Banking*. Douglass contributed a number of pamphlets to the controversy then taking place, the principal ones being his *Essay* of 1738 and

trade with the mother country being against them, must suffer a constantly decreasing quantity of silver money; *a certain quantity of paper-money* is necessary." *Administration of the British Colonies* (5th edition, 1744), i, 194.

[1] "Objections to the Bank of Credit," etc. (1714), *Reprints*, i, 253, 254. The quantity theory had first been definitely stated by Locke in 1691. (See J. L. Laughlin, *Principles of Money*, p. 227.)

[2] "Addition to the Present Melancholy Circumstances," etc. (1719), *Reprints*, i, 386, 387.

[3] Felt, *Historical Account of the Massachusetts Currency*, p. 91.

the *Discourse* of 1740.[1] He repeatedly denounced the authorization of paper money as debtor-class legislation, a "cheat" and a "fraud." [2] Douglass accepted the view that it was the paper money that caused an unfavorable balance of trade by encouraging extravagance, and that it was necessary only to reduce the amount of the bills in circulation to bring and retain an adequate supply of specie in the country.[3] He used the history of the colonial bills of credit at considerable length [4] to prove his point, that "large and frequent Emissions of Paper Money, sink their own Credit, and increase the Necessity of making more, by continued increasing Quantities to make good the depreciating Qualities of the same: And thus by a continued Progression, render the Quantity vastly great, and the Quality or Value contemptibly small." [5] Douglass, in common with several of his predecessors, understood the quantity theory, and urged that inflation renders the balance of trade unfavorable by leading to extravagant expenditures for imported goods. But he does not seem to have seen clearly the part higher prices play in making the balance of trade adverse. Another writer, however, just before the close of the half-century, did give a fairly good explanation of this.[6]

With the appearance of modern banks of deposit, discount, and note issue, whose notes, convertible into coin upon demand, served, apparently, the same purposes as metallic money, the

[1] "This accursed affair of plantation paper currencies," he confessed in one of the frequent tirades that are found in his historical *Summary*, "when in course it falls in my way, it proves a stumbling-block, and occasions a sort of deviation." *Summary, Historical and Political* (1751), ii, 13n.

[2] *Ibid.*, ii, 86n. Not only did the loan banks aid debtors by depreciating the currency, but, when public, they seem to have commonly advanced their funds at less than market rates of interest. A further complicating circumstance lay in the fact that the bills frequently circulated in neighboring provinces, so that, when they were redeemed at constantly increasing depreciation, the issuing province gained at the expense of its neighbors.

[3] Douglass, "Essay Concerning Silver and Paper Currencies" (1738), *Reprints*, iii, 233–235.

[4] *Discourse* (Professor Bullock's edition), 1740, pp. 302–320.

[5] "A Second Letter to a Merchant in London" (1741), *Reprints*, iv, 126.

[6] "Brief Account of the Rise, Progress . . . of the Paper Currency of New England" (1749), *Reprints*, iv, 390, 391.

doctrine that banks can increase the country's currency gained renewed vogue. Pelatiah Webster, sound as his views were in general, urged that one of the gains to be derived from banks is that they can issue notes, upon the basis of a partial reserve, which circulate as the equivalent of metallic money. In this way, "a good bank may increase the circulating medium of a State to double or treble the quantity of real cash, without increasing the real money, or incurring the least danger of a depreciation." [1]

Hamilton wrote in similar vein, and his *Report on a National Bank* (1790) unquestionably exerted a mischievous influence upon the literature and practices of the succeeding decades. The establishment of a bank, he asserted, results in the "augmentation of the active or productive capital of a country. Gold and silver, where they are employed merely as the instrument of exchange and alienation, have been, not improperly, denominated dead stock; but when deposited in banks, to become the basis of a paper circulation, which takes their character and place as the signs or representatives of value, they then acquire life, or, in other words, an active and productive quality." Money kept in a chest pending investment produces nothing meanwhile. But, deposited in a bank, it yields a profit to someone, and, when the opportunity for investment arises, can be withdrawn for use by the owner.[2]

Thus far, Hamilton seems to have had in mind the gathering together of idle surpluses of monetary capital, resulting in a more effective utilization, rather than an actual creation, of capital. It is not unlikely that he had been influenced by a reading of Smith. But his further elaboration of the point is more dubious.

"It is a well-established fact," he states, suggesting, perhaps, the influence of the passage that we have just quoted from Webster's essay, "that banks in good credit can circulate a far greater sum than the actual quantity of their capital in gold and silver. The additional employment given to money [through the deposit of spare cash in banks], and the faculty of a bank to lend and

---

[1] Pelatiah Webster, Essay on Credit (1786), in *Political Essays*, p. 436. The essay was a contribution to the controversy over the repeal by Pennsylvania of the charter of the Bank of North America.

[2] Hamilton, Report on a National Bank (December 13, 1790), *American State Papers, Finance*, i, 67, 68.

circulate a greater sum than the amount of its stock in coin, are, to all the purposes of trade and industry, *an absolute increase of capital.*" [1]

Again, Hamilton believed that the establishment of a bank would facilitate the payment of taxes, by "the increasing of the quantity of circulating medium, and the quickening of circulation." The quickening of circulation is another instance of what, "to the purpose of business, may be called greater plenty of money and it is evident that whatever enhances the quantity of circulating money, adds to the ease with which every industrious member of the community may acquire that portion of it of which he stands in need." [2]

Views no more sound than those of Hamilton persisted for some time, buttressed, in many cases, by resort to the favorite assertion of the writers of the colonial period, that the supply of metallic money was insufficient. Thus, the committee on banks of the House of Delegates of Virginia reported in 1816:

> It has been said, that the currency of any country bears a fixed proportion to its commerce, and consequently that a Bank cannot circulate notes, to a greater value than the gold and silver coin which it displaces. But the institution of a Bank, not only promptly supplies any pre-existing defect of specie, but increases the commerce and circulating medium of the nation, by the same operation.[3]

And Raguet's committee of the Pennsylvania legislature reported, in rueful retrospection of the period following 1811:

---

[1] Hamilton, p. 68. The italics are mine.

[2] *Ibid.* Hamilton reasons similarly in his *Argument on the Constitutionality of the Bank of the United States* (February 23, 1791), p. 26. Yet in opposing "paper currency issued by the mere authority of the government" as distinguished from convertible bank notes, he observes that "in the first case, there is no standard to which an appeal can be made, as to the quantity which will only satisfy, or which will surcharge the circulation; in the last, that standard results from the demand. If more be issued than is necessary, it will return upon the bank." The Government's issue of paper money is limited only by the government's discretion. (Report on a National Bank, *American State Papers, Finance*, i, 71.)

The apparent inconsistency between this view and that in the text, which holds that banks increase the volume of media of payment, is probably removed by his support of the old contention that the country was suffering from lack of an *adequate* supply of money.

[3] *Niles' Register*, ix (Sup.), 157.

It was supposed that the mere establishment of Banks would of itself create capital, and that *a bare promise to pay money* was money itself, and that a nominal rise of the price of land and commodities, ever attendant upon a plenty of money, was a real increase of substantial wealth.[1]

Even Cooper, who was at best but a half-hearted supporter of banking, pointed out that banks can lend their notes to three times the amount of coin on hand, and added: "This is a creation of new capital equal to two thirds of the loans."[2] Elsewhere he asserted that notes issued in excess of specie reserves

are in fact fresh capital thrown into the market, and occasion interest and profit to fall. . . .[3] If the labor and skill of the country has not full employment for want of capital, and the circulating medium of metallic money is fully employed, then an addition of paper money will have no effect on the circulating coin, but will be absorbed by new means of employing capital productively, [with the same] stimulating and productive effect, as so much additional capital brought into operation.[4]

Not all were so scrupulous as to assume a deficiency of media of payment when urging that large issues of bank notes were desirable. Thus, during the period of suspension of specie payments attending the War of 1812, one writer maintained that an abundant currency brings prosperity and a low rate of interest. He opposed making bank notes convertible, on the ground that the amount of notes issued had to be limited under such circumstances in accordance with the movements of specie out of the country. He quoted the opinions of Englishmen who held the Restriction Act, permitting a large note circulation, to be a great boon to their country.[5] The pamphlet is typical of several that

---

[1] Report, Jan. 29, 1820, in Gouge, *Short History of Paper Money and Banking in the United States* (1833), part II, p. 56. See also the crude views of A. B. Johnson (a prominent banker of the period) in his *Inquiry into the Nature of . . . Banking Institutions* (1813), pp. 16–18, 49.

[2] Cooper, *Lectures on Political Economy* (1826), p. 43.

[3] *Ibid.*, p. 153. Cp. p. 138. [4] *Ibid.*, p. 146

[5] *Suggestions on the President's Message* (Anon., 1815), pp. 4, 8–10. Cp. Report of Select Committee on Banks (Michigan, 1839), in United States House of Representatives, 26th Congress, First Session, Document No. 172, p. 1305. More entertaining than instructive is the opinion of another naïve inflationist of 1829. "I thank God," he assures his readers, "that I am no political economist. I know nothing of those visionaries, Adam Smith, Say, Ricardo, McCulloch, etc., and what is more, I want to know nothing of them." Additional bank notes, he asserts, augment wealth in exactly the same degree as new gold from the mines. And how

appeared at this time reflecting the principles of the English antibullionist school.

It is more surprising to find a fallacy of this sort in one of the ablest and most original of the writers with whom we have to deal. Stephen Colwell, writing at the close of our period, brought to bear upon the problems of banking theory an analysis that probed deeper, in many respects, than that of any predecessor. Yet, with reference to the matter of increasing the media of payment, he fell into the tyro's error. So largely had the use of metallic money been dispensed with, through the use of bank notes and of checks operating through mere transfers of deposit accounts on the books of banks, that but a fraction of one per cent of the payments of the world's commerce, in Colwell's estimation, were effected through the transfer of coin or bullion.[1] Yet the magnitude of the world's commerce had increased to such an extent that the precious metals were fully employed in the sphere still reserved for them — the settlement of balances. "So full is this employment, that it may be said that all the commercial business which is now done without the aid of the precious metals in the payments, is so much of an addition to what would be done if they were exclusively employed."[2] To return to the use of metallic money alone would be possible only through the reduction of commerce to a fraction of one per cent of its existing volume.[3]

Sounder views, such as had earlier been reached by some of the colonial pamphleteers, received the weighty support of the *Wealth of Nations*. "It is not by augmenting the capital of the country, but by rendering a greater part of that capital active and productive than would otherwise be so,[4] that the most ju-

one can doubt that the wealth of a country is in proportion to the quantity of its circulating medium, he is unable to understand. "No Political Economist," *Free Trade Advocate* (October 10, 1829), ii, 232, 233.

[1] Colwell, *Ways and Means of Payment* (1859), pp. 259–262.

[2] *Ibid.*, p. 262.

[3] *Ibid.*, pp. 170, 171. MacLeod falls into a similar fallacy. *Dictionary of Political Economy* (1863), i, 72, 73.

[4] Smith explained that banks make existing capital more active and productive by: (1) substituting an inexpensive currency for coins, thus permitting the latter to be sent abroad in exchange for other wealth; (2) enlivening idle surpluses.

dicious operations of banking can increase the industry of the country,"[1] was Smith's judgment upon this troublesome problem in banking theory. "The whole paper money of every kind which can easily circulate in any country never can exceed the value of the gold and silver, of which it supplies the place, or which (the commerce being supposed the same) would circulate there, if there was no paper."[2] Any excess is promptly returned to the bank for conversion into specie to be sent abroad.

Smith's opinion was quoted at the time of the controversy in Philadelphia over the repeal of the charter of the Bank of North America,[3] and it must have been well known in America at practically the beginning of the period we are studying. Yet there seems to have been but little intelligent opposition, in the early years, to the mischievous notions to which Hamilton, not without some wavering, had given his support. There were plenty of invectives against the "rag money" of institutions that "never raised a single bushel of wheat, nor even a single head of cabbage," but virtually no serious attempt to refute on logical grounds the doctrine that advances of credit by banks are additions to the country's capital.

About 1820 discussions of banking reached a decidedly higher plane. This improvement showed itself in the discussion of the issue with which we are now dealing. Thus Raymond, after taking Hamilton to task for his doctrine that bank notes provide more ample media of payment, thereby increasing the country's capital, pointed out that "a paper currency has no more effect in augmenting the capital of a country than changing the denomination of the coin would have."[4] In proportion as the quantity of circulating medium is increased, its value per unit is decreased. If the banks serve the public by loaning to double the amount of

[1] *Wealth of Nations*, book II, chap. 2 (vol. i, p. 303).
[2] *Ibid.*, book II, chap. 2 (vol. i, p. 283).
[3] James Wilson, "Considerations on the Bank of North America" (1785), *Works*, iii, 418, 419.
[4] Raymond, *Elements of Political Economy* (1823), ii, 137. But see the importance that Raymond attaches to a rapid circulation. *Thoughts on Political Economy* (1820), p. 301. See also, *Letter to the Secretary of the Treasury* (1819), by Aristides, pp. 18 ff.

their capital, they would perform an even greater service, upon the same principle, by loaning to ten times the amount of their capital, and, indeed, to any extent to which the finding of solvent borrowers would permit.[1]

Condy Raguet, in a report as chairman of a committee of the Pennsylvania Senate, disposed in similar fashion of the opinion, "almost universally entertained," that the issue of bank notes increases the community's capital. A bank note, or bank deposit, is not in itself real capital. Nor does the issue of a promise to pay that is acceptable as money make the latter more plentiful, except to the borrower and during the interval in which prices are rising to the new level indicated by the enlarged currency.[2] Raguet dilated upon the point in the many writings his prolific pen has given us.[3] Gallatin, in an essay that seems to have served as a more or less authoritative statement of the sounder views prevalent at the time, adopted the same position;[4] as did Gouge, in a work no less influential than Gallatin's, though far less favorable toward banks.[5]

Writers who regarded the inflation of the currency by means of bank notes as an augmentation of the country's capital, could hardly have failed to accept, occasionally, the somewhat more deceptive fallacy that makes the rate of interest dependent upon the supply of money. The notion, commonly held by the Mercantilists, that increasing the quantity of money reduces the rate of interest, was used by many of the colonial writers as an argument for the issue of paper money. One of them based upon it the interesting suggestion that the value of money be stabilized

[1] *Elements*, ii, 132.
[2] *The Examiner and Journal of Political Economy* (1835), ii, 337–339, contains the report, which was made in 1821.
[3] "Principles of Banking," *Free Trade Advocate* (July 4, 1829), ii, 7; *Currency and Banking* (1839), pp. 95, 96.
[4] Gallatin, *Considerations on the Currency and Banking of the United States* (1831), pp. 20–23.
[5] Gouge, *Short History of Paper Money and Banking in the United States* (1833), p. 45. Cp., for further examples, Amasa Walker, *The Nature and Uses of Money and Mixed Currency* (1857), pp. 41, 42; C. H. Carroll, "Specie Prices and Results," *Hunt's Merchants' Magazine* (October, 1857), p. 429.

by so regulating the issue of bills of credit as to keep the rate of interest at six per cent.[1]

Hamilton was one of the victims of this economic heresy. He approached the problem in attempting to combat the contention of some writers [2] that banks tend to raise the rate of interest because of their insistence upon punctual repayment of loans. Hamilton conceded that this requirement by banks sometimes obliges "those who have adventured beyond both their capital and their *credit*, to procure money, at any price, and, consequently, to resort to usurers for aid." But, by inculcating habits of punctuality, banks reduce the number of occasions upon which traders are forced to resort to usurers due to the failure of their creditors to make prompt payments.[3] Moreover, he added,

> If it be evident, that usury will prevail or diminish, according to the proportion which the demand for borrowing bears to the quantity of money at market to be lent; whatever has the property just mentioned [of increasing the quantity of media of payment], whether it be in the shape of paper or coin, by contributing to render the supply more equal to the demand, must tend to counteract the progress of usury.[4]

The view that banks reduce the interest rate by increasing the quantity of currency was in harmony, of course, with Hamilton's belief that capital is created in the process of inflating the circulating medium.

For some time we continue to meet with such statements as that, "Increasing the quantity of money to be lent, without a similar increase in the quantity to be borrowed, must necessarily reduce the interest." [5] Gallatin, however, after stating that bank

---

[1] [Hugh Vance], "Inquiry into the Nature and Uses of Money" (1740), in *Reprints*, iii, 402, 420.

[2] See Gouverneur Morris, Address on the Bank of North America (1785), Sparks's *Life of Morris*, iii, 440.

[3] Hamilton, Report on a National Bank (1790), *American State Papers, Finance*, i, 69.

[4] *Ibid*.

[5] Davies, *Bank Torpedo* (1810), p. 35. For further illustrations of the opinion that banks reduce the interest rate by making money more plentiful, see *Suggestions on the President's Message* (1815), p. 4; Blodget, *Economica* (1806), p. 161. An early example is to be found in the paper which Benjamin Franklin contributed, as a young man, to the cause of paper currency. See "A Modest Inquiry into the Nature and Necessity of a Paper Currency" (1729), in the *Works* of Franklin, ii, 272.

notes enhance a country's wealth directly only by displacing costly metallic currency, adds that any issue of notes beyond that which results in the export of a like amount of specie, effects but a depreciation of the monetary unit, and does not affect the interest rate, which depends on the amount of loanable capital and the demand for it.[1]

That banks raise the interest rate by increasing the volume of debts was the curious theory of a writer in the late eighteen-fifties, who brought more of stimulating originality to bear upon the problems of banking than he did of ability.[2] Bank notes and deposits, he observed, are but bank debts, and are invariably accompanied by a counter-debt on the part of the community. "To this incubus of debt," he added, with less cause for commendation, "we owe the exorbitant rate of interest, so constantly prevailing in this country, and the constant scarcity of money for all the purposes of life."[3]

William Douglass shared with his contemporaries the opinion that the interest rate varies with the supply of money, but qualified this with a remarkable contribution to the theory of interest. Increase in the amount of *silver* money lowers the interest rate, he granted, but increase in the amount of *paper* money

> sinks the value of the Principal, and the Lender to save himself, is obliged to lay the growing Loss of the Principal, upon the Interest. Rhode-Island who have much exceeded us in their Emissions, have for some Time rose their Rate of Interest to 10 or 12 per Cent and *give this very Reason for so doing.*[4]

While retaining, then, the fallacy of confusing money and other forms of loanable capital, and of regarding the rate of interest as dependent upon the supply of money, Douglass is probably to be credited with being the first to state clearly the

---

[1] Gallatin, *Considerations on the Currency and Banking of the United States* (1831), p. 23.

[2] Charles H. Carroll wrote no book upon money and banking, but expressed his views at considerable length, and with frequent repetition, in a number of articles in *Hunt's Merchants' Magazine.*

[3] Carroll, "Money and Banking," *Hunt's Merchants' Magazine* (January, 1858), xxxviii, 36.

[4] Douglass, "Essay," etc. (1738), *Reprints*, iii, 243. The italics are mine.

relation between depreciation of the currency and the rate of interest.[1]

[1] Irving Fisher, *Appreciation and Interest* (1896), p. 4, and *Rate of Interest* (1907), p. 356. Fisher bases his opinion that Douglass was the first to observe the influence of depreciation on the rate of interest upon a passage in the *Discourse* of 1740 (Bullock's edition, p. 336). He evidently had not seen the better and earlier statement, which I have just quoted, in the "Essay" of 1738. Had he done so, he would have found that Douglass suggests that the matter had already been commented upon with reference to the depreciation of Rhode Island's paper money. The only other contemporary reference to the principle that I have found, is in a "Communication to the Author of the Weekly Rehearsal," in the issue of March 3, 1734. Here mention is made of the exorbitant interest rate allowed by Rhode Island law, "which nothing can give Colour for, but their Consciousness of the ill Foundation their Bills are upon, and the Expectation of a Discount necessarily following, which this excessive Interest gives some Relief against." *Reprints*, iii, 62.

For later explanations of the influence of depreciation of the currency upon the rate of interest, see Rantoul, Speech in the Massachusetts House of Representatives (March 22, 1836), p. 8; and the *United States Magazine and Democratic Review* (December, 1843), xiii, 661.

In regard to the doctrine that the interest rate varies with the quantity of money, it is to be noted that Barbon confuted it in 1690 (*Discourse of Trade*); as did Massie and Hume in 1750 and 1752 respectively. See note to Professor Bullock's edition of Douglass's *Discourse*, p. 336.

CHAPTER IV

BANKS PROVIDE AN INEXPENSIVE SUBSTITUTE FOR METALLIC CURRENCY

Smith's statement of the doctrine. — Minor corrections at the hands of American writers. — Critics of this alleged benefit of banking. — Summary.

THE crude notion that expansion of the currency by means of bank notes implies a direct increase of capital became more and more generally discredited after 1820. Doubtless the orgy of inflation introduced by the suspension of specie payments during our second war with England helped to emphasize the absurdity of the error. At about the same time that this earlier doctrine was being abandoned, the claim that the issue of bank notes effects an increase in the amount of capital in the country began to be made upon quite a different basis. This newer thesis contended merely that banks afford an inexpensive substitute for the costly currency of gold and silver, thereby introducing an economy which, to all intents and purposes, increases the nation's wealth to a like extent.

That bank notes (and government paper also) are a circulating medium far less costly than one of the precious metals, and yet, within certain limits, equally effective, seemed an obvious observation at an early date. Adam Smith laid stress upon the manner in which banks cause metallic currency to be replaced by their own paper, and made this their chief service. It was the doctrine as formulated by Smith that bulked large in later discussion of the merits of banking, in America as in England.

> The substitution of paper in the room of gold and silver money [Smith explained] replaces a very expensive instrument of commerce with one much less costly, and sometimes equally convenient. . . . Let us suppose, for example, that the whole circulating money of some particular country amounted, at a particular time, to one million sterling, that sum being then sufficient for circulating the whole annual produce of their land and labor. Let us suppose too, that some time thereafter, different banks and bankers issued promissory notes, payable to the bearer, to the extent of one million,

reserving in their different coffers two hundred thousand pounds for answering occasional demands. There would remain, therefore, in circulation, eight hundred thousand pounds in gold and silver, and a million of bank notes, or eighteen hundred thousand pounds of paper and money together. But the annual produce of the land and labor of the country had before required only one million to circulate and distribute it to its proper consumers, and that annual produce cannot be immediately augmented by those operations of banking. One million, therefore, will be sufficient to circulate it after them. The goods to be bought and sold being precisely the same as before, the same quantity of money will be sufficient for buying and selling them. The channel of circulation, if I may be allowed such an expression, will remain precisely the same as before. One million we have supposed sufficient to fill that channel. Whatever, therefore, is poured into it beyond this sum, cannot run in it, but must overflow. One million eight hundred thousand pounds are poured into it. Eight hundred thousand pounds, therefore, must overflow, that sum being over and above what can be employed in the circulation of the country.[1]

Though this sum cannot all be employed at home, the excess will not lie idle, but will be sent abroad to seek employment. As paper currency is useless abroad, it is part of the gold and silver that must go. And goods will be returned in exchange; goods that are, for the most part, materials, tools, and the things necessary for the maintenance of labor.[2] To but a minor extent are articles received of the sort that promote prodigality and consumption, rather than production.[3]

The principle set forth by Smith, in the pages that we have thought important enough to quote at length, exercised a very great influence upon the literature of banking theory in America. Benjamin Franklin had, in 1774, made the elementary observation that among the advantages of paper money is that it costs less for "coining or making," besides being subject to less wear and tear.[4] But Smith's thesis, that the issue of bank notes in excess of the metallic money withdrawn from circulation into reserves displaces a like amount of specie from circulation, caus-

[1] *Wealth of Nations*, book II, chap. 2 (vol. i, pp. 275–277).

[2] This must qualify the statement made by Smith on the preceding page, that banking operations do not result in the need of a larger volume of circulating medium.

[3] *Ibid.*, pp. 277, 278.

[4] Franklin, *Works*, ii, 417. Similar statements are found in several colonial pamphlets.

ing it to be exported in exchange for productive goods, does not seem to have received any attention in America until after the beginning of the nineteenth century.[1] From this time on we meet it continuously, and it was usually made one of the major arguments in favor of banks, if not the principal one. Thus McVickar stated that the gain to a country from the substitution of paper money as a cheaper "instrument or machine" of exchange, "is the surplus coin which is sent abroad in productive exchanges." [2] Condy Raguet made much of this point in his many works,[3] and indicated the importance that he attached to it when he added that banks, aside from their deposit operations, are beneficial only when they occasion the export of specie and issue fiduciary notes to the amount exported and no more.[4] Should all the commercial countries have banks that issue credit currency (that is, notes or deposits in excess of reserves) *pari passu*, no exportation of coin would occur, and the substitution of paper money for metallic money would lose its sole advantage. Depreciation of the world's currency would be the only result.[5]

This thesis that the saving effected by the release of specie for export is one of the major advantages resulting from the establishment of banks was probably the most generally accepted tenet of

[1] The earliest work in which I have found the point is Baldwin, *Thoughts on the Study of Political Economy* (1809), p. 63. Douglass suggested a somewhat similar explanation of the advantage of a paper currency, judiciously issued, in his "Essay" of 1738. (Davis's *Reprints*, iii, 224.)

[2] McVickar, *Outlines of Political Economy* (1825), p. 77n. McVickar was professor of moral philosophy and political economy at Columbia College, and devoted considerable attention to the dissemination of the doctrines of money and banking developed in England, together with some notions of his own. The present citation is to a footnote in an American reprint, edited by McVickar, of an article by McCulloch taken from the *Encyclopædia Britannica*.

[3] Beginning with the first, *An Inquiry into the Present State of the Circulating Medium* (1815), p. 7.

[4] *Free Trade Advocate* (July 4, 1829), ii, 4; *Currency and Banking* (1839), pp. 77, 78.

[5] Raguet, *Currency and Banking* (1839), pp. 83, 84. See also, p. 158. After indicating so unequivocally that he regarded the economy of the precious metals as the sole benefit to be derived from the use of bank notes, Raguet inconsistently recognized, a few pages further on, the merits of the "elasticity of the banking principle." (*Ibid.*, p. 92. See *infra*, Chapter VII.)

American banking theory in the decades following 1820.[1] It was repeated in almost all of the writings of the period, and not a few writers thought that it indicated the sole benefit to be derived from the institution of banking.[2]

Raguet made a slight correction of Smith's position by explaining that the issue of bank notes is followed by the exportation of an amount of specie somewhat less than the quantity by which the note issues exceed the reserves held against them, because the world's total supply of currency has been added to, assigning a larger volume to each country.[3] A more significant correction, first suggested by Raguet, apparently, was that which recognized the similarity between bank notes and bank deposits. "The right to draw a check upon a bank, payable on demand, is as much a part of the currency as a bank note," [4] Raguet insisted, in a report of 1821 as chairman of the committee on banks in the Senate of Pennsylvania. It should follow, then, that the extension of bank credit in the form of deposits economizes gold and silver in a manner exactly similar to that in which note issue does so. And this is the conclusion that Raguet later drew.[5] Gallatin followed him, as did Tucker.[6]

Another modification of Smith's principle rested on the influence that banks have upon the amount of money, whether metallic or paper, necessary to perform the payments of a country. Smith

---

[1] See, for example, Barnard, *Speeches* (1838), p. 168; Hildreth, *History of Banking* (1837), p. 120, and *Banks, Banking and Paper Currencies* (1840), p. 128; Wayland, *Elements of Political Economy* (1839), p. 292.

[2] Gallatin, *Considerations on the Currency and Banking* (1831), p. 19; Putnam, *Tracts on . . . Political Economy* (1834), pp. 9, 10.

[3] Raguet, *Currency and Banking* (1839), p. 77. The *American Quarterly Review* (1827), xv, 509, contained an earlier statement of this. The advantage gained by the substitution of a paper currency was usually computed as equal to the interest, at current rates, on the quantity of metallic money dispensed with. Gallatin and other writers attempted to give estimates of this.

[4] *The Examiner and Journal of Political Economy* (1835), ii, 340. The discussion of the question whether bank deposits subject to payment on demand form a part of the currency is reviewed in Chapter XI.

[5] *Free Trade Advocate* (July 4, 1829), ii, 4.

[6] Gallatin, *Considerations on the Currency and Banking of the United States* (1831), pp. 19, 20; Tucker, *Theory of Money and Banks Investigated* (1839), p. 176. See also, "The Public Distress," *American Quarterly Review* (June, 1834), xv, 508.

and his followers erred, thought Rae, in failing to take into account "the superior efficiency of the money which the banker puts into circulation, whether paper or gold, as compared with that which exists where the art of banking is unknown."[1] Where banks exist, business men are relieved of the necessity of keeping large amounts of cash on hand by the facility of depositing them until need for their use arises, and by the ease of borrowing should any exceptional demands have to be met. The greater activity of the currency renders a smaller quantity of it necessary.

The point as phrased by Rae is virtually another of the major advantages of banks, to which we have soon to turn; namely, that banks enliven idle surpluses of capital. The "superior efficiency" of bank currency was alluded to by others, however, in a somewhat different sense. An earlier writer had remarked that bank notes, in common, apparently, with government paper money, facilitate exchanges and render them more rapid; "and if, according to the ingenious speculations of a late writer on the subject, the quantity, or amount of the circulating medium must be in inverse proportion to the rapidity with which it moves, and effects exchanges, a far greater sum in coins will be necessary for the purpose than in paper money."[2]

Vethake, also, referred to the fact that bank notes, because of "the greater facility of transporting or remitting them from one place to another," dispense with more than an equal amount of coin.[3] And Gallatin found that banks "lessen the amount of currency wanted for commercial transactions by increasing the rapidity of its circulation by that concentration of payments and by those exchange operations which, both on the spot and between places, substitute a transfer or exchange of debts and credits

---

[1] Rae, *Sociological Theory of Capital* (1834), p. 322. See also pp. 301, 323.

[2] Porter, "Review of Cardozo's Notes on Political Economy," *North American Review* (1827), xxiv, 184. Hamilton had maintained that, by furnishing "a more convenient and more expeditious medium of payment" than heavy coins, banks quicken circulation and thus afford what "to the purposes of business, may be called greater plenty of money." Report on a National Bank (1790), *American State Papers, Finance*, i, 68. Raymond, *Thoughts on Political Economy* (1820), pp. 301, 302, regarded this as of particular importance. But neither tied the point up with a greater displacement of costly currency.

[3] Vethake, *Principles of Political Economy* (1838), pp. 147, 166.

for actual payments and transportation of either specie or paper currency proper."[1]

We have already referred to the assertion of a later writer that the punctuality in meeting one's obligations which banks induce economizes currency by enabling the same piece of money to effect many more payments in a given period of time.[2]

While we may probably say, then, that none of the other professed benefits of banks was more widely granted than that of providing an inexpensive means of payment, thereby releasing specie for export, agreement was by no means universal. Some denied that the advantage existed; others objected that it was trivial. Jefferson computed the addition of capital, according to Smith's reasoning, as one of but three-quarters of one per cent of that previously in the country. Such a gain, he held, was not worth the attendant loss of stability in the currency.[3] Nor was the point ill taken, in the light of our early experiences with banks, if no other gain be attributed to their operations. Gouge and Amasa Walker advanced similar objections.[4] And Gallatin, after asserting that the gain of capital by dispensing with part of the coins in circulation was the "principal advantage of a paper currency," expressed the belief that "in countries saturated with capital the addition to it by the issue of bank notes does not compensate for the perpetual fluctuations and alarms growing out of that system."[5] In newly settled countries, such as the American colonies and the Western states, the resort to bank notes is most justified, but Gallatin confessed himself unable to understand

[1] Gallatin, Letter to Maison (1836), *Writings*, ii, 515.

[2] *Southern Quarterly Review* (1854), xxvi, 223.

[3] Jefferson, Letter to Eppes (November 6, 1813), *Writings*, ix, 409.

[4] Gouge, *Journal of Banking* (1841), p. 52; Amasa Walker, *The Nature and Uses of Money and Mixed Currency* (1857), pp. 42, 43.

[5] Gallatin, "Suggestions on the Banks and Currency," etc. (1841), *Writings*, iii, 378, 379. Cp. Witherspoon, *Essay on Money* (1786), pp. 45, 46. Witherspoon was dealing with another social benefit of banks, but likewise concluded that their disadvantages warranted their maintenance only in a new, capital-poor country. This was essentially the colonial defence of a confessedly inferior currency on the ground that a better but costlier one was unavailable. The gold-exchange standard affords a present-day example of an expedient to solve this difficulty.

their continued use by Great Britain. Charles Francis Adams came to a like conclusion.[1]

Of those who denied the very claim that bank notes are a less costly currency than coins, Gouge was one of the most notable. Bank notes cost little only to those who issue them, he contended; those who receive them must give as much for a paper dollar as for a silver one. Nor does the nation, as a whole, gain. "For a specie medium, but one mint would be necessary. To maintain a paper medium, we have from 300 to 400 paper mints."[2] Furthermore, banks discount notes to perhaps treble the amount of their capital, and thus earn eighteen per cent interest upon the latter, instead of six. The additional twelve per cent constitutes a tax upon the public exacted for the support of the banks.[3]

Amasa Walker maintained that banking operations swell the quantity of the currency, causing the community to pay interest "on mere inflation, of no possible utility." Add this consideration to that of the expense of maintaining banks, and a bank-note currency, he held, may no longer be regarded as inexpensive.[4]

The contention that the currency which banks furnish is, after all, not an inexpensive one, since bank notes, unlike specie currency, get into circulation through loans at interest, was quite common.[5] It was frequently accompanied by the thesis that the burden of paying the "tax" that banks exact for their currency falls ultimately upon the laborer.[6] This was especially true of a number of writers whose general sentiments were socialistic. Several writers, like Gouge and Walker, further contended that the costliness of bank currency is greater than at first appears, for

[1] *Hunt's Merchants' Magazine* (1840), ii, 199.
[2] Gouge, *Short History of Paper Money*, etc. (1833), pp. 65, 66. Cp. Vethake, *Principles of Political Economy* (1838), pp. 166, 169; *Democratic Review* (1841), ix, 195.
[3] Gouge, *op. cit.*, pp. 68, 69.
[4] Walker, *Nature and Uses of Money and Mixed Currency* (1857), p. 43.
[5] Gouge, *Short History of Paper Money* (1833), pp. 84, 85; William Allen, Speech in the United States Senate (February 20, 1838), p. 5; Duncombe, *Free Banking* (1841), p. 134; Hooper, *Specie Currency* (1855), p. 6; Carroll, "Money and Banking," *Hunt's Merchants' Magazine* (1857), xxxvii, 310.
[6] "The Paper System," *Niles' Register* (1818), xiv, 242, 243; William Hale, *Useful Knowledge for the Producers of Wealth* (1833), pp. 7, 13, etc. Cp. *Enquiry into the Principles and Tendency of Public Measures* (1794), p. 76.

banks collect interest on an inflated currency that serves society no better than the much smaller volume that would obtain were it not for the interference of banks.

Gallatin alone seems to have taken the trouble to reconcile the fact that interest must be paid to banks for the use of their currency with the doctrine that banks substitute a cheap for an expensive medium of payment, and he thought that the interest which banks receive by virtue of the substitution is of a nature that justifies appropriation of a part of it by the public.

> No change may be said to be produced that affects the community by the substitution of convertible and not depreciated paper to [for] gold and silver. In both cases the community loses (each individual in proportion to his share of it) the interest on the total amount of the circulation, and may be considered as paying an annual tax to that amount (which, being received, in the case of a metallic currency, by nobody, is a dead loss to the country); and as, in the case of such non-depreciated paper currency, the amount of the whole currency in circulation cannot be materially increased, the tax remains the same. But in this case the proceeds of that tax, or at least a considerable portion, instead of being lost to everybody, are actually received by those who have the privilege of issuing the paper; and this is in fact the principal advantage arising from the substitution of paper for gold and silver, a privilege in which there is a common, universal feeling, founded, as I think, in justice, that the community or the government has a right to participate.[1]

Thus we have found, on the one hand, a group that regarded the furnishing of a relatively inexpensive currency as one of the chief contributions of banking, and, on the other hand, a group that urged as one of the drawbacks of banking that it tends to monopolize the function of providing the media of payment, and taxes the community by charging interest for its issue. This second point of view overlooked what those who regarded bank notes as a saving device emphasized; namely, that while there is no apparent payment of interest for the use of metallic currency, the community is actually losing interest in the sense that a certain portion of its capital, that might otherwise be used, is invested in a costly currency. With respect to the interest paid to the bank in the lending operation through which its media of payment get into circulation, we are interested in the point of view

[1] Gallatin, Letter to Biddle (August 14, 1830), *Writings*, ii, 436, 437.

of the community, not of the individual. Were there no further significance to banking than the provision of a medium of payment, the problem would be simply that of determining whether the cost of maintaining the necessary establishments more than offsets the gain to the country from the releasing of capital invested in metallic money. But the benefits of banking cannot be comprehended in so simple a description of its services; the whole question of the bearing of its loans upon production is involved. This problem must be left for later consideration.

CHAPTER V

BANKS DRIVE SPECIE OUT OF THE COUNTRY

Colonial treatment of the doctrine. — Its influence at the end of the eighteenth century. — The views of later writers.

WHILE the votaries of the banking system urged as one of its greatest merits that bank notes tend to replace metallic money, many critics gave quite a different interpretation to this fact. The expulsion of specie by paper currency was to them one of the most severe indictments against banks.

Colonial writers had commonly argued that the issue of paper money was made necessary by the want of a sufficient supply of metallic money, and had explained this lack by saying that the balance of trade with England was adverse, necessitating the return to the mother country of such specie as was received. There were a few, however, who combatted this reasoning, and asserted that the withdrawal of specie from the provinces was in reality caused by that very issue of bills of credit for which it was offered as a pretext. "As to Silver and Gold," wrote one, in 1720, "we never had much of it in the Country; but we can very well remember, that before we had Paper Money, there was a sufficiency of it Currant in the Country, and as the Bills of Credit came in and multiplied, the Silver ceased and was gone." [1]

Several later writers adopted this view, in particular that staunch disciple of hard-money doctrines, Dr. Douglass. Although most of the writers of this group recognized also that prices were raised as the quantity of paper money was increased, the tendency of bills of credit to expel specie from the country does not seem to have been correlated with their price influence, if we except one pamphlet of 1749.[2] Douglass, for example, simply explained that "by the chimæra of a fallacious Cash,

---

[1] "The Country-Man's Answer," etc. (1720), in Davis's *Reprints*, i, 410.
[2] "Brief Account of the Rise, Progress . . . of the Paper Currency of New England" (1749), in *Reprints*, iv, 390, 391.

Extravagances are encouraged in favor of a great Consumption of British goods,"[1] turning the balance of trade against the colonies. Money was made to seem more plentiful, stimulating the purchase of domestic and foreign products alike.

Benjamin Franklin, on the other hand, in trying to dissuade the Board of Trade from extending the prohibition of bills of credit to those colonies outside of New England, dismissed the objection that paper money drives gold and silver out of the colonies as a "merely speculative" opinion. "The truth is, that the balance of their trade with Britain being greatly against them, the gold and silver is drawn out to pay that balance; and then the necessity of some medium of trade has induced the making of paper money, which could not be carried away."[2]

The committee appointed by the Pennyslvania Assembly in 1785 to consider the advisability of repealing the charter of the Bank of North America, made much of the criticism that the bank tended to "banish specie" from the country. In the debate that ensued, this argument seems to have been the one most frequently advanced by the bank's opponents. The discussion of the point was hardly edifying. One legislator argued that the bank was "an engine of trade that enabled the merchants to import more goods than were necessary, or than there was money to pay for, [and that] by means of a bank the European merchants were enabled to procure and carry off money for their goods: and to

---

[1] Douglass, *Discourse* (1740), p. 322 (Bullock's edition).

[2] Franklin, "Remarks and Facts" (1764), *Works*, ii, 342. In a letter to Joseph Galloway, written in London in 1767, Franklin seems to have had some misgivings concerning his espousal of the view that an unfavorable balance of trade made the issue of paper money necessary in the colonies. The English merchants, Franklin thought, misunderstood their own interests when they protested against the further issue of paper money in America. For, "should a scarcity of money continue among us, we shall take off less of their merchandize and attend more to manufacturing and raising the necessaries and superfluities of life among ourselves which we now receive from them. And perhaps this consequence would attend our making no paper money at all of any sort, that being thus by a want of cash driven to industry and frugality, we should gradually become more rich without their trade, than we can possibly be with it, and by keeping in the country the real cash that comes into it, have in time a quantity sufficient for all our occasions. But I suppose our people will scarce have patience to wait for this." Letter to Galloway (August 8, 1767), in *Private Correspondence of Franklin*, edited by W. T. Franklin, pp. 142, 143.

fix the payment thereof upon the purchasers in that hasty manner which the rules of the bank required. ... Whereas if it were not in existence, they would be obliged to take produce in exchange for them."[1] Others thought that it is only in countries having an unfavorable balance of trade that banks are disadvantageous in this respect.[2] Nor were the sponsors of the bank more resourceful. One professed himself unable to understand how the bank could possibly facilitate the export of specie by lending money that had to be repaid at the end of a short period.[3] "Only a foolhardy borrower," said Robert Morris, "would risk a shipment of money which must soon be repaid."[4] The balance of trade is unfavorable, he admitted, "but why bring this in as a charge against the bank? Has the bank engaged in commerce?"[5] The opinion of Benjamin Franklin, in his reply of 1764 to the Board of Trade, was invoked in support of the idea that, instead of the issue of paper money driving out gold and silver, it is the loss of metallic money through an adverse balance of trade that always brings the necessity of substituting some medium that cannot be drawn away.[6] Thomas Paine contributed a pamphlet in which he scathingly ridiculed the report of the committee of the Assembly. As for the committee's contention that a bank induces the export of specie, he argued that the reverse would rather be true. "Specie may be called the stock in trade of the bank, it is therefore in its interest to prevent it from wandering out of the country," for without hard money a bank cannot carry on its business. The bank "serves as a sentinel over the specie."[7] This attitude was taken by several of the controversialists: banks are institutions which at once find it most to their interest to retain a large amount of specie in the country and are at the same time best able to effect that purpose.[8]

[1] M. Carey, *Debates and Proceedings* (1786), p. 15. See also, *Remarks on a Pamphlet by James Wilson*, etc. (1785), p. 10; Nestor, "Thoughts on Paper Money," *American Museum* (1787), ii, 40, 41.
[2] Carey, *Debates and Proceedings* (1786), pp. 15, 24.
[3] *Ibid.*, p. 31.   [4] *Ibid.*, p. 51.   [5] *Ibid.*, p. 90.
[6] Barton, "True Interest of the United States," *American Museum* (1786), ii, 32.
[7] Paine, "Dissertations on Government" (1786), *Writings*, ii, 155–168.
[8] Carey, *Debates and Proceedings* (1786), p. 52.

Many of these early disputants, Paine being the principal exception, made no distinction between bank paper and government paper money in discussing the export of specie. Nor did they usually refer to the price phenomena underlying specie movements. One of the essayists at Philadelphia did explain the part played by prices in causing gold to leave the country upon an inflation of the currency with bank paper,[1] and a critic of a contemporary proposal in Maryland for the emission of bills of credit by the state gave a very creditable statement of the theory of gold movements since associated with the names of Hume and Ricardo.[2]

Hamilton, in his *Report on a National Bank*, dealt with the objection that banks "tend to banish gold and silver out of the country" as "the last, and heaviest charge against them." The current reply, "that it is immaterial what serves the purpose of money, whether paper, or gold and silver; that the effect of both upon industry is the same; and that the intrinsic wealth of a nation is to be measured, not by the abundance of the precious metals contained in it, but by the quantity of the productions of its labor and industry," he found inadequate. The precious metals are too important a species of wealth to permit of treating the country's supply of them as a matter of such indifference. But the objection, he thought, admits of a more conclusive answer, controverting the fact itself. Banks augment the active capital of a country, animating and expanding its industry; with the result that more commodities are produced for export and an inflow of gold and silver is induced.[3] Hamilton avoided the error, into which many of the early writers fell, of confusing temporary and permanent movements of specie. With respect to the former, he granted that banks facilitate the export of gold, but this he

---

[1] Witherspoon, *Essay on Money* (1786), pp. 43, 44. John Witherspoon was a Scotch clergyman who emigrated to America in 1768 to assume the presidency of Princeton College. He was an ardent colonial patriot and by his counsels played a conspicuous part in the struggle for independence.

[2] Hanson, *Remarks on the Proposed Plan of an Emission of Paper*, etc. (1787), pp. 22, 23.

[3] A similar opinion was expressed by William Barton, "True Interest of the United States" *American Museum* (1787), ii, 32.

considered a merit, as it enables us to pay our foreign indebtedness when no other form of remittance is possible.[1]

Like many of his predecessors, Hamilton failed to explain the influence of banks on the amount of specie in a country through the mechanism of prices. Later writers, who charged banks with the expulsion of the precious metals, gave this matter its due. Quite frequently the aspect stressed was not the loss of specie, but the relation of banks to domestic industry. A paper currency, raising domestic prices, was held to burden home producers with a disadvantage in a manner similar to that in which a tariff protected them. By raising manufacturers' costs it enabled the foreign producer to undersell the domestic product. The argument was used alike by those who would return to a metallic currency alone,[2] and by the friends of protection, who found in the existence of banks in this country a reason for demanding a high tariff.[3]

The use that Smith, and, about 1810, a number of his American followers, had made of the argument that bank notes do indeed tend to displace specie, but that they thereby effect an economy, could hardly be ignored, however. Nor did it escape criticism. Raymond, after quoting Smith at length, objected that consumers' goods, rather than productive capital, are returned for the specie exported; so that the exchange is that of a spendthrift.[4] J. N. Cardozo, editor of the *Southern Patriot*, a free-trade organ published in Charleston, South Carolina, offered a specious argument to the effect that the country using bank paper suffers an unfavorable balance of trade due to the inability of the country from which it had been obtaining its gold and silver to continue to purchase imports at its accustomed rate.[5] Charles

[1] Report on a National Bank (1790), *American State Papers, Finance*, i, 70.
[2] *Niles' Register* (1818), xiv, 194; Samuel Hooper, *Specie Currency* (1855), pp. 1–6; C. H. Carroll, "Money and Banking," *Hunt's Merchants' Magazine* (September, 1857), xxxvii, 309; Amasa Walker, *The Nature and Uses of Money and Mixed Currency* (1857), p. 39.
[3] A P. Peabody, "Financial Crisis," *North American Review* (January, 1858), lxxxvi, 176; "Speech of Buchanan in United States Senate," 1837, *Ibid.*, p. 184.
[4] Raymond, *Elements of Political Economy* (1823), ii, 152. See, also, p. 135n.
[5] Cardozo, *Notes on Political Economy* (1826), pp. 80–89.

H. Carroll devoted to the problem the major part of a number of acute articles in *Hunt's Merchants' Magazine*. Smith's reasoning, he asserted, overlooks the fact that our mixed currency of metal and paper is not such a combination as occurs in an alloy of two metals. The elements are readily separated. Thus when the currency is temporarily debased twenty per cent by bank-note inflation, the foreign merchant "sells us the value to himself of $5, and takes $6 away for it, first separating the paper from the gold, and taking only the gold."[1] If the coin were debased twenty per cent with pewter, or some worthless compound, he would take away the whole mixture and the exchange would be one of equivalent values. As it is, the foreign tradesman will take none of the mixture, but, separating the dross from the substance, he leaves the dross with us, and takes the solid gold at the value we place upon the mixture. The issue of bank notes "degrades the value of money, locally, causing a loss in the capital of the community invested in money, precisely like the loss to a merchant by the fall of price of the goods in his warehouses."[2] We must pay a larger amount of gold for our imports, exactly in proportion to the inflation of the currency, and thus the paper currency costs us the loss of its whole sum in standard gold.

One more attempt to confute the theory that bank notes tend to expel specie must be considered — the familiar one of Henry C. Carey. Carey contented himself with no half-way job; denial of the Ricardian theory of gold movements itself was his purpose. In its accomplishment he was aided by his habit of formulating generalizations, easily dubbed "laws," as superficial as they were novel, and not infrequently equally fantastic.

"Every commodity, as yielded by nature to man, tends toward those places at which it has the highest utility, and there it is that the labor value of the finished article will be found the smallest. Wheat tends toward the gristmill, and there it is that flour is cheapest." Thus do the precious metals tend toward those places

---

[1] Carroll, "Gold from California and Paper Money," *Hunt's Merchants' Magazine* (1856), xxxvii, 168. Cp. "The Banking and Currency Systems," *Ibid*. (October, 1858), xlix, 448, 449.

[2] "Financial Heresies," *Ibid*. (September, 1860), xliii, 318; cp. "Specie Prices and Results," *Ibid*. (October, 1857), xxxvii, 430–433.

at which they have the highest utility, and at which the interest rate is lowest. Bank notes increase the utility of gold and silver and accordingly attract them.[1] It is to England, that one of all the countries in Europe in which the use of bank notes has been most universal, that the precious metals have flowed.[2]

The belief that bank notes tend to supersede gold and silver failed, in Carey's opinion, to regard "the real Man — the being made in the image of his Creator. . . . The desires of *that* man are infinite, and the more they are gratified, the more rapidly do they increase in number."[3]

"Money tends to diminish the obstacles interposed between the producer and the consumer," Carey further argued, in a belated defence of the balance of trade doctrine, "precisely as do railroads and mills — all of them tending to the raising the value of labor and land while cheapening the finished products of labor."[4] While increase of the supply of money tends to raise prices, it augments also the "power of association," causing so large an increase of the supply of manufactures and of food as more than to offset the tendency toward a rise in prices.[5]

[1] H. C. Carey, *Money* (1855), p. 21.
[2] *Ibid.*, p. 14.
[3] Idem, *Principles of Social Science* (1858), ii, 332.
[4] *Ibid.*, ii, 327.
[5] *Money* (1855), p. 10. Although Carey had direct reference here to metallic money, similar reasoning is apparently implied with respect to bank paper. Compare with the point Carey has just made, Hamilton's reply, earlier in the chapter, to the doctrine that banks expel specie.

CHAPTER VI

BANKS CAUSE DISTURBING FLUCTUATIONS IN PRICES

Introductory. — The charge that banks cause price fluctuations. — The doctrine that convertibility prevents overissue. — Criticism of this thesis. — Theory that the manner in which notes are placed in circulation prevents overissue. — And that the amount of notes in circulation is a *result* of conditions of trade. — A just adjudication of the dispute. — Colwell's well-considered views. — Summary.

THE most mischievous of all the heresies of early banking theory was that which attributed to banks the power of adding to the nation's capital through the simple process of inflating the currency. To this the reply was soon made that such inflation does not affect the real capital of the community in the least; that it signifies, in fact, but a depreciation of the monetary standard. The direction in which this criticism leads is obvious, and it was not long before the possibility of increasing the quantity of media of payment through note issue, with resultant price fluctuations, became the ground for the gravest of all the charges against banks. The effect of temporary, rather than permanent, increase in the volume of currency was the point at issue here.

The remarkable controversy that occurred in England during the Restriction Period, continuing until the Bank Act of 1844 had more or less definitely secured the victory of one of the opposing schools, dealt almost exclusively with the matter of the influence of banking on prices. American writers did little more than to adopt one or another of the conflicting views to which their English brethren were giving so exhaustive a study. In England two different trends had been taken by those who opposed the doctrine, later labeled the *currency principle*, that bank notes are subject to mischievous overissue. The first was that convertibility precludes the possibility of notes being issued in excess. Any redundancy would promptly be returned to the bank. The second was that bank notes can never be overissued, provided only that the banks emit them in the process of discounting none but real commercial paper. The proffer of such paper for discount, it was claimed, shows that there has already taken place a *bona fide* transaction that makes the issue of notes for its completion desirable. In other words, bank notes issued against real commercial paper can never be excessive, inasmuch as they are put into circulation in response to the needs of trade.

These two doctrines are quite distinct, and need not go together. The Bullionists of the Restriction Period, for example, were opposed, not only by writers who believed that convertibility is not in itself a sufficient check against overissue, but also by those — the so-called anti-Bullionists — who regarded convertibility as too suppressive a check. These latter urged that notes issued in the discount of real commercial paper can never be excessive, and that convertibility is not merely superfluous, but harmful, in that it prevents banks from meeting all the requirements of trade.

Both theses had received the weighty sanction of the *Wealth of Nations*. And all the various shades of opinion found in England were reflected in the American literature.

The colonial pamphleteers did not, in general, distinguish between bank notes and government issues with respect to their bearing upon prices, nor did they usually contemplate convertible notes put into circulation by the discounting of short commercial paper. Their price theories had, accordingly, but little relation to the later doctrines.[1]

In the very earliest criticisms of banks after the close of the colonial period, the question of their influence upon prices played a curiously inconspicuous part.[2] Much more was heard of the menace of a "monied aristocracy," and of the tendency of banks to drive specie from the country. The charge that banks produce troublesome changes in prices was not long delayed, however. In 1792 we find a writer asserting that the proprietors of the Bank of Massachusetts had the power "to govern the medium of commerce in and about the metropolis of the state. By emitting

[1] See Chapter XII, however, in which inconvertible notes are discussed.
[2] See Witherspoon, *Essay on Money* (1786), pp. 43, 44, for a notable exception.

large sums they have raised the price of public securities, and of other articles in the market; and by refusing again to loan, have brought on an artificial scarcity of money, and sunk the price of the same articles." [1]

With this alleged power still concentrated in relatively few banks, it was inevitable that some should believe that it was being exercised in the speculative interests of the owners of the banks and of their friends. Such a charge was first made, apparently, against the Bank of the United States. Having "a monopoly of the bulk of the circulating medium," the bank, it was asserted, might readily reduce prices by contracting its note issue, purchase property, then raise prices by a policy of expansion, and sell, at greatly enhanced prices, what it had previously purchased.[2]

The causing of price disturbances became, from this time on, the most frequent and the most serious count in the indictment against banking. A currency of bank notes was said to be subject, not only to the "natural" variations in value characteristic of a metallic medium, but to "artificial" variations as well.[3] That a government which regulated minutely the quantity of bullion in

[1] Sullivan, *Path to Riches* (1792), p. 47.

[2] Anon., *Enquiry into the ... Tendency of Public Measures* (1794), p. 73. Similar charges, that bank directors arbitrarily alter prices in their own interest, continued to be made after the great increase in the number of banks must have made the necessary unity of action seem highly improbable. Raymond, *Elements of Political Economy* (1823), ii, 12, after explaining that banks can determine the price level through their control over the volume of the currency, added, "Whether bank directors will exercise this power, with a view to their own speculations, is not for me to say — If they do not they exercise a very unusual degree of forbearance." Vethake was more dogmatic (*Principles of Political Economy*, 1838, p. 178). On the other hand, George Bancroft ridiculed the opinion of the McDuffie Committee of Congress (*Report*, 1830, p. 11) that banks can so manipulate the currency, and observed further that, even if they were able to do so, to distress their customers in the manner contemplated "would be but a sorry imitation of the woman of classic celebrity who killed her best hen. The golden eggs are worth more than the carcass." A later writer (George Dutton, *The Present Crisis*, 1857, pp. 18–21) made the more plausible explanation that it is only the great capitalists, such as the controllers of the Second United States Bank and of the Bank of England, who wield such a power; the ordinary banker is victim, rather than participant, in the scheme.

[3] Baldwin, *Thoughts on the Study of Political Economy* (1809), pp. 39–43; Gouge, *Short History of Paper Money* (1833), p. 58; etc.

its coin should leave the creation of paper money "to the sport and caprice of petty corporations," became the despair of many.[1] Analogy between the banker and the counterfeiter was frequently drawn.[2] Amasa Walker regarded the variations in prices introduced by a mixed currency as the chief cause of bankruptcies, laying it down as a "fixed law" that "the bankruptcies which take place in any community are just in proportion to the expansibility and contractibility of its currency."[3]

Meanwhile the theory, developed in England, that convertible bank notes admit of no overissue, was not without its American adherents. Smith, the starting-point for the English and American discussion alike, had denied that paper money can depreciate the currency as a whole, contending that it can but become depreciated itself with respect to gold and silver coins. As for convertible bank notes, they can never increase the total circulation.

> The whole paper money of every kind which can easily circulate in any country never can exceed the value of the gold and silver, of which it supplies the place, or which (the commerce being supposed the same) would circulate there, if there was no paper. . . . Should the circulating paper at any time exceed that sum, as the excess could neither be sent abroad nor be employed in the circulation of the country, it must immediately return upon the banks to be exchanged for gold and silver.

The latter would be exported, promptly restoring the currency to its original quantity.[4]

---

[1] Baldwin, *op. cit.*, p. 64.

[2] Davies, *Bank Torpedo* (1810), p. 17; Committee of Philadelphians, Report (1829), *Free Trade Advocate*, i, 313; etc. Ricardo was occasionally cited as authority for this view. (See T. Cooper, *Lectures*, p. 144; Fisk, *Banking Bubble Burst*, p. 41; etc.)

[3] Amasa Walker, *The Nature and Use of Money and Mixed Currency* (1857), p. 33. Cp. Gouge, *Short History of Paper Money* (1833), p. 33.

[4] *Wealth of Nations*, book II, chap. 2 (vol. i, pp. 283, 284). Franklin, in an essay dated 1774, of which George Whatley was joint author, combated as erroneous "the idea of the too great extension of credit, by the circulation of paper for money." . . . For "were it not certain, that paper could command the equivalent of its agreed-for value," it would not be used. The paper is as useful as coin, "since the issuers or coiners of that paper are understood to have some equivalent to answer for what the paper is valued at, and no metal or coin can do more than find its value." How much or how little of Smith's doctrine was implied, is not evident. Sparks, *Works of Franklin*, ii, 417.

In his *Report on a National Bank,* Hamilton urged that
among other material differences between a paper currency issued by the mere authority of government, and one issued by a bank, payable in coin, is this: that in the first case, there is no standard to which an appeal can be made, as to the quantity which will only satisfy, or which will surcharge the circulation; in the last, that standard results from the demand. If more be issued than is necessary, it will return upon the bank.

The issues of a bank "must always be in a compound ratio to the fund [reserves] and the demand: — Whence it is evident, that there is a limitation in the nature of the thing." Government paper, on the contrary, is limited in quantity only by the government's discretion.[1]

This is not, of course, a complete adoption of Smith's doctrine, with which Hamilton was no doubt familiar. He could not, indeed, have adopted it, because of his opinion that banks increase the quantity of media of payment — the very principle that Smith was seeking to refute, and upon the denial of which Smith's own reasoning rested. But, while Hamilton thought that convertibility does not prevent the increase of the volume of the currency, he held that it does preclude any danger of an excessive increase — a position that becomes more intelligible when we recall Hamilton's acceptance of the favorite notion of colonial days, that banks may be used to remedy an inadequacy of media of payment.

The doctrine that bank notes cannot alter the total quantity of media of payment because of their convertibility seems to have received scarcely any attention before the second quarter of the century. A Congressional committee did declare in 1816 that it would be superfluous to "intrude upon the House a disquisition on a proposition so plain as to be at present almost received as an axiom, — that an excessive issue of notes will furnish its own check, if banks redeem with punctuality the notes they send into circulation."[2] But the literature of the period

[1] Hamilton, Report on a National Bank (1790), *American State Papers, Finance,* i, 71.
[2] Report of Committee on Unchartered Banking in the District of Columbia (March 25, 1816), United States House of Representatives, 28th Congress, First Session, Executive Document, No. 15, p. 683.

certainly does not bear out the assertion of the committee as to the prevalence of such a view.

After 1825 a number of writers began to contend that bank notes cannot influence prices so long as convertibility is maintained.[1] The historian, George Bancroft, in a forceful criticism of the *McDuffie Report* of 1830, regarded as ridiculous the assertion of the report that banks can cause great fluctuations in prices through expansion and contraction of their note issue. "A *redundancy* of *convertible paper* is a contradiction in terms — if it were *redundant*, it would be *converted*."[2] The notion that convertible bank notes can depreciate the monetary standard was to him pure "sophistry."

On the whole, however, the theory that convertibility of bank notes is a complete guarantee against their being issued in excess received no great support in this country. As in England, the most common objection was that convertibility does, indeed, prevent a permanent excess of currency, but that it cannot prevent temporary overissue.[3] It operates as a curative, rather than as a preventive; "its effect is consequential, not immediate and direct."[4] The familiar criteria of the state of the currency — the foreign exchanges, the price of bullion, and the export of specie — each received a little attention, and Eleazar Lord, a scholar whose writings and reform activities embraced the rather curious combination of religious and economic interests, made the significant suggestion that the "fact of an excess or deficiency of currency in a country is to be proved by a comparison of the cash prices of exportable commodities in that and other countries."[5] Samuel Hooper, also, attached particular importance to the prices of articles that enter into foreign trade.[6]

---

[1] Porter, Review of Cardozo's "Notes on Political Economy," *North American Review* (1827), xxiv, 184–186; Phillips, *Manual of Political Economy* (1828), pp. 265, 266; "On Currency," *Free Trade Advocate* (July 25, 1829), ii, 56; [David Henshaw], *Remarks on the Bank of the United States* (1831), pp. 19–21; Bowen, *Principles of Political Economy* (1856), pp. 318, 360.

[2] Bancroft, in *North American Review* (1831), xxxii, 29.

[3] Publicola, *Letter to Gallatin* (1815), pp. 33, 34; Eleazar Lord, *Principles of Currency and Banking* (1829), pp. 49–51.

[4] Lord, *ibid.*, p. 50.   [5] *Ibid.*, p. 24.

[6] Hooper, *Currency or Money* (1855), p. 59, *passim*.

Many believed that the currency may become very considerably inflated before the export of specie, operating through convertibility, begins to exert its corrective influence.[1] And the most common explanation of commercial crises, as we shall later see, was that they result from the alternating expansion and contraction of the media of payment which occurs wherever a currency of convertible bank notes exists.[2]

Several writers, of whom Secretary William H. Crawford was perhaps the first,[3] placed the emphasis not so much on the possibility of an inflation of the currency by bank notes, as on the necessity of more intense contraction when an outflow of specie does occur than would be required were there no credit currency. Bank credit is based on a fractional reserve, and the loss, through export, of a given quantity of gold accordingly calls for the contraction of bank credit in similar proportion to that which the specie exported bears to the total amount of specie available for bank reserves. Thus, under a régime of paper money involving an element of credit, specie movements result in a shrinkage of the media of payment to a multiple of their amount.[4] Hildreth and Francis Bowen attempted, rather unconvincingly, to controvert this thesis that the use of credit currency gives a multiple influence to gold exports.[5]

The rather meager support given in the earlier decades to the doctrine that convertibility precludes the possibility of overissue may well have been due in large measure to the great difficulties in the way of actually securing the redemption of notes. This was,

[1] Raymond, *Elements of Political Economy* (1823), ii, 151; Gouge, "Convertible Paper," *Journal of Banking* (1842), p. 369; cp. p. 275; C. F. Adams, *Reflections upon the State of the Currency* (1837), p. 14.

[2] See Chapter XVI, infra.

[3] Crawford, Report on the Currency (February 24, 1820), *American State Papers, Finance*, iii, 499.

[4] C. F. Adams, *Reflections upon the State of the Currency* (1837), pp. 8, 9; Fisk, *Banking Bubble Burst* (1837), p. 55; Tucker, *Theory of Money and Banks* (1839), pp. 184, 185; Vethake, *Principles of Political Economy* (1838), pp. 180, 181; Amasa Walker, *Nature and Uses of Money* (1857), pp. 27, 28.

[5] Hildreth, *Banks, Banking, and Paper Currencies* (1840), pp. 195, 196; Bowen, *Principles of Political Economy* (1856), p. 454; also J. S. Ropes, "Currency, Banking, and Credit," *Bankers' Magazine* (1859), xiv, 166.

in fact, offered as an objection to the doctrine when it did appear.[1] The poor homing power that bank notes then had, owing to the absence of channels through which they could be readily presented for redemption, is, of course, notorious. Nor were the banks reluctant to add to the difficulties. "Some new writer upon the wealth of nations," C. F. Adams observed, "might make an edifying chapter by explaining in more detail all the tricks that have been resorted to for puffing up the circulation." [2] Not only were there no facilities, prior to the spread of the principle involved in the Suffolk Banking System, for sending home notes that came from many and widely scattered banks, but the practice of demanding payment for notes was as unpopular as it was difficult. It was but recently, Appleton wrote in 1831, that "brokers, who sent home the bills of country banks, were denounced as speculators and bloodsuckers, whose extirpation would be a public benefit." [3]

Ere we pass from the matter of convertibility, it should be noted that the importance of clearing operations — virtually a means of aiding the community in presenting notes and checks for payment — as a preventive of unsound expansion by any one bank, was well understood. Mathew Carey was full of mournful forebodings of the general contraction on the part of all banks that the liquidation of the first United States Bank would necessitate.[4] Bollman gave similar warning.[5] "It is a fact corroborated

---

[1] See, for example, Report of New York Bank Commissioners, United States House of Representatives, 25th Congress, Second Session, Document No. 79, p. 236.

[2] Adams, *Reflections upon the State of the Currency* (1837), p. 16.

[3] Nathan Appleton, *Examination of the Banking System of Massachusetts* (1831), p. 4. "The habit of calling for specie," Sumner informs us, "had never been formed, and it was sternly discountenanced by public opinion." [*History of American Currency*, p. 157.] "A polite fiction" is the term the same writer applies elsewhere to the convertibility of our bank notes during these decades. [*The Forgotten Man*, p. 376.] When "good temper exists among them," wrote the president of the South Carolina State Bank, "banks do not present each other's notes for redemption, but rather reissue them over the counter. To do otherwise is to 'manifest a spirit of hostility.'" (*Report to the Senate and House of Representatives of the State*, November 1, 1819, p. 67.)

[4] M. Carey, *Letters to Seybert* (1810), pp. 45–50; *Desultory Reflections* (1810), pp. 10 ff.

[5] Bollman, *Paragraphs on Banks* (1810), pp. 29 ff.

by the experience of all banks," the president of the second Bank of the United States wrote, "that their operations must necessarily be regulated by those of the banks in their immediate vicinity; otherwise those which are the most prudent or parsimonious, will become the creditors of those who are the most liberal or extravagant; the consequence of which is an immediate specie responsibility."[1] That no check on an inflation by all the banks in common was involved, was equally clear. Many regarded increase in the number of banks as a boon, in that it multiplied the agencies that found it to their interest to send home the notes of each bank. No one seems to have recognized that diffusion of the power of issuing notes made the securing of their redemption so difficult, and the efforts of any one bank so insignificant, as to take away the incentive of competition in returning the notes of rival institutions.

Those who denied that bank notes cause price disorders, we have suggested, did so not only on the ground that convertibility prevents overissue, but also in the belief that the manner in which the notes are put into circulation obviates any such possibility. "There is no more danger of the nation's being overstocked with bank credits," thought Dr. Eric Bollman, "than there is of its being overstocked with loaves of bread.... A bank, therefore, can make no mistake as long as it discounts *good paper*, and this it will do for its own sake."[2] That the demand for circulating medium is limited, and in turn limits the supply, was his opinion.

Raymond, on the other hand, thought that "so long as banks are permitted to manufacture as much money as they can loan with safety, there will be an excessive issue of paper currency, unless some further restraint than that of paying specie for their

---

[1] William Jones, "Letter to the Secretary of the Treasury" (November 11, 1818), *American State Papers, Finance*, iii, 289. Oliver Wolcott, Hamilton's successor as Secretary of the Treasury, observed that the banking systems of the several countries must tend to expand and contract *pari passu*, so that any strenuous deflation by the Bank of England affects us and may cause a depression here. *Remarks on the State of the Currency*, etc. (1820), pp. 4, 5, 32.

[2] Bollman, *Paragraphs on Banks* (1810), p. 59.

notes, shall be placed upon the banks." Borrowers will never be lacking "weak enough to believe that they can make profitable use of the money" at the bank's terms.[1]

In harmony with the theory that the notes of banks, since they enter circulation in response to the requests of the business community for loans, cannot be overissued, a number of writers insisted that the tendency of higher prices and increased note circulation to accompany each other is due to the fact that higher prices give origin to a larger note issue, rather than to the reverse relationship. The quantity of currency was made the result, not the cause, of the price level; and the explanation of price changes, it was urged, must be found in changes in the conditions of supply and demand with respect to goods.

Thus Thomas R. Dew, professor of political economy (among other subjects) and later president of William and Mary College, took Gouge to task for mistaking what is more often the effect for the cause, in attributing price changes to the fluctuating quantity of bank notes. He did concede, however, that the increased note issue which higher prices initially stimulate, "immediately becomes in turn a powerfully operating cause" of still higher prices and more speculation.[2] Hildreth considered the volume of bank currency a consequent, rather than cause, of the price level, and addressed a satirical public letter to the Governor of Massachusetts for venturing to suggest otherwise in an address.[3] John A. Lowell took similar issue with an essay by Samuel Hooper in which the latter maintained that price movements are determined by the liberality with which banks issue their notes.[4] The volume of bank notes in circulation, Lowell contended in his criticism, depends upon the amount of money people keep on hand for meeting their needs, and he found it "difficult to see how any action of the banks can induce any man to increase materially the sum which he chooses, or is obliged, thus to keep

[1] Raymond, *Elements of Political Economy* (1823), ii, 154.
[2] Dew, *Essay on Interest* (1834), p. 16.
[3] Hildreth, *Letter to Marcus Morton* (1840), pp. 4 ff., and *Banks, Banking, and Paper Currencies* (1840), p. 157.
[4] Hooper, *An Examination of the Theory of Laws Regulating the Amount of Specie in Banks* (1860).

in his possession." [1] Never was there a more curious substitution of cause for effect, thought Lowell, than that evidenced by those who, like Hooper, attributed the crisis of 1857 to the reduction of bank credit, made necessary by lack of adequate reserves. Instead, the crisis rendered the use of capital unprofitable, and it was for that reason, and not because of scant reserves, that bank accommodations shrank. "It was not capital that was withdrawn or annihilated; the difficulty was, that nobody could be found to employ it." [2]

Hooper found a supporter in Charles H. Carroll, who insisted that the part played by banks in expanding and contracting the media of payment is by no means passive. Declaring that it is a poor rule that fails to work both ways, he asked, "Is it a decline of 'local dealing and expenditure' [as asserted by Lowell] which causes the contraction of bank loans, or is it the contraction of the loans which causes the decline of the dealing and expenditure?" [3]

A just adjudication of the issue had already been offered, at a much earlier date, by several writers who held that the increased note issue, which greater business activity calls forth, in turn occasions a higher price level, stimulating business still further. Thus, whichever gives the original impetus, the "needs of trade" and the volume of currency react upon each other until the export of specie, bringing a threatening drain of reserves, calls a halt.[4] The point was made, not in combating the theory that banks cannot influence prices, but in dealing with the doctrine that banking could have no harmful effects if its discounts were restricted to short commercial paper arising out of actual transactions, and we shall trace it at greater length in considering that thesis.[5]

One important writer, whose views form a closely knit body of

[1] John A. Lowell, *Review of Hooper's Pamphlet* (1860), p. 18. Lowell was, during the greater part of his life, a director of the Suffolk Bank, and is said to have been the first to suggest the system that bore its name.

[2] *Ibid.*, p. 11.

[3] C. H. Carroll, "Mr. Lowell *vs.* Mr. Hooper," *Hunt's Merchants' Magazine* (April, 1860), xlii, 581.

[4] Dew, we have seen, had shown some recognition of this in 1834. It had been stated by Raguet in 1829.

[5] See Chapter XV, below.

principles, remains to be dealt with. Not only did Stephen Colwell[1] deny any appreciable influence upon prices to bank notes, but he attached little importance to the quantity theory with respect to metallic money as well. "There is no strict or determinate relation," he contended, "between the quantity of [metallic] money in a country, and its range of prices. They act and react upon each other in a way, and to an extent, that it is well to mark and study; but these influences are too undefinable, and too much blended with other causes, to be exactly appreciated. Of all the causes which materially affect the range of prices in a country, the changes in the quantity of money are, perhaps, the least influential."[2]

It is too generally taken for granted that prices are the naming of so many pieces of money, or coins. But the larger payments are made almost exclusively by means of credit in units of abstract money of account. These credits cancel each other at the bank without the intervention of money, directly or indirectly, at any stage of the process.[3] Colwell gave an extended list of conditions affecting prices through their influence on the market,[4] cited statistics of prices to prove that the quantity of metallic money plays but a minor part in their determination, and concluded that no immutable laws can be laid down with respect to the influence of the currency upon prices, because "that which depends on the minds, temperaments and passions of men, and the casual occurrences of life, can never be reduced to laws like those which govern bees and ants."[5]

[1] Colwell's *Ways and Means of Payment* (1859), the most impressive single work on banking produced in America before 1860, stamps him as a writer of the first rank. He was born in Virginia in 1800, and began the practice of law there. Later he moved to Philadelphia, and soon left the bar to become an iron merchant. He acquired considerable wealth and gave liberally of it to endow professorships and libraries. After the Civil War (in which he was a staunch Unionist, though born a Southerner) he was appointed special commissioner to study the internal revenue system, with a view to suggesting revision. He wrote little except his *Ways and Means of Payment*, parts of which were forecast in a few articles in *Hunt's Merchants' Magazine*.

[2] Colwell, *op. cit.*, pp. 523, 524.
[3] *Ibid.*, pp. 541 ff.   [4] *Ibid.*, pp. 525–528.
[5] *Ibid.*, p. 535. That prices vary more or less directly with the quantity of money, whether metallic or convertible paper, was denied by very few. Two minor writers

If the quantity of precious metals employed as money exercises so little influence on prices, we may safely infer, Colwell believed, that bank currency has no greater power in that respect. He by no means rested his case on analogy to specie currency, however. There are special reasons why bank notes should affect prices but little, since

for all the currency issued by the banks, there is a special and constant demand from the debtors of the banks, which prevents it from having as much influence as it might otherwise have. The debtors of the banks having in their possession the whole range of commodities to which prices apply, are offering them for this currency, to secure it for their constantly recurring payments. Their constantly maturing obligations do not permit them to hold out for extra prices.[1]

The paper currency cannot depreciate (that is, cannot raise prices), because the manner in which it is issued ensures a demand for it commensurate with the supply; namely, the demand of the bank's borrowers, whose notes are maturing in orderly procession.[2] Colwell apparently overlooked here the fact that the customer of the bank does not need the bank notes for use in cancelling his obligation to the bank until 60 or 90 days after he has received them. Meanwhile they enter the general circulation, effecting a number of payments, and thus increasing the number of monetary units available for making purchases. Yet he recognized as much elsewhere, in urging the deposit of securities for bank notes.[3]

In further support of his view that bank notes are but a minor determinant of the general level of prices, Colwell resorted to the familiar doctrine that the volume of bank currency is the consequence, rather than the cause, of the price level. A rise in prices,

did contend that paper money can have no influence upon prices. D. M. Balfour, "A Decade of the Gold Plethora," *Hunt's Merchants' Magazine* (1860), xlii, 587; and George Ward, "Causes of the Crisis of 1857," *Ibid.* (1859), xl, 20. H. C. Carey was characteristically unconventional in this respect. We are told that price fluctuations are caused by the use of bank notes, he observed. "In every other case, however, in which the utility of a commodity is increased, the supply becomes more steady, and the price more regular. . . . That being the case, the use of circulating notes — tending as they do to increase the utility [efficiency] of [metallic] money — must tend to the production of steadiness in its supply, and regularity in its value." *Principles of Social Science* (1858), ii, 407.

[1] Colwell, *op. cit.*, p. 17.   [2] *Ibid.*, p. 434.   [3] *Ibid.*, pp. 463, 464.

he warned, is often ascribed to expansion of the currency, when the two are in fact joint products of speculation. In seasons of confidence, business men are at once prone to buy in large quantities,[1] and afforded the facility of doing so by liberal credit terms. There is "a great issue of bills of exchange and promissory notes of merchants and dealers, who thus multiply their engagements, without immediately increasing the quantity of goods in the market." Many of these bills are discounted at the banks and thus converted into bank notes, but the issue of the latter is an alleviation of the evil, rather than an aggravation, for it aids the sale of the goods purchased, upon which the solvency of the speculators depends. To be sure, the high state of confidence which gave rise to such large purchases on credit would not have existed but for the possibility of converting the commercial paper into bank currency. But the initial fault lies with the business men, and not with the banks. "That an increased issue of bank notes, consequent upon over trading, may stimulate prices, especially in the retail trade, is very probable, but not to the extent, nor in the way many suppose." [2]

To summarize the discussion: It was generally accepted that changes in the volume of convertible paper money affect prices quite as directly as variations in the supply of specie currency. Some held, however, that bank notes can produce no mischievous price fluctuations because convertibility prevents their overissue. But the advocates of this view were not very numerous. Nor was the doctrine that bank notes admit of no excessive issue because they are put into circulation only in accordance with the needs of trade any more popular. For the most part, it was believed that

---

[1] Colwell, *op. cit.*, p. 567.

[2] *Ibid.*, pp. 534, 535. Like many others who attached but minor importance to the influence of an expanding currency upon prices, Colwell viewed a contraction of bank credit with less equanimity. To maintain the convertibility of their demand obligations, he repeatedly remarked, imposes upon banks the necessity of drastically contracting the currency whenever a considerable loss of gold threatens. A collapse of prices results. He would, presumably, attribute this to the psychological influence of curtailed bank accommodations rather than to the operation of the quantity theory itself. *Ibid.*, pp. 483 ff.

they do cause temporary price disturbances, and differences of opinion were mainly as to the magnitude which the latter can assume before correction, called for by dwindling reserves, takes place.

A thesis that received far greater support was that bank notes would, indeed, vary in quantity exactly with the needs of trade (and usually, although not always, this was taken to mean that they would not diverge from the standard of a purely metallic currency), if properly issued — that is, if issued only in the discounting of short, real bills. This doctrine, however, since it begs the question whether or not banks do, in actual practice, conform to the approved principle, is quite different from asserting that banks cannot introduce currency disorders. We have postponed its consideration, accordingly, to the pages dealing with matters of banking policy.[1] Not a few accepted the theory, but argued that in point of fact the prevalence of accommodation loans and other abuses resulted in grave disturbances of prices.[2]

[1] *Infra*, Chapter XV.
[2] *E. g.*, Thomas Cooper, *Lectures on* ... *Political Economy* (1826), pp. 43, 44, 151.

CHAPTER VII

BANKS RENDER THE CURRENCY ELASTIC IN RESPONSE TO THE NEEDS OF TRADE

The elasticity of bank currency, except in its mischievous aspects, generally ignored. — But a few writers did give attention to it.

THE elasticity of the media of payment that banks furnish occupies a prominent place to-day among the benefits attributed to them. This consideration played a most conspicuous part in the criticism of the National Banking System and in the discussion that attended the framing of the Federal Reserve Act. Such was not the case, however, in the literature which we are reviewing. For here the elasticity of bank currency, except in its mischievous aspects, received very little attention. In large measure, no doubt, the prominence of troublesome expansions and contractions accounts for this. And the prevalence of long loans, frequently subject to renewal, may have contributed to obscure the function of banking in giving a desirable flexibility to the volume of media of payment.

It was almost universally agreed that the best currency is one composed wholly of specie, or one consisting in part of bank notes [1] but conforming in quantity exactly with the norm of a purely metallic medium. There were few to take a stand against notes secured by government stocks, or against the currency principle as embodied in the English Bank Act of 1844, on the ground that the desirable elasticity of the currency was interfered with.[2] The adherents of the "commercial principle" of banking, as the English "banking principle" was frequently called in this country, argued, for the most part, simply that convertible bank

[1] Of course, the elasticity of bank deposits is of no less significance than that of bank notes. But the early writers were concerned chiefly with the latter, and in this chapter, as elsewhere, we shall frequently use the term bank notes, reserving for a later chapter consideration of the question to what extent the similarity of deposits was recognized.

[2] *Infra*, Chapter XIII.

notes issued in discounting short and real commercial paper can have no disastrous elasticity. Bank notes when so issued, it was commonly stated, cause the currency to vary in quantity exactly as it would were it entirely metallic, and any divergence from this was regarded as harmful.[1] Not a few were skeptical of achieving the ideal of a currency composed partly of bank notes that would at all times conform in quantity to what would obtain were the currency of precious metals alone. These, accordingly, proposed a return to purely metallic money, or urged that bank notes be issued only against an equivalent amount of coin. The dominant theory was that "in every respect the law of money is the same, whether it exist in the shape of metal or in the shape of paper."[2]

No less indicative of failure to apprehend the province of a properly elastic bank currency were the views of those who urged the issue of a fixed amount of government paper. The notion, to which Adam Smith had subscribed, that the volume of currency which every country needs bears a more or less definite proportion to the magnitude of its annual trade, or to its population, was widely accepted. One fifth of the annual product of industry seems to have been a fairly popular standard,[3] while a committee of the Rhode Island legislature compromised on one eighteenth of the annual product, being the mean between one fifth and one thirtieth, the two extremes suggested.[4] Charles Carroll regarded one twenty-fifth of the aggregate property of the country as the correct proportion and thought that this ratio was "so well determined by natural laws, that if I would estimate the whole amount of property of the United States, I would rather know the sum of the currency, and multiply it by 25, than to have the most elaborate statistics otherwise prepared."[5]

[1] Appleton, *Remarks on Currency and Banking* (1841), p. 16; Lord, *Principles of Currency and Banking* (1859), p. 29.

[2] Barnard, *Speeches* (1838), pp. 168, 169.

[3] See Mississippi Governor's message accompanying the bank commissioner's report (1838), 25th Congress, Second Session, Senate Document, No. 471, p. 74; also 26th Congress, First Session, House Document, No. 172, p. 476.

[4] Rhode Island, *Report of Committee on Currency* (1826).

[5] Carroll, "New Views of the Currency Question," *Bankers' Magazine* (1859), xiii, 839.

Just as the champions of banking generally neglected the power of bank notes to conform to the fluctuations of the volume of trade, so its critics, with few exceptions, failed to recognize such a possibility. Decry the pernicious variations of bank notes they did, time and again, but they seemed wholly unaware that any other aspect of the matter was to be considered. Gouge was the principal exception. Unfortunately for the claim that banks expand and contract their issues to suit the wants of the community, he contended, they are compelled to contract when the demand for money is greatest, and are best able to expand when it is least. Not the needs of the public, but their own profit and safety guide them, as well as such untoward events as the outbreak of war, or whatever else may cause specie to flow out of the country.[1]

Let us turn now to the few who did claim for banks the merit of providing an elastic medium of payment. Bollman, writing in 1810, offers the first instance.[2] The needs of a country for circulating medium, he observed, vary with the extent to which credit is used, and with the rapidity with which property is transferred. A currency of gold and silver lacks the "inherent quality of adapting itself to the exigencies of the times."[3] The possibility, frankly

[1] Gouge, *Short History of Paper Money and Banking in the United States* (1833), p. 62. Colwell, who held in its most extreme form the doctrine that bank credit should improve upon a purely metallic currency through its elasticity, criticized convertibility on the basis of the perverse elasticity that Gouge emphasized. But Colwell's solution was the issue of inconvertible bank notes. *Ways and Means of Payment* (1859), pp. 12, 169, and *passim*.

I have found only two other critics of banking who dealt with the claim that elasticity is one of the desirable qualities of bank currency. Editor, *Democratic Review* (1837), i, 114; Fisk, *Banking Bubble Burst* (1837), p. 24.

[2] Probably no great significance is to be attached to the following words of Franklin: "It is impossible for government to circumscribe or fix the extent of paper credit, which must of course, fluctuate. . . . Any seeming temporary evil arising must naturally work its own cure." Franklin (in collaboration with Whatley), "The Principles of Trade" (1774), *Works of Franklin*, ii, 398. Cp. *Ibid.*, p. 417.

[3] Eric Bollman, *Plan of an Improved System of the Money Concerns of the Union* (1810), p. 9.

Bollman (1769–1821) was a physician and apparently no little of an adventurer. Born in Germany, he became successively a resident of France, England, Austria, and the United States. He came to this country toward the close of the eighteenth century, upon his release from an Austrian prison into which he had been thrown for an attempt to free Lafayette from just such a plight. He remained here

admitted, of an excessive quantity of notes being issued, would be avoided if one were but to allow "business itself to become productive of the means of its transaction — of money; and again, to cause the diminution of business to produce its absorption." This can obtain only when bank notes are used; metallic money and government paper money do not automatically adjust themselves in this way to the necessities of trade, because it is not through trade itself that they are brought into existence. But when bank notes are issued, as they should be, in the discount of short commercial paper arising out of actual transactions, they expand with the latter, and each note so issued returns to the bank at the maturity of the bill discounted, continuing in circulation only in the event that it is still needed, as evidenced by the offer of a new bill for discount.[1]

Condy Raguet,[2] whose writings, though able, contain a variety of views that slights but few, was one of those who insisted that banks were of no utility other than that derived from their substitution of an inexpensive for a costly currency, and from their service as intermediaries between borrowers and lenders. Yet with the same breath he paid tribute to the elasticity of their media of payment. The discounting of short real paper he regarded as the "legitimate operations of banking," whereby the quantity of currency is made to vary with the needs of trade. "Thus would the *elasticity* of the banking principle accommo-

until 1814, later paying us another brief visit. During his stay in America he became implicated in Aaron Burr's conspiracy of 1806.

[1] Bollman, *op. cit.*, pp. 11–13.

[2] Raguet (1784–1842) was one of the most interesting of all the writers on banking. He became a successful merchant in Philadelphia, then served as colonel in the War of 1812, after which he studied law and was sent as consul to Brazil. He later represented his district in the Pennsylvania legislature, and his reports as chairman of its committee on banking show a remarkable insight into some of the more difficult problems of banking theory. His versatile interests led him to become an ardent free-trader, and he published a series of economic journals devoted primarily to the doctrines of free trade and of banking reform. The fact that each seems to have been a financial failure makes them none the less valuable to us. In 1839, three years before his death, he published a small volume on *Currency and Banking*, containing a systematic exposition of his views, for the most part made familiar to us in earlier writings. It was reprinted in England in the same year and translated into French in 1840.

date itself to the state of commercial wants. . . . From this view of the subject, it may easily be seen, that all the benefit, which the public derives from banks of circulation, arises from their *elasticity*."[1] Elsewhere Raguet laid emphasis on the harm done by long-term loans through their rendering the banks incapable of properly adjusting the volume of media of payment. Bank currency thus loses the elasticity that is its peculiar merit.[2]

Richard Hildreth also regarded the elasticity of bank notes as one of their principal advantages. International trade, he observed, fluctuates considerably in amount, and if coin were its only medium of payment, prices would fluctuate correspondingly. But the use of bills of exchange, which vary in quantity with the seasonal needs of trade, modifies the price fluctuations. Being equally flexible with respect to their geographical distribution, bills of exchange lessen local price variations in similar manner.[3] Now a currency of convertible bank notes, Hildreth thought, represents merely an application of the same principles to domestic trade. By giving seasonal and local flexibility to the currency, causing the latter to expand and contract with the requirements of trade, bank notes, like bills of exchange, "greatly improve the quality of the precious metals as a measure of value."[4]

Stephen Colwell carried this view to its extreme. Bank notes should be governed as to their quantity, not by the supply of the precious metals, but by the necessities of the business for the use of which they are issued.[5] To regulate a currency consisting in part of bank credit so that it will operate like one composed wholly of specie, is as absurd as it would be to regulate the speed of locomotives by that of the horse and wagons that preceded them. The "whole substance of the positions taken in this vol-

[1] "Principles of Banking," *Free Trade Advocate* (July 4, 1829), ii, 5, 6.
[2] "The Currency," *Free Trade Advocate* (May 23, 1829), p. 321. Cp. *Currency and Banking* (1839), p. 92.
[3] Hildreth, *History of Banks* (1837), pp. 116, 117.
[4] *Ibid.*, pp. 121, 122. Cp. *Banks, Banking, and Paper Currencies* (1840), p. 142. J. N. C. [Cardozo?], *Southern Quarterly Review* (Sept., 1850), xviii, 132, also held that the "flexibility to the influences of movement and pressure from without" is the chief excellence of mixed currency.
[5] Colwell, *Ways and Means of Payment* (1859), p. 370.

ume," he added, in criticizing Peel's bank act, "are [sic] opposed to the principles propounded as grounds for the act of 1844."[1]

Though we have found, then, a few writers who gave heed to the need of modern business for flexibility in its media of payment, these writers were the exception, and the literature of the preceding half-century indicates that, at the time of the passage of the National Bank Act, the concept of an elastic currency was but little understood.

[1] Colwell, op. cit., pp. 162, 163.

PART II

THE UTILITY OF BANKS AS AGENCIES IN THE DISTRIBUTION OF LOANABLE FUNDS

CHAPTER VIII

BANKS SERVE AS INTERMEDIARIES BETWEEN BORROWERS AND LENDERS

The thesis that banks are mere intermediaries in their lending operations was the prevailing one. — Their alleged benefits as such. — Basis of the dogma that banks cannot lend more than they receive from depositors and shareholders. — The error into which the quantity theorists fell here. — Some inklings of a deeper insight. — The persistence of this issue even to the present day.

WE turn now from those considerations concerning the nature and utility of banks which regarded them in their rôle as creators of an important form of media of payment, to the analysis that dealt with them as special agencies in the distribution of loanable funds.

From the point of view of the currency they provide, the advantage most commonly claimed in behalf of banks was that of substituting a less expensive form of media of payment for the precious metals. Coupled with this benefit that banks were alleged to confer upon the community was generally the further one of gathering the surplus funds lying idle in the hands of their owners and distributing them among men who were in a position to give them productive employment. In other words, banks were thought to act as intermediaries between borrowers and lenders, thus making possible a more efficient utilization of the nation's capital.

It was inevitable that some should go further and assert that banking operations are not confined to lending to one set of individuals merely what is borrowed from another, but include, in addition and with equal advantage to the community, the loan by the banks of their credit in the form of notes. But let us consider first those who made the lending operations of banks purely intermediary. Banks, said George Tucker, who held the chair of moral philosophy and political economy at the University of Virginia, "put the money of the female or the minor into the hands of the active and capable man of business," thus giving existing capital greater "activity and a more enlarged sphere of utility."[1] They can no more increase capital, he added, than a mill-dam increases the amount of water when it gathers together many little rills that would otherwise serve no useful purpose, and causes them to turn the wheels of industry.

One of the principal benefits afforded by a bank, Thomas Paine had written at an earlier date, in a pamphlet prompted by the debate over the repeal of the charter of the Bank of North America, is that "it gives a kind of life to what would otherwise be dead money." Each merchant has frequently "remnant money," which can be of use to him only when more has been added. Half of the money in a city, Paine estimated, would lie thus in useless driblets, in the absence of banks to collect it and render it capable of being used.[2]

Throughout the whole of our period, the school that denied that banks can do more than lend on the one hand what they borrow on the other was very large.[3] Francis Bowen put the case succinctly when he said that banks, in their deposit and loan operations, "only play the part of brokers in this matter, bringing borrowers and lenders together."[4] Quite frequently this operation was coupled with that of providing a cheap currency in substitution for costly metallic money, and the two were held to exhaust the possible advantages to be derived from banks.

[1] Tucker, *Theory of Money and Banks Investigated* (1839), pp. 199, 200. This rather obvious doctrine was an old one. See, for example, Henry Robinson, "England's Safety, in Trade's Encrease" (1641), in W. A. Shaw's *Select Tracts*, etc., pp. 55, 56. It is also found in Benjamin Franklin's "Modest Inquiry into the Nature and Necessity of a Paper Currency" (1729), Davis's *Reprints*, ii, 347.

[2] Paine, *Dissertations on Government*, etc. (1786), pp. 167, 168. Cp. Mathew Carey, *Debates and Proceedings* (1786), p. 104, for a similar view.

[3] "The legitimate object of banking, if it has any object at all, is for those possessed of money to lend it on favorable terms to those who need it in the furtherance of their business, and who pay the lender a fair rent for its use. The incorporation of banks had for its object the collection of many small capitals into a common reservoir, to be applied in the same way." T. P. Kettell, "The Money of Commerce," *De Bow's Review* (1848), vi, 253. That bankers can do no more than this was the view of S. P. Newman, *Elements of Political Economy* (1835), pp. 113, 114; D. D. Barnard, *Speeches* (1838), p. 162; Vethake, *Principles of Political Economy* (1838), pp. 170, 171; and many others.

[4] Bowen, *Principles of Political Economy* (1856), p. 449.

To some it was quite sufficient that banks should do no more than this. Individuals with loanable funds would hardly know who merited their confidence, it was pointed out, and would frequently allow their funds to lie idle were it not for the intercession of the banks. These institutions "assume the responsibility of the debtor; they relieve the creditor of his anxiety and doubt; they enable him to divide into small portions, and transfer some of his risk to those with whom he deals."[1] Rae observed that banks remove three difficulties that would obtain were the borrowers of a bank to deal directly with its cash depositors: the two parties would but infrequently know of each other's needs and character; the amounts which the one wished to lend and the other to borrow would hardly be likely to be equal; and, finally, the two might not care to have the loan extend over the same period of time.[2]

There were a few writers who denied that any benefit results from the action of banks in placing at the disposal of borrowers the funds received from depositors (and shareholders). Thus Gouge asserted that banks "do not increase the loanable capital of a country, but only take it out of the hands of its proprietors, and place it under the control of irresponsible Bank Directors."[3] This raised the significant question whether or not the banker is wise in the distribution which he makes of the purchasing power entrusted to his care. Since the problem has equal bearing on his lending operations when they are regarded as advances in part of the banker's credit, and not merely as the loan of money received from depositors, it will be dealt with after the former viewpoint has been considered. Of course, the assumption that the judgment of the banker in selecting borrowers is sound was more or less implicit in the argument of those who, with Rae,

---

[1] Porter in *North American Review* (1827), xxiv, 183. From the point of view of creditor's risks, it should be observed, banking involves on a smaller scale the same principle that underlies the insurance business: each bank makes so many loans that loss from any one becomes proportionately less disastrous, the risk being more or less calculable through the theory of probability as applied to large numbers.

[2] Rae, *Sociological Theory of Capital* (1834), p. 311. Cp. pp. 298, 299, 310.

[3] Gouge, *Short History of Paper Money and Banking in the United States* (1833), p. 45. Cp. minority report on banks in the Pennsylvania Constitutional Convention (1837), *Niles' Register*, lii, 217.

urged that banks intercede in behalf of people who have funds to loan but do not know who deserves their confidence.

Meanwhile the writers on banking were not, of course, blind to the fact that banks lend notes which they themselves freely manufacture. Indeed, it was this very characteristic of banks that brought upon them the greatest condemnation. "By being loan offices," Daniel Raymond complained, "they are enabled to loan all the money they can make, or, at least, as much as they please; and by being the manufacturers of a paper currency they are enabled to make as much money as they can loan."[1] Recognition of this ability to lend units of media of payment of their own creation did not interfere, however, with the conception of bank loans as entirely intermediary. For the quantity theory was invoked to show that, while banks may make advances of more dollars than they have received from depositors and shareholders, proportionate depreciation of the monetary standard is involved, so that the banks really return no greater *effective* purchasing power than they had previously taken in from the public.

Indeed, this very tendency of banks to lend more dollars than they receive was frequently used as a basis for declaring their intervention between borrower and lender mischievous. Nothing was more puzzling to early students of banking than the proportions of a bank's operations as compared with its reserve. On the one hand, we find men, like Hamilton, who regarded bank loans of credit in excess of actual cash on hand as an increase of capital; on the other hand were those who regarded the matter as a bit of financial legerdemain, in which the public played the rôle of docile victim. Thus one early writer, as perplexed as he was aggrieved by the ability of banks to lend to perhaps five times the amount of their specie holdings, argued that they were in effect receiving thirty per cent upon their money, "while the rest of the community were under heavy penalties if they should take more than six per cent for the loan of their monies."[2] The incorpora-

---

[1] Raymond, *Elements of Political Economy* (1823), ii, 129.
[2] Sullivan, *Path to Riches* (1792), p. 49. This seems to have been one of the more influential booklets on banking published at the time of its infancy in America.

tion of a bank, in his opinion, "is an open, express privilege of taking more interest for their money than other people have a right to take."[1]

This notion was common. Daniel Raymond subscribed to it, urging that

every dollar of paper money put in circulation above their [the banks'] actual specie capital, depreciates the value of the currency in proportion, so that the public derives no benefit from a bank lending its notes to twice the amount of its capital, which it would not derive from its charging twelve per cent interest on its actual capital, without issuing notes, except the greater conveniency of a paper over a metallic medium.[2] ... There is no more reason why a man, or a body of men, should be permitted to demand of the public, interest for their reputation of being rich, than there would be in permitting a man to demand interest for the reputation of being wise, or learned, or brave.[3]

Several of the later writers chose to regard bank notes issued in excess of reserves as a loan made by the community to the bank. Thus one wrote: "Every dollar of paper carried by the people represents a loan to some bank, varying in amount according to the ratio on which that bill is issued. Thus if a bank circulates two dollars of paper to one of specie [in its reserve], every individual who receives that two dollars indirectly lends to the bank a credit of one dollar, on which the bank earns its interest."[4] The bank thus receives "double interest."

These writers who used the quantity theory to controvert the belief that banks can create capital refuted one of the crudest fallacies of banking theory. But they in turn fell into error in attaching no further significance to an increase of the quantity of media of payment than a more or less proportionate depreciation

---

Sullivan (1744–1808) was the member of an eminent family and led a distinguished life in Boston as lawyer, magistrate, statesman, and scholar.

[1] Sullivan, *op. cit.*, p. 57.

[2] Raymond, *Elements of Political Economy* (1823), ii, 145. Like statements may be found in Davies, *Bank Torpedo* (1810), p. 18; Fisk, *Banking Bubble Burst* (1837), p. 40; Gouge, *Short History of Paper Money*, etc. (1833), pp. 68, 69.

[3] Raymond, *op. cit.*, ii, 144.

[4] Thomas B. Hall, *Gold and the Currency* (1855), p. 15; L. McKnight, "Free Banking," *De Bow's Review* (June, 1852), xii, 611; also xiv, 156; Hooper, *Specie Currency* (1855), p. 3; A. P. Peabody, *North American Review* (1858), lxxxvi, 178.

of the value of each unit. Many of them, with that inconsistency which often characterizes the development of economic theories, made suggestions which, had they been followed through, would have resulted in a complete revision of their views.

With few exceptions, those who denied the possibility of creating capital, or of rendering the media of payment more abundant, by the issue of bank notes, recognized only two major advantages to be gained from banking. The first was displacement of costly forms of currency through the substitution of relatively inexpensive types; the second was that gained through what we may term the utilization of idle surpluses of cash. In the latter view banks were regarded as mere intermediaries between borrowers and lenders.

The two notions were not mutually consistent. If banks, by temporarily inflating the currency, crowd specie out of circulation to be exported in exchange for other forms of capital, they cannot be regarded as mere lenders of what they themselves borrow. To consider them such is to confuse the matter of the aggregate purchasing power of the existing media of payment with the distribution of that purchasing power. It is true, broadly speaking, that inflation of the media of payment by banks ultimately results in restoring the aggregate purchasing power of the media to its former level, through the depreciation of each unit and the exportation of gold from bank reserves, making contraction necessary.[1] But inflation takes the form of granting the borrowers of the banks a larger fraction of the total quantity of monetary units than they had before, thus giving them command of a greater proportion of the community's wealth. This is effected by nibbling a fraction of the purchasing power of every preëxisting unit of media of payment, and placing it at the disposal of those who receive the newly added units.[2] And unless it can be shown that, in the restoration of the purchasing power of the sum

---

[1] The subtleties of the quantity theory, and the qualification that the issue of bank credit raises the normal level of quantity of circulating medium for each country, need not concern us here.

[2] It is not supposed, of course, that the preëxisting units of media of payment can be nicely distinguished, in the physical sense, from the new ones. But the necessity of differentiating, in the abstract, elements that are mechanically indistinguishable, is a familiar one in economic reasoning.

total of media of payment to the level indicated by international conditions, those who were thus favored finally relinquish, by yielding them up for exportation, the monetary units they have acquired, the old distribution of purchasing power is not restored. Nor, of course, is it in fact restored. Without pursuing the subject into too treacherous realms of abstraction, we may safely say that it is the community at large, as consumer of the imported articles (or, perhaps, of the products of imported capital goods), which yields a claim upon the nation's goods, by purchasing some foreign goods instead.[1]

Thus banks do more than simply transfer to their borrowers the "claim checks" upon the community's wealth of which depositors do not for the moment care to make use. The theory that such transfers exhaust the significance of their lending operations is illogical in yet another respect. It resorts to the quantity theory to prove that any attempt on the part of banks to lend more monetary units than they have actually received from depositors and shareholders, can result but in depreciation of the monetary standard. Yet precisely the same line of reasoning would indicate that no advantage is gained from the service of banks in intervening between borrowers and lenders to prevent the spare cash of the latter from lying idle. Exception must be made, of course, of the benefit derived from the facts that media of payment are costly and that more effective use of the supply already in existence renders a smaller quantity of them necessary. But most of the writers had in mind, not the economy of money, but its more constant and effective use. From this point of view, adding to the money in active circulation those funds which, but for banking, would lie idle, is essentially the same in its influence as increasing the currency through bank-note expansion. With reference to the activities of banks as intermediaries between borrowers and lenders, media of payment were commonly regarded as real capital in a sense in which the same writers did not so regard them when referring to the increase of their quantity through the expansion of bank credit.[2]

[1] For some further discussion, see Chapter X.
[2] John R. Hurd stated that one of the evils resulting from the depreciation of bank notes that are distant from their place of issue is that they are frequently still

While we are indebted, then, to those who called a halt to the discreditable notion that expansion of the circulating medium through the issue of bank notes implies a direct creation of capital, we must hold that they did not fully dispose of the matter by saying that a mere depreciation of the monetary standard is involved. That not a few who held this view seem to have seen, though dimly, a little further, has already been indicated. Thus Condy Raguet maintained most staunchly that banks can but lend the money which their stockholders and depositors could, with somewhat greater trouble, lend directly, and that credit expansion on the part of banks has no significance other than the depreciation of the monetary standard. Yet he opened the way to a more satisfactory analysis of bank credit when he suggested that a bank note might be considered as "a draft in favor of the borrower, given by a bank upon the public at large, to deliver him a certain amount of capital of any description he may want."[1] A rather important qualification, this, of his statement on a later page of the same work that "nothing but capital, that is, something possessing an intrinsic value [such as metallic money], can possibly be the means of setting industry in motion."[2]

So severe a critic of banking as was Gouge in his earlier writings[3] contended at one moment that banks can but lend what they have received, and at the next moment explained that the expansion of bank credit gives the borrowers a larger purchasing power, forcing prices upward through keener competitive bidding. Industry and speculation are stimulated, and business prosperity prevails. "So far it has the same effect as an increase of *real money* — as an increase of real wealth"; and nothing could be finer, in Gouge's opinion, if prices could only continue to rise in-

accepted at par in trade when local banks receive them only at a discount. Hence, small surpluses of them will be kept at home, representing so much *idle capital*, instead of being deposited in banks to seek active employment. *A National Bank or No Bank* (1842), p. 27.

[1] Raguet, *Currency and Banking* (1839), p. 96. Cp. *The Examiner and Journal of Political Economy*, ii, 339.

[2] Raguet, *op. cit.*, p. 124.

[3] Gouge was one of the most thorough students of our early banking and also one of its keenest and most influential critics. In later life he modified to some extent his antipathy toward banks.

definitely.[1] But in due time all prices rise to conform to the new quantity of media of payment, and money becomes no more abundant than it had been originally. It is only during the period in which the volume of bank notes is expanding, he concluded, that the community gains, and the benefit is finally lost in the inevitable reaction.[2] Yet he has admitted enough to damage materially his own assertion that banks can but advance what they have in turn received from others. And many shared this inconsistency with him.

I turn now to a writer who avoided the absurd dogma that expansion of bank credit is a direct creation of capital, and yet took a conscious stand against the doctrine that a bank is but the go-between for borrowers and lenders. Robert Hare was a chemist of Philadelphia whose scientific investigations gained him an honorary degree of Doctor of Medicine, first from Yale in 1806 and then from Harvard a decade later. From 1818 to 1847 he occupied the chair of chemistry at the University of Pennsylvania. He found time, amid scholarly researches in his own subject, to write several articles and pamphlets of merit on currency problems, and had already interested himself in finance in 1810. It is his *Brief View of the Policy and Reosurces of the United States* of that date which we have now to examine.[3]

Credit, said Hare, must not be regarded as merely subsidiary to specie, in the place of which it occasionally serves as a representative. It is rather to be said, that "credit constitutes an original, and in some respects a peculiarly beneficial medium of interchange in trade." It frequently enables those who can utilize certain things most advantageously to gain possession of them.

[1] Elsewhere Gouge recognized, as did many of his contemporaries, the hardships of maladjustments in incomes that attend a rising price level.
[2] Gouge, *Short History of Paper Money and Banking in the United States* (1833) p. 24.
[3] This work was published anonymously, but its authorship was acknowledged in the preface of a later one, *Proofs that Credit as Money . . . is Preferable to Coin* (1834). Besides these pamphlets, Hare wrote several other essays on money and banking during the rest of his life. (See the *Bibliography* of this study.) His total contributions to the subject were not great in volume, but they include many significant points.

This renders a given quantity of land, labor, and capital, more effective, "hence credit under all its productive forms, should be comprised in any estimate of wealth." [1]

Credit is in certain respects to be preferred to money as a medium of payment. The mechanic with one hundred dollars in cash can live without working, so long as his money lasts. On the other hand, the mechanic who can command credit to the extent of a hundred dollars "has nearly the same capacity to earn money, as the other; but his privilege will not sustain him in idleness, or dissipation. It can only be of use to him, through the medium of his industry," unless he be dishonest and does not contemplate repayment.[2] Honesty, skill, and industry are the conditions of high credit. The presumption that productive goods will be put to good use is greater, therefore, when they are in the control of one who has secured his command of them through credit, than when they are placed at the disposal of another who has gained his purchasing power, let us say, through inheritance.[3]

But individuals with loanable funds are not likely to know in whom to repose their confidence. "Hence, to give a more general efficiency to the credit of individuals, banking institutions are established; which by the notoriety of their wealth and punctuality, obtain universal credit; and by their extensive means of information, are enabled duly to estimate the degree of confidence to which traders may be entitled." [4]

To be sure, evidences of credit cannot be added to the nation's aggregate capital, since an offsetting debit exists in every case. But, while it is true that "the nominal aggregate of the commercial capital is not increased, the efficiency of the whole, and consequently the real value is increased." Existence of the possibility of borrowing the purchasing power that one can profitably employ enhances the wealth of a country over what it would otherwise be, "although the quantity of substantial capital, and the field of profitable employment be equally great." [5]

---

[1] Hare, *Brief View of the Policy and Resources of the United States* (1810), pp. 51–54.
[2] *Ibid.*, p. 55.
[3] *Ibid.*, pp. 58, 59.
[4] *Ibid.*, p. 60.
[5] *Ibid.*, pp. 67, 68.

Here is recognition of the service of banks in advantageously distributing the purchasing power of a country, free of the fallacy of regarding bank notes as substantial capital.[1] Nor are banks treated as mere intermediaries.

In 1834, Hare virtually republished his early pamphlet under the title, *Proofs that Credit as Money . . . is to a Great Extent Preferable to Coin.* In the preface of this later work, he offered an explanation of the failure of his novel line of analysis to have greater influence upon other writers. He believed that "the sentiments with which the opinions in question were originally associated [public borrowing to build a large navy], were too independent, to be relished by either of the prevailing parties; and hence, although approved by some distinguished men, they had only a limited circulation." Yet this reiteration of his earlier views on banks and credit, divorced from all questions of navy and public policy, seems to have received no greater attention.

Hare again urged his doctrines in 1852, in an article devoted to the specific purpose of refuting the opinion of Gouge, typical of the period, that "Banks do not increase the amount of loanable capital in a country," and that, "All that banking can do is to take the loanable capital out of the hands of its owners and place it in the hands of irresponsible corporations."[2] Hare thought that Gouge neglected to observe that "the establishment of a bank *creates a credit* which otherwise would not exist; and that the bank credit thus created, in the form of notes and bookcredits transferable by checks, is in utility superior to hard money."[3] No mere passing on of the money received from stockholders and depositors is involved.

[1] Hare is less sound in his views with reference to government certificates of indebtedness. This results partly from his object — to induce the government to borrow in order to build a large navy. *Op. cit.*, pp. 74-83.
[2] Hare, "Do Banks Increase Loanable Capital?" *Hunt's Merchants' Magazine* (June, 1852), xxvi, 702. The quoted words are those of Gouge, *Short History of Paper Money and Banking in the United States* (1833), p. 45.
[3] *Op. cit.*, p. 703.

In 1854 a contributor to *Hunt's Merchants' Magazine* dealt with Hare's thesis, although he did not refer to Hare. "Now we may admit," he argued, after explaining how bank inflation redistributes purchasing power, "that under the excitement of extended paper issues, many speculative projects have been commenced, and that,

The view that banks are limited in their operations to the lending of money received from stockholders and depositors, is by no means one of mere antiquarian interest. We read in a leading dictionary of political economy:

> The business of banking, generally speaking, consists in taking money on deposit, and also, in issuing notes and drafts, by which the transfer of loanable capital is facilitated. The funds thus obtained, together with those supplied by the capitals of the banks themselves, are employed in making advances. [Thus capital is] transferred from those persons by whom, and from those places where it is not required for active use, to those requiring it.[1]

And in a more recent book [2] we read:

> In a progressive community the steadily growing demands for capital must be met by a continued saving. Fresh savings are placed daily at the disposal of those having fresh capital requirements. In this the banks only act as intermediaries. They can increase their loans only in proportion to the amount of fresh savings that are available. Lending on the part of the banks, however, is done in bank currency, to the creation of which there are no absolutely definite limits.

The criterion for a sound bank policy, the author adds, is that the quantity of bank currency should increase only as the needs of the country for such currency increase.

> The banks, however, must constantly see to it that the quantity of bank currency is never unduly increased — *i. e.*, that bank currency is not arbitrarily created merely to meet capital requirements which cannot be met with available savings. . . . A complete daily adjustment between demands for capital and fresh savings is scarcely possible. It is therefore of advantage

---

even when the state of collapse has arrived, the *whole* of the benefits have not been lost to the public; but it is probably no exaggeration to say, that in all cases, *twice* as much has been lost as has been gained; in addition to the evil and injustice of its being a previous tax upon the community, for the benefit of a few. In this sense, then, the banks encourage trade. They issue paper promises, and circulate them as money, and by so doing increase prices, and therefore the assumed amount of capital which they lend to the grasping or enterprising, is taken out of the pockets of the prudent and honest for the benefit of the lender [borrower?]; and becomes real capital to him, beyond the loss that may accrue from the revulsion that takes place; and under ordinary circumstances was certain to follow." Richard Sulley, "Currency and Banking," *Hunt's Merchants' Magazine* (1854), xxxi, 193.

[1] Palgrave, *Dictionary of Political Economy*, i, 91, 92. Cp. Labor's *Cyclopedia of Political Science*, i, 229, 238, and Cannan, "The Meaning of Bank Deposits," *Economica* (Jan., 1921), No. I, pp. 28–36.

[2] Gustav Cassel, *Money and Foreign Exchange after 1914* (New York, 1922). The quotations are all from pp. 102–104.

if the issue of bank currency is given a certain elasticity, so that demands for capital may be met without unnecessary disturbance. This elasticity, however, must not be taken advantage of to meet, during prolonged periods, demands for capital on a higher scale than the amount of savings effected within the same period permits.

Finally, the author summarizes his thesis by exhorting central banks so to regulate their discount rates that *"demands for capital must, by means of the rates of interest of the banks, be limited to the amounts of funds supplied by current saving, so that no artificial purchasing power, with its accompanying rise in prices, will be created."*

CHAPTER IX

BANKS DIRECT CAPITAL INTO UNDESIRABLE CHANNELS

Banks of no assistance to farmers. — Their loans encourage speculation primarily. — Possibilities of discrimination in making loans.

IN regarding banks as reservoirs into which idle surpluses of cash flow, to be distributed to those who are in a position to employ them profitably, it was usually implied, if not explicitly stated, that the distribution was such as to benefit the community. If banks were to be regarded as lending more than the funds they receive from stockholders and depositors, the wisdom, or lack of wisdom, with which their loans were made, became correspondingly more important. Not all were ready to grant their confidence in the judgment of the banker.

The late eighteenth-century critics found fault not so much with the positive aspect of bank loans, as with the type of borrowing that was denied. Thus, in the discussion of the Bank of North America, a criticism that received no little attention — and it has a familiar ring to-day — was the charge that banks are prejudicial to the farmer, partly because their scenes of operation must necessarily be in the city, and partly because their loans, it was already recognized, are too short for agricultural purposes. The pampering effect of colonial land banks and land-bank theory may well have lent intensity to this plaint. It was accompanied at times by a Physiocratic reverence for agriculture which Ricardian economics has not completely dispelled even to this day.

The opponents of the Bank of North America insisted that the attractive dividends which banks offered tended to lead to their usurping all investable funds, to the exclusion of all classes of loans other than those made by the banks themselves. This was held to affect the farmer, and landowners in general, most adversely.[1] Robert Morris, Pelatiah Webster, and Thomas Paine

---

[1] M. Carey, *Debates and Proceedings* (1786), p. 25; Barton, *True Interest of the United States* (1786), reprinted in the *American Museum*, ii, 33. James Sullivan

answered this criticism by urging that banks do aid the farmer, indirectly to be sure, by making advances to the merchants to whom he sells his products, thus giving him a broader and readier market.[1]

Soon the indiscretion with which bankers in the earlier decades permitted themselves to make loans of long duration gave farmers another cause for complaint. A committee of the New York legislature, in discussing banks in 1818, pictured "the ruin they have brought on an immense number of the most wealthy farmers, and they and their families suddenly hurled from wealth and independence into the abyss of ruin and despair."[2] Niles repeatedly warned the husbandman against the alluring pitfalls of accommodation loans and easy renewals, and insisted that "agriculturalists should avoid banks as they would scorpions."[3]

The attack upon banks did not long content itself with the assertion that they fail to benefit the farmer; their loans to merchants were soon held to be in themselves baneful. Merchants are useful while supplying a nation's wants, one pamphleteer maintained, but "dangerous whilst speculating indiscriminately on foes and friends for the acquisition of wealth, and aspiring to exclusive privileges and prerogatives." If banks do enable merchants to extend commerce, asserted one critic, it would be better to bestow the capital on agriculture and manufactures, "which alone create the real fund for an extension of commerce."[4] Bank loans are for too short periods, this writer believed, to be adapted to any other use than speculation; indeed they convert merchants from an honorable group of men, into "a set of contemptible gamblers." None but "speculating rogueries" could yield

proposed that the profit of banking be reduced so that some money would remain for loans to farmers by individuals. *Path to Riches* (1794), p. 67.

[1] Morris, in Carey's *Debates and Proceedings* (1786), pp. 93, 94; Webster, Essay on Credit (1786), in *Political Essays*, p. 443; Paine, "Dissertations on Government" (1786), *Writings*, ii, 168.

[2] See Gouge, *Short History of Paper Money and Banking in the United States* (1833), p. 5.

[3] *Niles' Register* (1829), xxxv, 346. Cp. Crawford, Report on the Currency (1820), in *American State Papers, Finance*, iii, 498.

[4] Anon., *Enquiry into the ... Tendency of Public Measures* (1794), p. 78.

such returns as to permit borrowing money at the rates that went to make up the high dividends that banks were paying.[1]

That bank loans are peculiarly adapted to the needs of the speculator was the opinion of many. In 1803 the governor and council of Vermont vetoed the grant of two bank charters by the legislature on the ground that such institutions, "by facilitating enterprises both hazardous and unjustifiable, are natural sources of all that class of vices which arise from the gambling system, and which cannot fail to act as sure and fatal, though slow poisons, to the republic in which they exist."[2] A contributor to *Niles' Weekly Register* wrote that "the facility of borrowing money of the banks, has multiplied the race of merchants to such an extent that the business is not worth following," and many merchants have become "brokers, shavers, speculators — in other words, blood-suckers of the community."[3] Commerce, manufacture, and agriculture, Raymond believed, do not yield such profits as to warrant their pursuit with money borrowed at the banks. "Speculation is the only business that can be followed with money loaned of banks, and hence we always find that speculation is most rife, where banks are the most abundant."[4] "Those who maintain that banks enrich a community, are bound to prove that speculation creates wealth," was the verdict of a committee of citizens of Philadelphia (including Raguet and Gouge in its membership) that was appointed in 1829 to report on the growing menace of banking.[5] And twenty-five years later Samuel Hooper wrote that the "effect of too much bank capital upon the industry of the country is injurious, by encouraging the investment of money in temporary loans for purposes of speculation, instead of inducing permanent and productive investments."[6] Banks put the spare cash of individuals to work, but too frequently it is speculative work.

[1] Anon., pp. 81, 82. [2] Knox, *History of Banking*, p. 345.
[3] "The Paper System," *Niles' Register* (May 2, 1818), xiv, 154, 155. See also, *ibid.* xv, 217.
[4] Raymond, *Elements of Political Economy* (1823), ii, 146, 147.
[5] Report of the committee appointed by a Meeting of Citizens (March 25, 1829), *Free Trade Advocate*, i, 315.
[6] Hooper, *Currency or Money* (1855), p. 92.

Speculation was but little understood at the time, and the boundary line between unwholesome speculation in commodities and their normal marketing was a perplexing one. There are limits within which speculation is doubtless legitimate and honorable, Colwell thought at the close of our period, but it is too tempting a field not to be occupied by many "actuated by fraud, by a greedy spirit, by rashness, by the spirit of competition, and by sheer infatuation." "The tendency of speculation," he added, less acceptably, "is undoubtedly to widen the range of fluctuations, not only in the prices of the articles operated upon, but also of many others." Prices may be enhanced "for many years."[1] Speculation was usually taken to imply little more than an enlarged scale of activity such as attended periods of prosperity and rising prices.[2]

Bank loans were criticized not only on the basis of objections to the classes of undertakings for which they were most readily available, but also with reference to the selection of individual borrowers. Those who regarded banks as the go-between of borrower and lender, usually explained that they remedy the defect that individuals with surplus cash to lend would not ordinarily know whom to trust. Not all were willing to concede the banks greater ability in determining this. Hamilton, who overlooked but few of the current objections and arguments in favor of banks, took the orthodox position that they would seek, in their own interests, to lend to those who would use the funds prudently and well; and that bankers were best able to determine who had the

[1] Colwell, *Ways and Means of Payment* (1859), pp. 532, 533.
[2] Antipathy toward speculation is, of course, reflected in the Federal Reserve Act, with its discrimination against the collateral call loan and its purpose to lessen the financial dominance of New York. To some extent this was intensified by the undoubted financial evils associated with the call-loan market as it developed under the peculiar circumstances of the National Banking system. The local banks of France appeal to prejudice against speculation in their attempt to cope with the encroachments of the great credit companies. Patronage of the local institutions is urged in order to avoid centralization of capital in Paris for use in encouraging speculation rather than commerce and industry. (See Liesse, *Evolution of Credit and Banks in France*, p. 220.) The early writers had commodity speculation in mind, however; the present-day aversion is rather to stock speculation.

necessary qualities.[1] Quite a different view was taken by the committee on banking of the Pennsylvania Senate in 1821. Having observed that banks can but lend what they receive from stockholders and depositors, the committee declared that it would be better were the latter to lend their money directly. Were it not for the intervention of banks, the people's capital would naturally find its way into the most profitable channels. Now, banks either merely assist what would be done even if they were not in existence, or they divert capital from its most productive employment. The committee believed the latter to be more probable.[2] That the views of its chairman, Condy Raguet, were largely adopted in the report in this respect, as in most others, is shown by Raguet's later writings, in which he held that banks, through their loans, place the unskilled and the reckless on a par in purchasing power with the skilled and cautious.[3]

Gouge held the same opinion. "All Banking can do, is, to take this loanable capital out of the hands of its owners, and place it under the control of irresponsible corporations," the directors of which have little regard for any but their own personal interests and those of their favorites. "Great facilities are thereby afforded to many men for borrowing, to whom no man ought to lend. They are led by Bank loans to engage in business for which they are not fitted by either nature or education."[4] Combined with the notion of poor judgment in lending, we have here the charge of partiality. This criticism of banks was made from the

[1] Hamilton, Report on a National Bank (1790), *American State Papers, Finance*, i, 69, 70.

[2] The report is to be found in the *Examiner and Journal of Political Economy* for 1835, ii, 337–343. Direct loans by the owners of the capital were also favored because they would permit of long loans on personal security, suitable to the financing of permanent enterprises.

[3] Raguet, "Principles of Banking," *Free Trade Advocate* (1829), ii, 7. Adam Smith thought that "a bank which lends money, perhaps, to five hundred different people, the greater part of whom the directors can know very little about, is not likely to be more judicious in the choice of its debtors, than a private person who lends out his money among a few persons whom he knows, and in whose sober and frugal conduct he thinks he has good reason to confide." (*Wealth of Nations*, book II, chap. 2, vol. i, p. 138.)

[4] Gouge, *Short History of Paper Money*, etc. (1833), pp. 36, 37, 45.

first, and, for good reason, was a persistent one. It has to do, however, with banking practice, rather than banking theory.[1]

[1] A classic example was that of the Farmers' Exchange Bank, of Gloucester, Rhode Island, which failed in 1809 with $86.50 in specie in its vaults, after having loaned $845,771 on the basis of $100,000 capital, upon unendorsed notes reading: "I, Andrew Dexter, Junr., do promise the President, Directors, and Co. of the Farmers' Exchange Bank, to pay them, or order, —— dollars, in ... years, from this date, with interest at two per cent. per annum; it being, however, understood that the said Dexter shall not be called upon to make payment *until he thinks proper*, he being the principal Stockholder and best knowing when it will be proper to pay the same." Davies, *Bank Torpedo* (1810), p. 57.

CHAPTER X

SUMMARY OF THE VIEWS ON THE NATURE AND UTILITY OF BANKS

The dual rôle of commercial banking. — The utility of banks as source of a form of currency. — The utility of banks as distributors of loanable funds.

WHETHER consciously or otherwise, banks were regarded in their dual rôle: first, as the institutions that provide the community with a large part of its media of payment; secondly, as establishments for the lending of purchasing power. When it was asserted that banks provide an inexpensive currency, that they increase capital in the guise of circulating media, or that they lend elasticity, be it pernicious or desirable, to the media of payment, it was their rôle as a source of currency that was being primarily referred to. But when they were being considered as intermediaries between borrowers and lenders, or as lenders, in addition, of a peculiarly significant credit of their own, it was their function in directing the resources of the country that was being contemplated. Not, of course, that these two aspects of banking permit of separation, except in the abstract and with due consciousness of the limitations of such treatment. It is in placing purchasing power in the hands of this or that entrepreneur that banking brings media of payment into existence. Unfortunately, many (I think we may say the great majority) of the writers of the early nineteenth century, did, to a large degree, regard these two functions of banking separately; and in this mode of treatment lay the source of a number of their errors.

The first notable experience of Western civilization with paper money began in 1690, with the emission of bills of credit by the colony of Massachusetts Bay. The problem at once arose of determining the economic significance of an increase in the quantity of media of payment, whether through the issue of government paper, or of bank notes. Not a few believed that a net addition to existing capital was the result. To this was opposed the quantity theory, and among our own colonial writers appeared a number of sound thinkers, like Douglass, who urged that an increase in the quantity of units of currency but depreciates each unit, so that the enlarged circulation does no more work, and does it no more effectively than the smaller supply that previously obtained. The appearance of the modern type of bank note, issued in excess of reserves and yet convertible into specie on demand, gave the earlier view renewed popularity; but after 1825 the naïve doctrine, to which even Hamilton had fallen victim, that bank-note inflation signifies added capital, was quite thoroughly discountenanced.

Adam Smith, reasoning on the assumption that a given quantity of media of payment is necessary to effect the exchanges of each country, had held that bank notes do augment the nation's capital, in the sense that they displace a like amount of the precious metals from circulation, all of which, save what must be kept as reserves against the notes, is exported in exchange for other forms of wealth, chiefly productive capital. That banks secure this advantage, became, with some qualifications, quite generally accepted at about the time that the cruder doctrine confusing inflation and the creation of capital began to be abandoned. Even this more moderate view was rejected, however, by a relatively small group who insisted that the community exporting specie receives no compensation, thus recurring to something like the earlier simple opinion that the use of bank notes is harmful in that it causes the expulsion of gold and silver. Smith's thesis was opposed also by those who asserted that bank notes are even more costly than metallic money, since many large establishments are needed to issue them. In its least tenable form this objection emphasized the cost in the form of interest paid for the loans through which the notes are put into circulation. It was frequently complained, furthermore, that this cost is increased by the fact that banks make loans in excess of the amount of money they actually possess, thus imposing a larger interest charge upon the community, while depreciation of the monetary standard prevents the enlarged circulation from doing any additional work.[1]

That banks furnish an inexpensive substitute for metallic currency, as explained by Smith, was, however, one of the major advantages most frequently ascribed to them after 1825. But Smith's doctrine was based on the belief that any tendency of bank notes to become excessive in quantity would immediately bring about a readjusting specie outflow. Not all were ready to concede this. Many thought that serious price disturbances took place before the redundant currency was drained off. Banks thus provided an inexpensive currency, but one that fluctuated in value.

Smith had dealt with this contention himself, and had maintained that convertibility precludes the possibility of a bank-note currency becoming excessive. This view, adopted by the Bullionists of England, received rather little support in America. Convertibility, it was commonly thought, does indeed prevent a permanent excess of bank notes, but not a temporary one. And this excess, even though short-lived, may be very considerable. A number of writers observed that, when the corrective export of specie occurs, the banks, in order to sustain their reserve ratio, must contract their note issue by several times the amount of the loss of specie, thus multiplying the depressing effect of a gold outflow.

Another theory, likewise transplanted from England, was that bank notes cannot be overissued because they are emitted only in response to the demands of trade. So sweeping a thesis had little support; but the more modest claim that bank notes do not admit of overissue if emitted only against real commercial paper (as distinguished from accommodation bills) was rather widely accepted. A few writers recognized, however, that the needs of trade, as indicated by the volume of bills of exchange offered for discount, may themselves become unhealthily inflated as the result of a rising price level.

The votaries of the theory that the quantity of bank notes is

[1] This reasoning involved the fallacy of overlooking the fact that the interest itself is paid in the depreciated currency.

automatically regulated by the requirements of business generally meant thereby that the currency is thus made to vary in amount exactly as it would were it entirely metallic.[1] There were a few, however, who saw that the ebb and flow of modern commerce call for a more elastic currency. In this respect, they held, a mixed currency of bank notes and specie is better than one composed of specie alone. Yet the verdict of an overwhelming majority was that the ideal norm is that of a metallic currency, and that neither their convertibility, nor the manner in which they are issued, prevents a currency of which bank notes compose a part from deviating from this standard. In part the prevalence of this view may be attributed to the fact that accommodation loans figured largely in American banking practice, and in part to the obstacles in the way of the prompt redemption of bank notes. Even Gallatin, a sane and friendly critic of banking, was inclined to think that the use of bank notes, because of their fluctuating character, is attended by a net disadvantage.

On the currency side, then, banking was credited by most of the writers with offering an economical substitute for coins of the precious metals, and to this advantage a half-dozen writers added that of introducing a desirable elasticity into the media of payment. Against this was placed the disadvantage of a fluctuating monetary standard.

With respect to those aspects of banking that have to do with the provision of general media of payment, the most important and most wholesome influence was exerted by the doctrine that bank-note inflation merely raises prices. With respect to banking as the source of loans to business men, the influence of the quantity theory was to hamper the development of sound principles. Even to the end of the period but few freed themselves from the notion, illogically derived from the quantity theory, that banks can lend to their customers only so much effective purchasing

[1] The doctrine that a currency composed of both paper and specie should at all times correspond in quantity to one wholly metallic is often denominated the currency principle. (*E. g.*, see Palgrave's *Dictionary*, i, 472.) But not all the disciples of the banking principle would have dissented; the two schools differed mainly in their opinion as to the need of regulation to achieve the desired end.

power as they receive from stockholders and depositors. If they lend any more monetary units than they have thus taken in, they are returning into circulation more than they withdrew from it, and the sole result (if we neglect the confusion attending the transition) is a depreciation of each unit, which restores the purchasing power of the aggregate of media of payment to its former level. Time after time it was reiterated that the only important advantages which banking confers are those of providing a substitute for costly gold and silver currency, and of gathering idle surpluses of cash and placing them at the disposal of those who can give them active employment. That the reasoning underlying each of these two views is inconsistent with that of the other has already been suggested.[1]

In reasoning, on the basis of the quantity theory, that banks cannot lend more than they have received from depositors,[2] the early writers passed incautiously from the way in which banks make loans to individuals to the way in which they provide a general circulating medium. They failed to give adequate attention to the mechanism through which media of payment are furnished. They assumed that the added media of payment brought into existence when the bank expands its loans are diffused throughout the channels of circulation, but virtually neg-

[1] See Chapter VIII. The alleged advantages and disadvantages of banking might conveniently be divided into two groups according to whether they deal with the influence of banks upon prices, or with their relation to the effective supply of capital in the country. The three major views on the effect of banks upon prices have already been given; namely, that bank currency causes price fluctuations; that either convertibility or the manner in which they are issued prevents bank notes from deviating from the norm of a metallic currency; and, thirdly, that bank notes improve upon a purely metallic medium of payment by introducing a desirable type of elasticity. The ways in which banks were said to increase the effective supply of capital in a country were also three in number. First came the naïve notion that confuses an increase in the amount of media of payment with that of wealth itself. This was superseded by the doctrine that banks provide an inexpensive substitute for costly currency of gold and silver, thereby, to all intents and purposes, increasing the nation's wealth to a like extent. And, finally, banks were said to gather surpluses of capital, temporarily idle in the hands of their owners, and place them at the disposition of those who can employ them productively.

[2] For simplicity in exposition we may here regard stockholders as permanent depositors.

lected the redistribution of purchasing power attending the process of diffusion.

In some measure, probably, the confusion may have been incidental to the fact that banking theory emerged out of the doctrines built upon government coins and government paper money. If a government finances its needs by the simple resort to the printing press, the added monetary units enter the general circulation and raise prices without a great and direct increase in the relative purchasing power of any particular individuals.[1] At least there is no such direct shifting of purchasing power as when banks add to the media of payment by lending. In this latter process, certain individuals receive claims upon the community's wealth which are added to the preëxisting claims. This was commonly recognized. But the result, it was argued, is that each claim must be assigned a smaller segment of the unchanged amount of national wealth, so that there might just as well have been fewer claim checks, each more highly honored. The error in this objection lies in its overlooking the fact that the borrowers of the banks now hold a larger *proportion* of the total number of checks than they did before. The aggregate purchasing power of the whole body of claimants may be unchanged, but its distribution among the several members of that body has been altered.[2]

[1] Of course, changes in relative purchasing power do result indirectly; *e. g.*, there is the familiar maladjustment of incomes that accompanies alterations in the price level. Moreover, the seductive ease with which the printing press pays for public expenditures may cause certain lines of industry to prosper more than they otherwise would.

[2] Even to this day it is probably not an unjust criticism of many textbooks on banking to say that they hail the economical *creation* of media of payment as one of the great advantages of commercial banking and leave it to the student to wrestle with the apparent paradox that he is elsewhere insistently warned that multiplication of the media of payment signifies merely depreciation of the standard. With reference to our own thesis that a measure of involuntary saving on the part of the community is involved, through redistribution of purchasing power favoring producers at the expense of consumers, it is, of course, to be observed that such benefits accrue only when bank expansion is properly limited. Briefly, the productive capacity of a country is relatively inelastic, so that indiscreet expansion of bank loans tends to be absorbed to an increasing degree by higher prices rather than by enlarged production. Stimulus is then being given less to productive industry and trade than to unwholesome speculation. Furthermore, ill-advised bank expansion tends to bring about such abrupt gold movements, in consequence of rising prices,

Granting that those who thought that banks can, for a considerable period at least, raise prices by inflating the currency, were inconsistent when they denied banks the ability to lend more effective purchasing power than they received from depositors, is the same to be said of those who held that the export of specie promptly checks the tendency of bank notes to alter the volume of media of payment and prices? Their self-contradiction was no less real, if, perhaps, a little less obvious. They conceded that banks, while they may not enlarge the currency, supplant a part of its metallic portion by their own issues. Now, unless the individuals who receive the bank notes simply hand over the specie that is displaced and exported, a readjustment of relative purchasing power has occurred. But, obviously, these individuals do nothing of the sort. The specie that is exported represents the relinquishing of command over the nation's wealth, not by these individuals, but by the community at large, as ultimate consumer of the foreign products that are accepted, in the stead of domestic products, by virtue of the price changes resulting from the inflation of the currency through the issue of bank notes. Gold movements may restore the preëxisting number of units of media of payment, but the banks' borrowers now hold a larger proportion of them.

Again, if all the leading countries in the world were to enlarge their media of payment *pari passu*, practically no gold movements would follow. The laws governing the international distribution of currency would merely indicate a higher level for each country. A few writers discussed this case, and asserted that "no result of any moment would ensue, except an universal rise of prices." [1] In believing that banks would still serve but as intermediaries between borrowers and lenders, they made the same

that sudden contraction, perhaps precipitating numerous business failures, becomes necessary. Whatever benefits resulted from the preceding expansion are then liable to be offset. At best no nice quantitative determination of the influence of bank loans upon a country's wealth is possible. Our thesis probably has its clearest significance in explaining the advantages of having a well-regulated commercial banking system as compared with having none at all.

[1] Eleazar Lord, *Principles of Currency and Banking* (1829), p. 18. Cp. Raguet, *Currency and Banking* (1839), pp. 83, 84.

error as those who held a similar view while thinking that banks can exercise a considerable influence over the volume of currency and the level of prices.

With respect to the lending activities of banks, then, we notice first that there were very few who recognized that anything more was involved than the passing on of what had been received from depositors. The question next arose whether banks committed these funds to the custody of those who would use them to the best interests of the community. In general, the assumption that bank loans are wisely directed underlay the statement that banks bring idle surpluses into active employment. Some expressly stated that banks overcome the difficulty that those with spare cash frequently do not know who is worthy of a loan, and all who advanced this intermediary function of banking as one of its beneficial services implied that the country's capital was more advantageously used than it would have been in the absence of banks. But there were some, like Gouge and Raguet, who believed that bank loans were detrimental to society. Sometimes it was asserted that the short duration of the loans made them available chiefly for undesirable speculation; in other cases the judgment, if not the impartiality, of bank directors in passing upon prospective borrowers was questioned.

PART III

BANK NOTES AND BANK DEPOSITS

CHAPTER XI

THE NATURE OF BANK DEPOSITS

Early recognition that deposits constitute part of the currency. — Failure generally to realize that deposits may be created by the banks. — A few instances in which this was understood. — Conclusion.

IN reviewing the theories that prevailed before 1860 with respect to the nature and utility of banks, we have inquired merely whether it was believed that banks, in making loans with their notes, lent only what they had in turn received from shareholders and depositors; and whether it was thought that by the operations of banking any capital was created, prices disturbed, or specie driven from the country; but we have so far avoided raising the correlative question how far bank deposits were held to share these several characteristics with notes. We now turn to this other problem.[1]

Two questions arose here: are deposits to be regarded as a part of the currency? and are they ever created by the banks themselves? That demand deposits subject to withdrawal by check constitute a part of the currency on an equal footing with notes was apparently recognized by American writers somewhat in

[1] The practice of drawing checks upon demand deposits came in with the beginnings of banking in this country. In 1786 Pelatiah Webster commented upon it as so convenient that "it is almost universally adopted by people who keep their cash in our present bank" (the Bank of North America). See *Political Essays*, p. 434.

The volume of notes exceeded that of deposits in the aggregative balance statements for all the banks of the country until 1855, although in Massachusetts the total amount of deposits passed that of notes (not, to be sure, permanently) as early as 1806. (See *Report of the Comptroller of the Currency* (1876), pp. 95, 98, 99 and *passim*.) The relative sparseness of population, and, no doubt, the less complete development of the banking habit, told against the use of checks, with its implication of frequent visits to the banks. The greater attention accorded to notes can hardly be accounted for on the ground that deposits were as yet little used; the explanation seems to lie rather in a misapprehension of the nature of deposits, discussed in the text, and in the fact that the more spectacular evils of banking were connected with the function of note issue.

advance of their English contemporaries. Of the latter, James Pennington, in 1829, seems to have been the first to insist that deposits be given a coördinate importance with notes as a part of the currency.[1] The contrary view was still so widely accepted as late as 1844 as to be generally assumed in the arguments made in behalf of the Bank Charter Act of that year, which sought to eliminate fluctuations in the volume of the currency by rendering bank notes inelastic in quantity.[2]

In the United States, on the other hand, the doctrine that bank deposits must be reckoned a part of the currency appeared much earlier. We find it in Hamilton's *Report* of 1790 and in Hare's significant essay of 1810.[3] A committee of the Pennsylvania legislature, headed by Condy Raguet, incorporated in its report of 1821 the principle that "The right to draw a check upon a bank, *payable on demand*, is as much a part of the currency as a bank note." [4] In all his later works [5] Raguet insisted upon the inclusion of bank deposits in the currency. Gallatin, in his *Considerations* of 1831, wrote: "We can in no respect whatever perceive the slightest difference between the two: and we cannot,

---

[1] Silberling, *British Theories of Money and Credit, 1776–1848*, pp. 124, 310. (Unpublished Harvard thesis.) See Tooke, *Letter to Grenville* (1829), pp. 117–127.

[2] Peel's Act, and the currency principle upon which it is based, are often said to have been founded upon failure to appreciate the fact that bank deposits, no less than bank notes, function as currency. (Cp. Pierson, *Principles of Economics*, p. 457; Andreades, *History of the Bank of England*, p. 276; Palgrave's *Dictionary of Political Economy*, i, 473.) To a certain extent this is true. But the currency principle might logically have been advocated by one who recognized that bank deposits share equally with bank notes the functions of currency, but who believed, as did many American writers, that while bank notes may be *created* by the banks more or less at their own discretion, bank deposits represent sums of preëxisting media of payment placed in the bank by its patrons. In that case there would be no reason to regulate deposits so as to prevent their volume from fluctuating; while there would be reason to restrict note issues.

[3] Hamilton, Report on a National Bank (1780), *American State Papers, Finance*, i, 68; Hare, *Brief View of the Policy and Resources of the United States* (1810), p. 63.

[4] The report was printed in virtually all of Raguet's later publications, *e. g.*, *Examiner* (1835), p. 340. It seems to have been little more than an expression of Raguet's own views.

[5] *Financial Register* (1838), i, 406, ii, 208, 209; *Currency and Banking* (1839), pp. 183 ff.

therefore, but consider the aggregate amount of credits payable on demand, standing on the books of the several banks, as being part of the currency of the United States."[1]

H. C. Carey contended, with wearisome repetition, that bank deposits are, indeed, the troublesome part of the currency that banks issue. The quantity of bank notes in circulation, being dependent upon the wishes of the public, is relatively stable; it is the book credits of banks that work mischief with their wide variations in quantity.[2] And Carey criticized Peel's Act of 1844 for overlooking the major cause of price disturbances.[3]

There were many, on the other hand, who discussed fluctuations in prices, the necessity of keeping large reserves, regulation of banking, and like problems, with reference to bank notes only. In part this marked a failure to perceive that deposits are an element of the currency; in larger degree, it seems to have arisen from a misconception of the nature of bank deposits (whether they be included in the currency or not) — namely, from the tendency to regard them in all cases as credits for money actually brought to the bank.

In England the inclusion of such items as bills of exchange in the currency had been urged by some writers, and the merits of the contention received some consideration in this country. Usually the wide circulation of bills of exchange in Lancashire was cited, and the whole discussion was but a frank echo of the English one. Professor Dew thought that it was an error, in discussing the currency, to "lose sight of those other items, bills of exchange, private promissory notes, bonds, stock, etc., which do, in fact, perform, though sluggishly, the functions of a circulating medium." Their great volume more than offsets their sluggish

---

[1] Gallatin, *Considerations*, etc. (1831), p. 31. Gallatin had reached the same conclusion in 1809. See Report to the Senate (March 3, 1809), *American State Papers, Finance*, ii, 351.

[2] H. C. Carey, *Past, Present, and Future* (1848), pp. 187–204; *Principles of Social Science* (1858), ii, 392, 421; etc. Cp. *Bank Notes and Specie* (Anon., 1856), pp. 5, 10.

[3] H. C. Carey, *Past, Present, and Future*, p. 180; *Principles of Social Science*, ii, 393.

circulation.[1] Vethake thought similarly.[2] Gallatin, on the other hand, preferred to regard bills of exchange and promissory notes as substitutes for currency. In his opinion,

> the essential distinction is, that the bills of exchange are only a promise to pay in currency, and that the failure of the drawers, drawees, and indorsers, does not, in the slightest degree, affect the value of the currency itself, or impair that permanent standard of value by which the performance of all contracts is regulated.[3]

Gouge, after endorsing this view with respect to ledger accounts, bills of exchange, and promissory notes, added:

> An increase of these three kinds of commercial medium may have the same effect on prices as an increase of money. Where the spirit of speculation is excited, men, after having exhausted their cash means, strain their credit. Cash and credit are then competitors in the market, and raise prices on one another.[4]

Raguet, Tucker, and Carroll followed Gallatin.[5]

No less significant than the problem whether bank deposits should be classed as currency was that of determining whether they were in any measure created by the banks themselves. We have seen that the overwhelming majority of the writers conceived of the lending operations of banks as confined in essence to the advance of capital left with them by stockholders and depositors. That such a view would tend to be more readily accepted by those who regarded all deposits as representing money brought to the bank by its patrons is evident, but the two points are by no means the same. The one involved the problem of the ability of banks to create bank notes and deposits; the other involved the problem of the significance of such a creation, if its possibility be granted. Some of those who assigned to banks only an intermediary function believed also that international gold move-

[1] Thomas R. Dew, *Great Question of the Day* (1840), p. 6; and *Essay on the Interest of Money* (1834), p. 16.
[2] Vethake, *Principles of Political Economy* (1838), pp. 148, 149. See also, Middleton, *The Government and the Currency* (1850), pp. 88-91.
[3] Gallatin, *Considerations*, etc. (1831), p. 29.
[4] Gouge, *Short History of Paper Money*, etc. (1833), pp. 19, 20.
[5] Raguet, *Currency and Banking* (1839), pp. 173-177; Tucker, *Theory of Money and Banks* (1839), p. 142; Carroll, "The Banking and Credit Systems," *Hunt's Merchants' Magazine* (September, 1858), xxxix, 311.

ments prevent banks from raising the quantity of circulating medium, and illogically saw in this a basis for their former opinion; but those who held that banks can inflate the currency for a more or less lengthy period, restricted their lending operations no less frequently to mere intervention between borrowers and lenders, arguing that the advance of more monetary units than were received from depositors effected but a depreciation of the standard. In escaping the confusion of monetary capital with capital in its other forms, they fell into another error. This problem has been dealt with in an earlier chapter;[1] my present purpose is simply to indicate that it would be equally logical, or rather, no more illogical, to recognize that bank deposits originate in part in the process of lending, and yet to hold that in lending the bank performs but an intermediary function. For, whether in the shape of notes or deposits, inflation implies depreciation of the purchasing power of the unit and has the same bearing upon the potentialities of banking.

Despite the prevailing theory with respect to the limitations of the lending power of banks, the fact that bank notes are units of media of payment created by the banks themselves was, of course, universally recognized. Niles railed incessantly against the institutions with the privilege of "creating, out of nothing, two or three hundred millions of paper-money, which they were authorized to pass away, at the value of silver and gold, and which the people were virtually obliged to take."[2] Raymond, Raguet, Gouge, and innumerable lesser writers heaped unstinted condemnation upon the "order of rag barons" who lived upon the labor of others by putting forth their vile money that rested upon "an idea called credit."[3] That many thought effective checks obtained against the abuse of this power to manufacture media of payment is another matter. The important thing to notice is that, as long as those liabilities were stated in the form of bank notes, it was recognized, necessarily, that the banker, in discounting bills of exchange and promissory notes, *created* liabilities against himself that formed a part of the currency, and that in so

---

[1] See Chapter VIII.   [2] *Niles' Register* (1818), xiv, 197.
[3] Anon., *Enquiry into the . . . Tendency of Public Measures* (1794), p. 16.

doing he *created* media of payment. On the other hand, only a small minority saw that liabilities taking the form of deposit credits upon the books of the bank could similarly be creations of the banker. The failure to distinguish in bank statements between deposits originating in the process of discounting and those arising from the actual lodging of cash in the bank led the great majority of writers to conceive of all such liabilities as of the latter type.

That deposits were regarded as representing money left with the bank is shown by the practice of speaking of notes as based upon the deposits of the bank. "A bank," one early writer insisted, "should not emit a single note beyond the sum of specie in its possession. The profits of a bank should arise only from shares and deposits."[1] Like opinions were expressed from time to time throughout the entire period. The liabilities of the first Bank of the United States were limited by its charter to the amount of its capital and of "the moneys actually deposited in the bank for safe-keeping."[2] doubtless on the assumption that all deposits were of such origin. The charter of the second Bank of the United States contained a similar provision,[3] and Connecticut limited the note issue of its banks to fifty per cent of capital and deposits combined.[4]

It was a similar misconception of the nature of deposits that led many American writers, in common with the English disciples of the currency principle, to distinguish sharply between a bank that did but a deposit and discount business, and one that added also the function of note issue. "A Bank of Issue," Lord Overstone maintained, "is entrusted with the *creation* of the circulating medium. A Bank of Deposit and Discount is concerned only with the use, distribution, or application of that circulating medium."[5] Raymond seems to have been of like opinion in 1823,

[1] Nestor, "Thoughts on Paper Money," *American Museum* (1787), ii, 40. Similarly, Sullivan, *Path to Riches* (1792), pp. 50, 65, 76, etc.

[2] Holdsworth, *First Bank of the United States*, p. 129.

[3] Catterall, *Second Bank of the United States*, p. 483.

[4] Dewey, *State Banking Before the Civil War*, p. 54. See also, Bissell, "Banking in Massachusetts," *Bankers' Magazine* (March, 1853), vii, 677, 678.

[5] "Reflections . . . on the Money Market" (1837), Overstone, *Tracts . . . on Metallic and Paper Currency, 1837-1857* (London, 1858), p. 31.

when he contended that the evils of banking arise entirely from the ill-advised union of the functions of loan office and of manufactory of paper money. "By being loan offices, they are enabled to loan all the money they can make, or at least, as much as they please; and by being the manufacturers of a paper currency they are enabled to make as much money as they can loan."[1] He would forbid the issue of notes by banks. Gallatin believed that "the proper banking business consists not in making currency, but in dealing in existing currency and in credit, or, as both are generally expressed, bankers are money dealers."[2] Banks should borrow and lend money. The New York law prohibiting private banking he deemed entirely desirable with respect to note issue, but professed himself unable to understand, "Why individuals should not be permitted to deposit their money with whom they please."[3] Gouge, Vethake, Walker, and many others as well, would have subscribed readily to the statement of a writer in *Hunt's Merchants' Magazine*, that

The business of banks and bankers is to borrow money from one class and lend it to another.... Credits they may issue, sight or time drafts, or any other means to accomplish the proper transfer of moneys or commodities from one place to another, but the issue of paper for the circulation of a country ought not to be connected with banks or banking privileges.[4] ... Take away from the banks of the United States the power of issuing paper money, and the whole difficulty of banking vanishes. Banks would borrow and lend money as individuals.[5]

That banks of deposit and discount are entirely different in character from banks that add the function of issuing credit in the form of circulating notes was very nearly the universal view.

The faulty conception of deposits was indicated, again, by the distinction drawn between them and bank notes with respect to

---

[1] Raymond, *Elements of Political Economy* (1823), ii, 129.

[2] Gallatin, Letter to Maison (December 20, 1836), *Writings*, ii, 515.

[3] *Ibid.*, ii, 514; *Considerations*, etc. (1831), p. 95, note c. In 1837 New York did in fact repeal the law of 1818 prohibiting unincorporated banking in so far as it referred to merely "keeping offices for the purpose of receiving deposits, or discounting notes or bills." Laws (1837), chap. 20, p. 14.

[4] Wilkes, "Banking and the Currency," *Hunt's Merchants' Magazine* (August, 1858), xxxix, 192.

[5] *Ibid.*, p. 193. See also, James Buchanan, First Annual Message (December 8, 1857), in Richardson, *Messages of the Presidents*, v, 441.

the need of legal regulation. Gallatin, for example, maintained that the business of deposit and discount calls for no more restriction than any other species of commerce.[1] It was frequently pointed out that bank notes circulate among individuals who accept them without being in the position to use much discretion in the matter; whereas the holders of bank deposits become such voluntarily and with the opportunity of informing themselves about the bank involved.[2] Accordingly, such safeguards as legal reserve minima, and regulation of the proportion of capital to liabilities, were usually proposed for bank notes only.[3] Now, it is true that protection of note-holders (whether by safety fund, prior lien, bond security, or what not), while depositors receive no such protection, has an entirely valid justification. It is, however, with respect to particular banks only that there is force in the arguments that bank notes meet the test of presentation for payment less frequently, and that their acceptance is far less voluntary. There is no reason for distinguishing between notes and deposits when machinery is being set up for the control of expansion on the part of the banking community as a whole. In urging that it is with reference to note issue only that charters should be required of banks, or minimum ratios of reserves and capital to demand liabilities insisted upon, the part that deposits play in causing fluctuations in the volume of media of payment was overlooked. And in general this was because of the failure to understand that deposits are created by the banks themselves in the process of making loans.

It is not improbable that the tendency to miss the true nature of bank deposits is in part to be explained by the relatively large volume of deposits of a more or less permanent sort that were held by commercial banks in the absence of any considerable development of savings banks. Before savings banks became preva-

[1] Gallatin, "Suggestions" (1841), *Writings*, iii, 428. Cp. iii, 374; and Letter to Maison (1836), ii, 516. This letter contains both the same view as that in the text and another apparently inconsistent with it.

[2] Gallatin, Letter to Maison, *Writings*, ii, 516; Hildreth, *Banks, Banking, and Paper Currencies* (1840), p. 155; Bissell, "Banking in Massachusetts," *Bankers' Magazine* (March, 1853), vii, 677.

[3] See Chaddock, *Safety Fund System*, p. 379.

lent, commercial banks were presumably made the depositories of much actual cash for safe keeping and the earning of interest. This may well have helped to obscure the fact that some deposits originated in the lending activities of the banks.

The belief that bank deposits arise wholly through the bringing of cash to the banks was the dominant one. But the other view, more orthodox to-day, that the banks also create deposits, as they do notes, was advanced by some writers at a significantly early date. Hamilton, apparently, perceived the dual nature of deposits in his *Report on a National Bank* of 1790. After explaining that banks can put a far greater sum into circulation than they have on hand as gold and silver, he remarked that every loan which a bank makes is, in its first shape, a book credit, and in many cases is merely transferred to different creditors, circulating as such and performing the office of money until someone, into whose possession it has come, decides to use it in cancellation of his debt to the bank, or to call for its conversion into coin or notes.[1] Bollman observed in 1810 that most large payments were already being made not in specie, but in "bank credit, rendered portable, transferable, and divisible into exact sums, by the contrivance of checks." These credits the bank "creates and multiplies at pleasure," becoming a "mine and mint."[2]

Raguet, in his report of 1821 to the Senate of Pennsylvania, classified banks, after a fashion already becoming orthodox, into banks of deposit, of discount, and of circulation. His definitions of the three types are significant, however. Banks of discount are limited in the amount of their loans to the amount of their own capital; banks of deposit merely issue convenient receipts for money received for safe keeping; but banks of circulation create part of the circulating medium that they lend by loaning their own credit in the form either of notes *or of book entries* payable upon demand.[3] Raguet repeated this in his later writings, refer-

---

[1] Hamilton, Report on a National Bank (1790), *American State Papers, Finance,* i, 68.

[2] Bollman, *Paragraphs on Banks* (1810), p. 21. I have found no other statements of this thesis between Hamilton's and Bollman's, nor a third before that of 1821 which follows in the text.

[3] Report of January 15, 1821, *Examiner* (1835), ii, 337, 338.

ring, on one occasion, to the deposits of banks of circulation as "createable at will."[1] He seems, however, to have freed himself but partially from the current fallacy, when, in a later definition of banks of deposit and discount, he failed to see that the loan by the bank of money left with it subject to payment on demand constitutes in itself an addition to the quantity of media of payment, inasmuch as both the original depositor and the recipient of his money (or of the notes or deposit credit based upon it) command purchasing power to the full extent of the money entrusted to the bank.[2]

Henry C. Carey recognized that deposits are created by the banks and that the "loan that is based upon a deposit doubles the *apparent* amount of currency — the power of purchase remaining with the real owner of the money, while being exercised, and to the same extent precisely, by him to whom the bank has lent it."[3] Carey believed, as we saw earlier in the chapter, that it is the deposits, rather than notes of banks, that introduce violent changes in the volume of media of payment; and he criticized Peel's Act of 1844 upon this ground.[4] It is more important, he thought, that the law prescribe an ample reserve against the fluctuating element of bank credit, namely, deposits, than that it do so against notes.[5]

Robert Hare, who objected strenuously to the theory that bank loans are in essence the loans of the depositors of the bank to its borrowers, was not deceived as to the character of deposits. The latter, like notes, are the product of the bank itself.[6] Charles H. Carroll agreed with Hare with respect to the origin of deposits, although he differed completely from him in maintaining that banks can serve only as intermediaries in their lending operations, since the advance to customers of more dollars than were re-

---

[1] *Currency and Banking* (1839), p. 71. See also, "Principles of Banking," *Free Trade Advocate* (July 4, 1829), ii, 3, 4.

[2] Cp. *Currency and Banking*, p. 71.

[3] H. C. Carey, *Principles of Social Science* (1858), ii, 421. See also, *Past, Present, and Future* (1848), pp. 180 ff.

[4] Carey, *Past, Present, and Future*, p. 180.   [5] *Ibid.*, p. 182.

[6] Hare, "Do Banks Increase Loanable Capital?" *Hunt's Merchants' Magazine* (1852), xxvi, 703.

THE NATURE OF BANK DEPOSITS 119

ceived as capital stock and time deposits signifies but a depreciation of the monetary standard, so that the actual purchasing power of the community remains unchanged.[1] The "fictitious" character of deposits, Carroll said, was better understood in this country than in England, where ignorance of it was illustrated by the Bank Charter Act of 1844.

> The "deposit," as I have already said, is created by the discount; it is not drawn from preëxisting funds, as most persons suppose; it is, of course, no deposit at all, but it is an inscribed credit for money and capital having no existence.[2]

It is a common error, Carroll added, to suppose that banks discount on the basis of previously existing funds,

> whereas, the discount creates the deposit, the discounted note forming the only fund out of which it is itself discounted, and the only question the bank needs to consider is, whether the reserve of coin is sufficient to meet the returning liabilities.[3]

Stephen Colwell was another important writer to adopt the view that deposits are frequently the product of the act of lending.[4] The Massachusetts bank commissioners did likewise in their report of 1860, asserting that deposits "grow out of the discount-

---

[1] This illustrates our point (see p. 110, note 2) that the problems of the nature of deposits and of the lending operations of banks (whether or not purely intermediary) are distinct. Raguet also held at once the opinions that banks can lend only what they receive from depositors, since the loan of further sums but depreciates the standard correspondingly, and that deposits are created by the bank.

[2] C. H. Carroll, "Congressional Movement in the Currency Question," *Hunt's Merchants' Magazine* (April, 1860), lii, 444. Cp. Carroll, "Bankruptcy in the Currency," *Hunt's Magazine* (June, 1859), xl, 677n.

In regard to Carroll's comment upon the backwardness of English banking theory in the matter of the nature of deposits, it should be said that MacLeod stated the proper view, somewhat confusedly, in 1855 (*Theory and Practice of Banking*, first edition, i, 209 ff.), and most ably in 1860 (*Dictionary of Political Economy*, pp. 72–75).

[3] "Mr. Lowell *vs.* Mr. Hooper," *Hunt's Merchants' Magazine* (April, 1860), xlii, 576. Carroll was reviewing a controversy between Samuel Hooper and J. A. Lowell (*Review of Hooper's Pamphlet*, etc.), in which Hooper had undertaken to explain the mystery that deposits, taken with note issue, increase and diminish with the loans of banks, by showing that notes are issued *and deposits created* in the act of lending. Hooper, *Specie in Banks* (1860), pp. 14–16.

[4] Colwell, *Ways and Means of Payment* (1859), pp. 12, 244, 245. See also, *Bank Notes and Specie* (Anon., 1856), pp. 25–27; and discussion in *Bankers' Magazine* (May, 1850), iv, 912, 913.

ing of paper, precisely as does the issue of bills."[1] "Discounts *create* deposits, curtailment destroys them," was the terse summary of George Opdyke.[2]

In the last decade before the Civil War, then, the fact that bank deposits are not merely the result of the actual lodging of cash with the bank was beginning to receive definite recognition. Such, of course, is the accepted theory to-day, due in no small part, probably, to the writings of Henry Dunning MacLeod in England, and of Charles Franklin Dunbar in America. The older view is not without its advocates, however. Professor Cannan furnishes us with its most notable recent statement.[3] The chief difficulty with this conception of bank deposits is that it fails to perceive that the loan of a sum of money payable upon demand to its depositor, or the extension of credit (whether in the form of notes or deposit account) upon the basis of such a sum, in itself constitutes an addition to the previously existing media of payment. So long as a bank lends no more than the funds actually received as capital and *time* deposits, it is returning into the circulation no more than it has drawn out of the circulation. But the same thing cannot be said of a bank that lends cash received in exchange for a checking account, or extends a deposit credit upon the basis of such cash used as reserve. In this case the original depositor has not decreased his immediate command of purchasing power (as he would have done in making a time deposit), but will continue to exercise it by the transfer of his claim upon the bank through the writing of checks. If, upon the basis of the cash it has received, the bank finds it possible to assume another like liability to pay cash on demand, the volume of media of payment is to that extent increased. For both deposits, the

---

[1] *Report* (1860), p. 130. Their predecessors of three years before entertained a different view.

[2] "New Views on the Currency Question," *Bankers' Magazine* (1858), xiii, 420.

[3] Edwin Cannan, "Meaning of Bank Deposits," *Economica* (January, 1921), i, 28–36. Cannan reverts to the earlier theory and denies that deposits are created or that banks can lend more than they receive from patrons. He seems hardly to appreciate the early date at which the doctrine that deposits are *created* by the bank itself made its appearance.

original one and the additional one which it has made possible, serve their respective holders just as well as would the cash which has been left in the bank. Where one person commanded a dollar of purchasing power before, two do so now.

The reader need hardly be cautioned that we are here concerned primarily with the operation of the banking system as a whole rather than with the individual bank. The significance of this distinction, long familiar to economists, has recently been thoroughly elaborated for us by Professor C. A. Phillips.[1] With reference to the individual bank, it is true that its ability to lend is contingent upon its receipt of deposits in the form of lawful money, bank notes, and checks upon other banks. Moreover, in a system of many banks, with highly developed clearing arrangements, the securing of an additional deposit permits the particular bank to extend new loans to little, if any, more than the amount of this deposit. Should all the banks receive additional reserves more or less simultaneously (as would tend to be the case, for example, during a period of general rediscounting with the central bank), each could gradually extend its loans to many times the amount of the fresh reserves. Care would have to be taken, simply, that the equilibria of clearing balances among the several members of the system should not be disturbed. But of this manifold expansion on the part of any one bank, the bulk would be feasible in consequence, not of its own initial receipt of reserves, but of the credit items it would be able to present at the clearing house as a result of the expansion of neighboring banks. The enlargement of its own reserve would in itself permit the bank to expand loans to only about a like sum. (For convenience of exposition let us in fact assume an exact one-to-one ratio between deposit received and loan of credit rendered possible on the part of the single bank.)

At first glance this would seem to invalidate my contention that bankers create deposits and perform a service beyond that of acting as middlemen. Such is not the case, however. In the first place, we are dealing here with the banking system as a whole. The acquisition by a bank of a given sum of money representing

[1] *Bank Credit* (1919), especially chap. 3.

an addition to the aggregate bank reserves of the country would not, to be sure, permit *that particular* bank to undertake a manifold expansion of loans. But after the cash had been more or less stably distributed among the different banks of the country, it would be found that the banks taken together had been enabled to extend their deposits, through loans, to as many times the original deposit as the prevailing reserve ratio of the country would indicate. Regarded from the standpoint of the banking system as a whole, Professor Phillips's analysis of the limited extent to which a single bank can make the receipt of cash the basis of loan expansion does not deny that a given cash deposit makes possible bank loans to perhaps ten times its amount, but merely explains the mechanism by which this process works itself out. The placing in a bank of a stated sum of specie newly imported into the country permits the bank receiving it to undertake further demand liabilities to approximately (we have assumed it to be exactly) an equal amount. For, as a result of the influence of the expansion of its deposits upon the clearing balances of the bank, most of the freshly acquired reserves will normally be withdrawn into other banks. But each of these other banks, as it thus receives some of the reserve newly introduced into the system, will in turn find it possible to expand its loans to the amount of this accession. This will tend to render necessary a further readjustment among the banks — and so on, until the original deposit will have enabled the banks to expand their deposits, by making loans, to several times its amount.

So much for the banking system as a whole. But the thesis that a given deposit permits the particular bank to increase its loans by only an equal amount in no wise contradicts the theory that deposits are created, *even from the point of view of the individual bank.* For we may grant that before a bank can undertake to increase its demand liabilities it must receive from a depositor an equal amount of cash (including checks upon other banks), and still we can protest the fallacy of regarding bankers as mere brokers, whose sole function is to enable borrower and lender to find each other.[1] The mere passing on to a borrower of a sum of

[1] See, for example, Irving Fisher, *The Rate of Interest*, p. 324.

money left with the bank subject to draft by checks involves in itself an act of creation. The man who deposited the money has not thereby lessened the amount of purchasing power, or media of payment, at his immediate disposal. He has simply converted the media of payment into another form, the possession of which makes him no less effective a factor in the market. He has loaned the bank nothing; he has postponed neither his right, nor, probably, his intention to spend. The fact that he is willing to accept a book credit at the bank in lieu of lawful money, in the confidence that he can make equal use of either, is another matter altogether: it merely explains *why it is* that the cash deposit enables the bank to make a loan that duplicates the original depositor's undiminished command of media of payment. The significant point is that, to the extent that the people of a community are willing to keep their current purchasing power in the form of balances in their check accounts, even the individual bank is able to cause two units of media of payment, each as active as legal tender money itself would be, to exist where there was one before. We might, to be sure, regard the check as merely transferring by proxy the primary deposit which made the created deposit possible, and insist that simply an increase in the velocity of circulation of the original deposit is involved. But there is no more reason to do this than there is to regard bank notes as mere proxies that accelerate the circulation of other forms of cash, instead of treating them as being themselves media of payment.

Nor is it a helpful point of view to contend that, since the initial depositor could, by pressing his demand claim upon the bank, destroy the latter's ability to continue the new loan, the bank has borrowed from this man that which it lends to another. For, aside from the fact that the bank has already given an equivalent for the cash received, it is with the deposit in the generic sense that we are concerned — with the sum totals of deposits and of cash reserves rather than with specific ones. If a depositor withdraws cash that is soon replaced by another patron, no essential change has been made with reference to the lending ability of the bank. To be sure, the bank is able to make loans only because its depositors as a group refrain from withdrawing the reserves upon which the deposits are based. But this is merely equivalent to saying that banking can extend credit upon the basis of certain cash reserves only so long as those reserves continue to exist.

Still again, — for the problem is a treacherous one, — if the *individual* bank could function simply as a middleman, passing on to borrowers funds that are left by cash depositors, it would be impossible for us to read into the operations of the banking system as a whole any more than this. For, obviously, if no single bank creates the deposits it lends, the group of banks taken together cannot do so.

By way of final argument — and we return now to the point of view of the banking system at large — let us ask what would happen were the habits of a community to change overnight and were checks to be used to a much less degree in making payments. To simplify the analysis, let us say that the government reserved for itself the privilege of issuing paper money. Assume that one million dollars were suddenly and permanently withdrawn from bank reserves, to circulate in making payments hitherto accomplished by the drawing and depositing of checks. The aggregate of bank deposits would immediately shrink by the amount of one million dollars through the action of depositors in exercising their rights against the banks. But would the matter stop there? Obviously not, for the banks would have to contract their loans by several million dollars until the proper reserve ratio had been restored by the resultant contraction of deposits. Surely one can hardly regard the banking system as serving simply in an intermediary capacity if the withdrawal by depositors of a given amount of cash, diminishing the aggregate of reserves in the system, causes a contraction of loans to several-fold the amount of the deposits cancelled.

CHAPTER XII

PRINCIPLES OF NOTE ISSUE — CONVERTIBILITY

The need of convertibility little understood in the colonies. — Convertibility was generally assumed in the later period. — Belated land-bank projects. — Other advocates of an inconvertible currency. — The banking principle as basis for such a proposal. — Stephen Colwell's notable statement of the thesis.

THE importance of maintaining the immediate convertibility of paper money was but little appreciated in the colonial period. One of the most interesting chapters in colonial banking literature is concerned with that problem, and the extent to which security, now in the form of real estate mortgages and now in the form of staple commodities as well, was substituted for specie reserves in the schemes of the day, is familiar knowledge to all students of colonial banking. The operations of the deposit banks of continental Europe (which virtually issued warehouse receipts, reduced to common denominations, for the sundry coins in circulation) were familiar to the colonists, and to many of them, as to monetary "reformers" of later periods, it seemed but a logical step to issue like receipts to circulate as media of payment against real and personal property of recognized value.

We find in some cases definite traces of the influence of the English land-bank schemes, and frequent references to John Law leave no doubt as to the extent of his influence. Franklin thought that land is a better basis for note issue than specie, in that the latter is liable to depreciate from sudden increase in its quantity, whereas land is more stable in value, and probably appreciates slowly with the gradual growth of population.[1] "The Earth endures forever," several tracts remind us, and must obviously be the best type of security.[2]

John Colman, one of the most ardent and best known of the friends of a plentiful currency, expressed a common disparage-

[1] Franklin, "Modest Inquiry," etc. (1729), *Works*, ii, 268.
[2] "Money the Sinews of Trade" (1731), Davis's *Reprints*, ii, 435; "A Proposal to Supply a Medium of Exchange" (1737), *Reprints*, iii, 174.

ment of the precious metals as the basis of paper money when he asked:

> What intrinsick value is there in Silver, or Gold more than in Iron, Brass, or Tinn, but only the common acceptation of it by men in Trade, as a Medium of exchange. . . . Is not every thing in this World, just as men esteem and value it: If a man give me his Bond, it is as good in my Opinion as Silver; and the only reason why it is so, is, because it will pay my Debt, or command wherewith to Pay it: Surely then if a Bank Note will answer for that end, and will purchase for me Food, Physick, and Cloathing, and all necessaries of Life, it answers all the ends, which Silver & Gold can answer for.[1]

A medium of payment, in the opinion of a later writer, is none the better for having "intrinsic value." The significant thing is the amount of goods for which a unit of the currency will exchange, and the writer rebuked the merchants for raising the prices, in terms of bills of credit, of coins and commodities. "The only Thing needful then to keep up its Value, is the making a proper and resolute Stand against that inconsiderate Folly."[2]

Such emphasis upon the mere customary exchange value of a paper currency, without question as to the source of that value, would lead, logically, to a minimizing even of the need of ultimate security, such as land mortgages. The fiat theory, however, did not usually stand by itself, but was used to buttress arguments for a currency secured by land. Franklin, for example, in his polemic addressed to the Board of Trade in 1764, urged that, although the colony bills lacked convertibility,

> the legal tender, being substituted in its place, is rather a greater advantage to the possessor; since he need not be at the trouble of going to a *particular* bank or banker, finding (wherever he has occasion to lay out money in the province) a person that is obliged to take the bills.[3]

The land-bank projects frequently provided that the subscribers were to bind themselves to receive the notes at a given value.

The advocates of inconvertible paper did not rest their case upon the claim of its absolute desirability. We have seen that the

---

[1] "Distressed State of . . . Boston Once More Considered" (1720), *Reprints*, ii, 88. Cp. "A Modest Apology for Paper Money" (1734), *Reprints*, iii, 91, 92.

[2] "A Letter Relating to a Medium of Trade" (1840), *Reprints*, iv, 20, 21. Similarly, "A Word of Comfort," etc. (1721), *Reprints*, ii, 193.

[3] Franklin, "Remarks and Facts" (1784), *Works*, ii, 348; cp. p. 354. See Davis's *Reprints*, ii, 85.

PRINCIPLES OF NOTE ISSUE

vogue of land banking and of paper currency, which became most extensive about the years 1714, 1720, and 1740, was intimately connected with cheap-money agitation; and in part the failure to provide for convertibility into specie was caused by the fact that the projects of the time were intended to remedy the very difficulty that the supply of specie was supposedly inadequate. Even if a convertible currency were to be preferred, it was commonly argued, the want of sufficient specie prevented its adoption. Paper money possessed this superiority over metallic money, namely, that the country could not be deprived of it by an unfavorable balance of trade.[1] This raised the question, with which we have dealt in a preceding chapter, whether the issue of paper money had caused the drain of specie, or the reverse.[2]

It must not be thought, however, that there was none to insist that paper money should be payable in specie. "I would thank no man," wrote one critic, "for his Note or Bond, obliging himself always to owe me a Thousand Pounds, for if he always owes it, he *never* pays it, and so I shall never be the better for it."[3] The land security given for notes, Governor Hutchinson observed, "is a sufficient Surety to the Province, that they shall be paid in again, but it is no Security to the Possessors or the Persons that give a Credit to them, that they shall purchase as much Silver or Gold the next Year, as it does the present."[4]

Most of the proposals for specie-paying banks contemplated notes redeemable in silver at some future date. The silver for this purpose was usually to be secured by requiring that the loans through which the notes had been put into circulation should be repaid in metallic money, perhaps by installments.[5] The found-

[1] "A Word of Comfort," etc. (1721), *Reprints*, ii, 167; "Inquiry into the Nature and Uses of Money" (1740), *Reprints*, iii, 412–423.
[2] See Chapter III.
[3] "Addition to the Present Melancholy State," etc. (1719), *Reprints*, i, 381. Cp. "Objections to the Bank of Credit," etc. (1714), *Reprints*, i, 252.
[4] "A Letter to a Member of the House," etc. (1736) *Reprints*, iii, 153.
[5] "A Project," etc. (1720), *Reprints*, ii, 140 ff.; "A Letter to a Member of the House," etc. (1736), *Reprints*, iii, 157; "Communication to the Weekly Journal" (Jan. 1, 1740), *Reprints*, iii, 289–297. An interesting suggestion, rejected by its author as impracticable, was that of Hugh Vance for a bank to issue bills "promising a certain Sum payable in 3 or 6 Months, to the Possessor, in Sterling-Drafts." "Inquiry into the Nature and Uses of Money" (1740), *Reprints*, iii, 413.

ing of a bank upon these principles, and the contemporaneous establishment of a land bank, brought the controversy between the advocates of each type to a climax in 1740. That post notes would be discounted with respect to demand notes was recognized by those who opposed the introduction of both silver bank and land bank. It was also conceded by some of those who sponsored the emission of post notes. These latter thought that the issue of such notes, on condition that those who received them repay the loans in silver, was the only feasible means of procuring sufficient specie to enable the return to a specie standard.

When we come to the period following the development of commercial banking in the United States, we find convertibility taken more or less for granted by most of the writers, as we should expect. Stoppage of specie payments by the banks, "unbanks them at once," declared Richard Hildreth, "and changes them into mere machines for manufacturing paper money of no particular value."[1] And, due allowance being made for rhetorical hyperbole, the great majority of his contemporaries undoubtedly agreed with him, that "non-specie-paying banks are the greatest nuisances with which a country can be cursed."[2] The systematic treatises on money and banking that began to appear about 1820, usually contained repetition of the trite commonplaces that explained the merits of the precious metals as the monetary standard and pointed out the necessity of requiring convertibility on demand in order to prevent excessive extension of bank credit.

Yet there was not the same insistence upon the matter that we find to-day. In actual practice it was not uncommon to place such obstacles in the way of getting gold and silver from the banks as to make a mockery of their promise to pay upon demand. Nor did local opinion fail, in many cases, to uphold the banks. And temporary suspension of specie payments was frequently tolerated with a measure of stoicism that seems strange to us to-day. William Crawford wrote in his *Finance Report* of 1820, that in "all great exigencies, which, in the course of human events, may

[1] Hildreth, *Banks, Banking, and Paper Currencies* (1840), p. 176.
[2] *Ibid.*, p. 177.

be expected to arise in every nation, the suspension of specie payments by banks, when the circulation consists principally of bank notes, is one of the evils which ought to be considered as the inevitable consequence of their establishment."[1] Apologists for the banks were numerous during the suspensions of 1837–1840. A select committee of the Michigan legislature made the absurd report that to require the banks to resume "would seem to imply the same moral obligation, on the part of the debtors of those institutions, to pay them in coin, that the banks are under to pay their debts in a like medium. Your committee can see no reason why the moral obligation is not strictly reciprocal." [2]

This seemingly lax attitude toward the obligation to maintain convertibility was often primarily an indifference of hopelessness — the product not so much of failure to perceive the importance of uninterrupted convertibility as of despair of achieving it, born of the wretched conditions that attended our early banking.

On the other hand, there were proposals aplenty for a definitely inconvertible bank currency. Projects for land banking, for example, were by no means lacking long after commercial banks had been well established in this country. Similar schemes are, to be sure, advanced to this day by those who, through comfortable ignorance, mistake the archaic for the novel. Mathew Carey's account of the debate in Pennsylvania in 1785 contains several suggestions that loan offices, to make advances upon land after the fashion of colonial precedent, be substituted for the Bank of

---

[1] *Reports of the Secretary of the Treasury on the State of the Finances*, ii, 491. Cp. C. F. Adams, "Theory of Money and Banks," *Hunt's Merchants' Magazine* (Aug., 1839), i, 115; E. C. Seaman, "Currency, Commerce, and Debts of the United States," *Hunt's Merchants' Magazine* (May, 1858), xxxviii, 549, 550.

[2] Report of Select Committee on Banks (1839), in United States House of Representatives, 26th Congress, First Session, Document 172, p. 1308. Apologists for the banks at times of suspension of specie payments commonly argued, as did this committee, for example, that such action was necessary in order that the banks might continue to furnish an adequate circulating medium. The Committee of Ways and Means of the House observed that, on the contrary, "the suspension [of 1837] . . . suddenly converted eighty millions of currency into merchandise, and it was withdrawn from circulation." The operation of Gresham's Law, in the committee's opinion, resulted in the first instance in contraction rather than relief of the pressure. Report (March 5, 1838), p. 3.

North America, whose short loans were largely unavailable to the farmer in particular.[1]

"Let us then," urged a contemporary pamphleteer, "coin our lands and thereby obtain from those most valuable of all mines, a sufficient circulating medium of commerce. For this purpose let loan-offices be instituted in the several states, on principles similar to those whereon the loan-office of Pennsylvania was established for many years."[2]

Alexander Hamilton had subscribed to the fallacies of land banking in two letters written to Morris in 1779 and 1781. He proposed a bank which was to issue notes against landed security, and among its advantages he included the stock attraction of all land-bank schemes — that the proprietors could at the same time have the use of their land and of a cash representative of its value.[3] Later, however, Hamilton saw that land was an improper basis for a bank of issue, and in 1784 he opposed a project (attributed to Chancellor Livingston) to found such a bank in New York. Six years afterwards, in his *Report on a National Bank*, he again explained the defects of landed security as the basis of banking.[4]

In the eighteen-thirties a number of the southern and western states established "property banks," which sought to aid the farmer by combining mortgage loans with the issue of circulating notes and met with varying degrees of disaster.[5] A committee of the Florida legislature, in rueful contemplation of the results of the experiment by that state along this line, harked back to the Massachusetts episode of 1740 and found that the outcome bore "a remarkable similarity to that of the same system in Mississippi, and in Florida, and other parts of the Union, within the last few

---

[1] Carey, *Debates and Proceedings* (1786), p. 25, *passim*.

[2] [William Barton], "True Interest of the United States" (1786), *American Museum*, ii, 31. The loan office of colonial Pennsylvania was, of course, notably successful. (Cp. D. R. Dewey, *Financial History of the United States*, pp. 26, 27.)

[3] Hamilton, *Works* (Lodge edition), iii, 61, 82.

[4] Report on a National Bank (1790), *American State Papers, Finance*, i, 73.

[5] See Sumner, *History of Banking in the United States*, pp. 244 ff., 390, and Knox, *History of Banking in the United States*, pp. 604, 612, *passim*.

years."[1] Yet suggestions for the public or private issue of paper money backed by land, in all stages of crude naïveté, continued to recur.

The necessity of maintaining the convertibility of bank notes was most frequently questioned during the period of suspension of specie payments by most of the banks outside New England that began in the fall of 1814. During the years 1815 and 1816 the advocates of an inconvertible currency became quite numerous. They sought to show that the premium on metallic money which existed at the time in terms of the notes of the suspended banks was to be interpreted, not as a depreciation of the paper money, but as an appreciation of gold and silver. The English writers of the Restriction Period, then drawing into its later stages, undoubtedly exerted a considerable influence in this discussion.[2]

[1] Florida, Committee on Corporations, Report (Feb. 5, 1842), in U. S. House of Representatives, 29th Congress, 1st Session, Document 226, p. 753.

Arkansas blithely established her own State Bank upon the thesis that, "as a correct test of an adequate circulating medium, properly proportionate to the demand of industry and commerce in every civilized society, we may assume it as a principle applicable to all stages of society, that the active capital of a country should bear a fair and reasonable proportion to that which is fixed and permanent; and whenever real estate is converted into active capital at a fair valuation, and money can be obtained readily, at a reasonable rate of interest, on secure mortgages of real estate, that country is making rapid advances in a commercial and agricultural point of view; and without banking facilities such cannot be the case." Report of the Special Committee on Banks (Oct. 4, 1836), in U. S. House of Representatives, 35th Congress, 2nd Session, Document 121, p. 173.

How tenacious is the lease on life of some primitive fallacies is illustrated by the Report to the Senate and House of the State, made November 1, 1819, by the Bank of the State of South Carolina. After dilating for some forty-six pages on the inadequacies of a specie currency in a country subject to an unfavorable balance of trade, the report urged that the government issue inconvertible paper money on the basis of real estate as security. "We believe," these responsible bankers declared, "that if it were once to be established as a principle of national economy, that such a currency should in no case be issued, unless on ample security pledged for its repayment, the government would no more be induced to depart rashly from such a principle, than to issue metallic money of a debased and depreciated standard." A sufficient safeguard would thus be present, it was thought, against overissue. (Report, p. 54.)

[2] The question whether a disparity between paper money and metallic indicated a depreciation of the former or an appreciation of the latter was discussed in the colonies three quarters of a century before the beginning of the English Restriction

Condy Raguet, in his first essay on money and banking, written in the year 1815, argued that the specie had risen in value and that paper money had not fallen.[1] He found no cause for concern in the fact that the banks had suspended specie payments. They had never been in a position to redeem all their notes at one time, and they had then the same means of discharging their notes that had been theirs before, namely, their claims on borrowers, "who are now as able to pay as they ever were, if not in specie, in merchandise of equal value. — Some banks may indeed be insolvent, but that insolvency cannot arise from mere inability to pay specie, but from the inability of their debtors to pay in anything."[2] He granted, however, that the absence of the check imposed by convertibility increased the danger that an excessive quantity of notes would be issued, but felt that, if the banks would exercise the same prudence in their issue of notes that they did when under the restraint of specie payments, nothing was to be feared.[3] In 1820 Raguet thought that the banks had not acted with this desired moderation, and he laid great stress upon the importance of retaining convertibility.[4] He later accepted the doctrine that the rates of exchange on foreign countries and the market price of specie were conclusive tests of the degree of depreciation of an irredeemable currency.[5]

"An inconvertible circulating medium of paper, resting on the real substantial property of the nation," asserted another writer

Period. Colman (*Distressed State*, etc., 1720), and others, urged that silver had appreciated because of an extraordinary demand for it. (See Davis's *Reprints*, ii, 68, 69, 198; iii, 421 and 429; and iv, 8.) On the other hand we find Wigglesworth contending in 1720 that the premium on silver was caused by depreciation of the bills (*A Letter from One in the Country*, etc., Davis's *Reprints*, i, 419). The most able exposition of this second opinion is found in Douglass's *Discourse* (1740). The colonial paper was not issued against commercial loans, and care must be taken in comparing the early discussion with that which referred to the later bank notes.

[1] Raguet, *Inquiry into the Causes of the Present State of the Circulating Medium* (1815), pp. 14, 15, 43.
[2] *Ibid.*, pp. 35, 36.
[3] *Ibid.*, pp. 44, 45.
[4] Report as Chairman of Committee on Banks, Pennsylvania legislature (1820), *Free Trade Advocate*, ii, 345-347. About 1815, the report tells us, the commonly received theory that the paper currency was not depreciated began to be abandoned.
[5] *Currency and Banking* (1839), p. 141.

of 1815, harking back to the notions of the colonial period, "would be, both for England and the United States, more desirable than one convertible in the usual mode and on the usual principles."[1] He saw no reason why suspension of specie payments might not be permanent, and urged a plan whereby notes would be convertible, not into specie, but into six per cent government bonds.[2]

This curious suggestion that a paper currency be issued, redeemable in the certificates of indebtedness of the national government, the latter being themselves payable in specie, was taken up by several persistent writers, and seems to have had considerable vogue throughout the next two decades. An anonymous contributor to the *Analectic Magazine* has been credited with originating the idea, but apparently he himself had merely borrowed it.[3] His proposal was that the banks, in the absence of sufficient specie to maintain its payment, should redeem their notes in six per cent bonds of the government, at par or market value, whichever was lower. Payment of the interest on the government bonds upon which notes were issued, could at most require specie to the amount of only six per cent of the volume of notes in circulation, whereas the maintenance of direct convertibility into specie would require a twenty-five per cent banking reserve, he thought. Though intended primarily for the period before resumption of specie payments could be effected, the plan, in the author's estimation, might well "be permanently adopted as an improvement in political economy."[4] Redemption in the

---

[1] *Observations on the Proposed Patriotic Bank* (1815), p. 11. Quotations from an article by "Homo" in the *National Intelligencer* make up the bulk of this pamphlet.

[2] *Ibid.*, p. 26.

[3] A. M. Davis (*Origin of the National Banking System*, p. 9) gives the credit to the author of the article in the *Analectic Magazine*. This article appeared in December, 1815; the *Observations* considered in the preceding paragraph of the text appeared in May of that year; and it in turn borrowed most of its material from an earlier writer (perhaps the same) in the *National Intelligencer*. See also, *Suggestions on the President's Message* (1815?), pp. 17–19.

[4] "Banks and Paper Currency," *Analectic Magazine* (Dec., 1815), vi, 514. Most of the advocates of this "patriotic bank" (as it was at times called) urged it as a substitute for specie payment while the latter was impossible, but thought it might well be permanently adopted. Recall that the first two issues of the Greenbacks were originally made convertible into six per cent government bonds. This feature was later repealed. See Dewey, *Financial History of the United States*, pp. 290–292.

six per cent bonds of the government would prevent overissue of the notes, since no prudent man would keep paper money for which he had no good use if he could convert it into such bonds.

Bollman, who would have preferred a paper currency completely divorced from the fluctuating metallic standard, thought that, since the adoption of such a completely inconvertible currency was politically impossible, the plan of the contributor to the *Analectic Magazine* should be followed.[1]

We turn now to those advocates of an inconvertible currency who saw in the nature of the lending operations of the banks themselves a sufficient safeguard against excessive issue and depreciation. The doctrine that bank notes, as distinguished from government paper forcibly injected into the circulation in payment of public expenditures, could not be issued in excess of the needs of trade, has already been discussed elsewhere.[2] It afforded an attractive argument to the anti-bullionists, in America as in England. Bollman inclined toward it, although he doubted that the directors of numerous independent banks could permanently be trusted to avoid forbidden accommodation loans.[3] If issued against real business paper, he contended, bank notes can never be redundant, since "their amount in circulation can never be greater than the amount of approved, discounted, commercial bills in the possession of the banks ... so that, in the regular course of things, banks are always ready to absorb all the paper which emanated from them."[4] The bank notes of the day, an anonymous writer asserted during the period of irredeemability, were not superfluous since they had been issued through loans at

---

[1] Bollman, *Plan of an Improved System*, etc. (1816), p. 33. See also, Thomas Law, and Thomas Mendenhall in my bibliography, and Robert Hare, *Suggestions Respecting the Reformation of the Banking System* (1837), for more or less fantastic presentations of like schemes. Mathew Carey pronounced Bollman's proposal for an inconvertible currency a "magnificent" one, which "would be a sovereign remedy for all the financial difficulties of the country." Carey later changed his views as to the desirability of inconvertible paper; not so Bollman. See Carey's *Letter to the Directors of the Banks* (March 27, 1816).

[2] See Chapter VI.

[3] Bollman, *Plan for an Improved System*, etc. (1816), pp. 4, 19–24.

[4] *Ibid.*, p. 14.

interest, and borrowers would have been able to obtain them at a lower rate than that charged by the bank had they tended to become excessive.[1]

The doctrine that bank notes need not be convertible, because the manner in which they get into circulation precludes the possibility of their exceeding the needs of trade, received but little support in this country, however. The one noteworthy statement of it came at the end of the period, at the hands of Stephen Colwell.[2] Colwell developed the argument for inconvertible bank currency in a large volume devoted to this problem, which showed him to be decidedly superior to any of his predecessors in capacity for sustained analysis. His *Ways and Means of Payment* (1859) is undoubtedly the most searching and original single treatise contributed to our subject during the period in which we are interested, and calls for a rather extensive treatment.

Colwell begins with an explanation of money of account, "the language in which prices are expressed, and books of account are kept."[3] Though the unit of money of account originates from some coin, or special weight of specie, it soon becomes so fixed in the consciousness of men as a unit of value, that they "carry the memory of that value in the mind, and use it with the same effect, abstractly, as if referring to the coin."[4] And it need have, nay, should have, no corresponding unit in actual coinage. "Whatever may be said of the policy of fixing the price of any article, even that designated for money by law, it cannot be questioned that it was a false step to endanger the steadiness of the money of account by fastening it to any coin or quantity of gold."[5] When gold depreciates as a result of its influx, it should be quoted at a correspondingly lower price per ounce in terms of money of account; instead of which the unit of money of account now shares

---

[1] *Suggestions on the President's Message* (1815), p. 12. Cp. Bollman, *op. cit.*, p. 35, and *Paragraphs on Banks* (1810), p. 59.
[2] For minor discussions of an inconvertible currency, see Mathew Carey, *Essays on Banking* (1816), pp. 163–181; A. B. Johnson, *Treatise on Banking* (1849), p. 20; Anon., *Currency Explosions* (1858), pp. 7–10.
[3] Colwell, *Ways and Means of Payment*, p. 2.
[4] *Ibid.*, pp. 31, 32.
[5] *Ibid.*, p. 50.

the depreciation of the specie with which it has been tied up by the legal-tender law fixing the latter's value.

Money is an important agency of exchange, but by no means essential to it. "When a man sells an hundred bushels of wheat for $150, and with that money purchases three tons of iron, the transaction is an exchange of the wheat for the iron." Money may be employed as a convenient agent, just as a wagon is used to transport the goods. But even when it is so employed, "its real value as an equivalent is not an essential ingredient of the exchange." [1]

And, in reality, the precious metals enter, whether directly or indirectly, into but a small fraction of all payments. It is through the credit system that most payments are now made, without resort to coin, bullion, or any similar equivalent. Commodities and services pay for commodities and services; men apply their credits to the extinguishment of their debts.[2] Money does not merely yield here to a substitute; it is dispensed with altogether. "It is dispensed with at the time a purchase is made, by stating the amount in money of account, and postponing the day of payment; it is dispensed with at the day of payment, because the debt is adjusted or paid by a process which does not require the aid of gold or silver." [3]

All this argument in support of the notion of an abstract money of account without tangible representative and in disparagement of the part played by the precious metals is preliminary to a proposal for the complete dissociation of the monetary standard from coins. Credits, through the cancellation of which payments are made, whatever be the shape they take, whether bank notes, bank deposits, or less important representatives of private credit, "become a general instrument of purchase, not because they are money, or representatives of money, but because they are the chief medium of paying debts." [4] As such they are in great demand by debtors, and it is from this demand that they derive their value. "It would require all the bank notes thus issued to purchase the goods, the sale of which created the paper in ex-

---

[1] Colwell, *Ways and Means of Payment*, pp. 27, 28.
[2] *Ibid.*, pp. 188–193.   [3] *Ibid.*, p. 193.   [4] *Ibid.*, p. 195.

change for which the bank notes were given. The goods are sufficient to redeem the notes issued upon them, and therefore sufficient to pay or redeem the bank notes substituted."[1] Thus the very merchants through whom the notes are placed in circulation, create a demand for them exactly equivalent to the whole amount extant. One accepts the notes in exchange for what he sells, not because of the specie into which they profess to be convertible, but because he knows that, by virtue of this demand, the notes will be received for what he purchases. "It is not, then, that bank notes may be useful, that they are payable on demand; it is, that they may be subjected to a constant test of their soundness." The British Restriction Period bears out the fact that, "The process of adjustment by which men are enabled to apply what others owe to them in satisfaction of what they owe to others . . . is in no way dependent upon money."[2]

Colwell did not rest his case with denial that convertibility is necessary to the proper functioning of bank currency, whether notes or deposits. The manner in which the notes are issued necessarily implies a demand for them, on the part of borrowers, that is sufficient assurance that they will have value, and that they will not be overissued; and insistence upon convertibility is as disastrous as it is dispensable. In demanding that bank notes be payable in specie on demand, as a test of their soundness, "we impose a criterion which, when the time of application arrives, forces the bank to admit failure, or to become a scourge to the community by inflicting the hardships of a drastic contraction." The only alternative would be the keeping of a reserve of one-hundred per cent against all demand liabilities.[3]

Banks whose notes and deposits are payable in specie on demand have no choice but to contract when specie is being with-

---

[1] Colwell, *Ways and Means of Payment*, p. 235. Cp. p. 195. Elsewhere he recognizes that the banks' borrowers may be unable to market the products at a sufficient price to enable them to meet their obligations.

[2] *Ibid.*, p. 390. Cp. p. 400. Colwell held the view that the disparity between bank notes and gold during the Restriction Period was the result of appreciation of the gold, expressed in terms of money of account, and not of depreciation of the notes.

[3] *Ibid.*, pp. 11, 12.

drawn for export. The logical action would be to increase the volume of other devices of payment at such times, in order to fill the void left by the outflow of specie. Our banking system is falsely predicated upon the assumption that whenever our importers, in consequence of having overtraded, must meet a heavily adverse balance, the business community as a whole should be denied its usual bank accommodation; that the whole country should be wrecked in order to save importers from the necessity of paying heavily adverse exchange rates.[1]

By way of solution of the problem, Colwell urged that a bank's notes should be receivable at all times in payment of debts to the bank, but that the latter should be bound to pay specie in no other respect than that in which payment is due from its patrons — at the maturity of the loans which brought the notes into circulation. Thus the bank notes would be absorbed in payment of debts to the bank, and such as were not so returned could be presented for payment only after the borrower had given the bank specie in lieu of the notes themselves. The issue of such post notes would offer some difficulties, but Colwell did not doubt that they could be surmounted.[2]

[1] Colwell, *Ways and Means of Payment*, pp. 162, 170, 221–228. Those who opposed any fiduciary currency whatever, also made much of the manner in which such a currency aggravated the hardships of an outflow of gold. Colwell's position bears a certain resemblance to that taken by the colonists who urged that it was lack of gold and silver which called for the issue of paper money, in that both tend to overlook, or deny, the relation between an enlarged circulating medium and the balance of trade. In this connection it is well to observe that Colwell assigns to bank credit but little influence on prices. See *supra*, Chapter VI.

[2] *Ibid.*, pp. 470, 492–495.

CHAPTER XIII

PRINCIPLES OF NOTE ISSUE (*Continued*)

The currency principle. — The question of small notes. — Bond-secured issue. — The safety-fund system.

1. THE CURRENCY PRINCIPLE

THE weightiest as well as the commonest criticism of bank notes was that they fluctuate in quantity, causing great variations in prices. An obvious method of preventing such disastrous changes in the volume of the currency was to require that notes be issued only against an equal amount of gold and silver, thus withdrawing one type of money from circulation just as rapidly as the other type was put into it. This principle was stated at the very outset of the discussion of commercial banking, but rather, it is probable, from a naïve prejudice against allowing banks to lend more money than they had in their actual possession than from an intelligent understanding of the difficulties of banking upon a partial reserve. A bank, in the opinion of an anonymous writer of 1787, "should not emit a single note beyond the sum of specie in its possession."[1] James Sullivan, in his *Path to Riches*, roused by the desire of those who wanted to establish banks "to spring a mine of wealth without labor," urged the same view,[2] and as much was implied by many of the early writers who opposed lending upon the basis of a fractional reserve largely because they were mystified by it.

Proposals for an inelastic currency began to be made in the eighteen-twenties. In 1823, the year in which Joplin first clearly stated the *currency principle* in England,[3] Raymond wrote that the government should never delegate to private individuals and corporate bodies its prerogative of furnishing the circulating

---

[1] Nestor, "Thoughts on Paper Currency," *American Museum* (1787), ii, 40. The article was a reprint, and may have been written a year or two earlier.

[2] Sullivan, *Path to Riches* (1792), pp. 71–73, *passim*.

[3] Silberling, *British Theories of Money and Credit, 1776–1848* (unpublished Harvard thesis), pp. 234–236.

medium, and urged that it issue paper money only against the deposit of a like amount of coin, thus avoiding fluctuations other than those incidental to a metallic currency itself.[1] Eleazar Lord recommended a limited issue by the government, the limitation being set "below the quantity of currency ordinarily required for circulation in the country."[2] He recognized, however, that there would be danger of tampering with the limit under political pressure.

Gouge, in the earlier of his writings, would have preferred to return to a completely metallic currency, as would many others, including the House Ways and Means Committee, as indicated by its famous report upon Andrew Jackson's message of 1830.[3] Even Gallatin would have favored such a course had it not been that the existence of many banks made reversion difficult.[4] Those who would deny to banks the privilege of note issue, whether in order to abolish paper currency entirely or to relegate its emission to the government, failed to see, in most cases, that bank deposits are likewise created by the banks and are equally capable with notes of introducing elasticity into the volume of media of payment.

In the later eighteen-fifties the movement for a specie currency, or for one containing only coins and specie certificates, received renewed impetus, owing in part to the crisis of 1857, and in part, perhaps, to the fact, commented upon by one writer, that the great output of gold by California now made it easier for the country to get the necessary amount of specie.[5] Charles Carroll wrote industriously in support of a return to the use of metallic money alone, or of bank notes representing an equivalent number of coins held in reserve. Unlike most of those who held such

---

[1] Raymond, *Elements of Political Economy* (1823), i, 248–252. See also, Vethake, *Principles of Political Economy* (1838), pp. 201 ff.; Malcolm, *Short Essays on a Gold Note Currency* (1858), pp. 11 ff.

[2] Lord, *Principles of Currency and Banking* (1829), p. 53.

[3] Gouge, *Short History of Paper Money* (1833), pp. 102–105; McDuffie, *Report* (1830), pp. 7, 8. The McDuffie Committee did not so definitely commit itself as to its choice.

[4] Gallatin, *Considerations*, etc. (1831), p. 38.

[5] Carroll, "Specie Prices and Results," *Hunt's Merchants' Magazine* (Oct., 1857), xxxvii, 429.

views, he recognized that deposits must also be taken into consideration, and would have the banks make loans and discounts only to the extent that they had received money in payment of capital stock and on time deposits.[1] Amasa Walker contributed the best known American argument for the currency principle in his *Nature and Uses of Money and Mixed Currency* (1857), which was largely made up of articles first published in *Hunt's Merchants' Magazine* on the very eve of the panic of 1857. He urged vigorously the defects of a "mixed currency," — that is, one involving an element of credit, being composed in part of bank notes in excess of reserves, — and would gradually prohibit "all bills not absolutely based upon an equal amount of specie in the banks." [2]

Colwell, who saw clearly the need of an elastic currency and wanted an inconvertible one for that reason, thought that banks should not incur demand liabilities to pay specie in excess of their immediate means of doing so. "Bank notes payable on demand should never be issued beyond the amount of specie actually in the bank." [3]

The English Bank Charter Act of 1844, which authorized a limited issue of bank notes against government securities and required the deposit of an equivalent in gold for each additional note issued, received frequent comment in America, but surprisingly little support. The purpose of the act was to retain to a limited and fixed extent the advantage that paper money confers of releasing specie from monetary use by furnishing an inexpensive substitute, and yet to avoid the evil of an unstable monetary standard. C. G. Memminger, later to become the Secretary of the Treasury of the Southern Confederacy, favored the adoption of the principle in the legislature of South Carolina,[4] but objectors

[1] Carroll, "The Gold of California and Paper Money," *Hunt's Merchants' Magazine* (1856), xxxv, 160–172; Mr. Lowell *vs.* Mr. Hooper, *Hunt's Merchants' Magazine* (April, 1860), xlii, 584.

[2] *Nature and Uses of Money and Mixed Currency* (1857), p. 52. Walker proposed to avoid too sudden a transition by abolishing the smaller notes first, then gradually increasing the minimum denomination until the total circulation did not exceed the specie in reserves. This suggestion was fairly common.

[3] Colwell, *Ways and Means of Payment* (1859), p. 495. Cp. pp. 11, 12, 368.

[4] Speech of C. G. Memminger in the House of Representatives of South Carolina, etc. (Dec., 1857). A special committee of the General Assembly of South Carolina

were far more numerous than supporters. Carey, in 1848, and, at a later date, Carroll, criticized Peel's Act on the ground that it made no attempt to regulate deposits, which are quite as variable in volume at the discretion of the banks, and which influence prices as much as do bank notes.[1] Amasa Walker thought that the act constituted a step in the right direction, but felt that it did not go far enough. "That any such exigency as that which existed in England in 1847 could have occurred," he wrote, "if its bank had not promised to pay specie for fourteen millions of notes without the specie to pay with, we presume that neither Lord Overstone, nor Lord Monteagle, nor any other Englishman — nobleman or commoner — will for a moment pretend."[2] Walker seems to have profited none at all from the contention of Carey, Carroll, and others, that deposits represent an equal source of danger.

2. Should Notes of Small Denominations be Prohibited?

The desirability of permitting banks to issue small notes had been seriously questioned in England before we had our first experience with modern banking. The relatively high denomination below which the Bank of England could not issue notes was reduced to £1 during the Restriction Period, and the problem of small notes received a great deal of attention until the act of 1829 established a £5 minimum. The controversy in England had its counterpart in the United States.

Smith had stated the principal objections to small notes in the *Wealth of Nations*. Such notes are received with less caution, and a person who does not enjoy a sufficient degree of credit to give

---

had rejected the principle in 1849, on the ground that it presupposed the restriction of the power of issue to one, or a few, banks, which savored too much of monopolistic privileges. South Carolina, Report of Special Committee, pp. 11–13. See also, Dwight, "The Progressing Expansion," *Hunt's Merchants' Magazine* (Aug., 1851), xxv, 151; W. G. Hunt, "Banking and Currency," *Bankers' Magazine* (July, 1858), viii, 2.

[1] See *supra*, Chapter XI.

[2] A. Walker, "Lord Overstone on Metallic and Paper Currency," *Hunt's Merchants' Magazine* (Feb., 1859), xi, 155.

his £5 note wide circulation may yet engage in banking if small enough notes be permitted. Small notes pass mainly into the hands of the poor and any loss from their unsoundness is, accordingly, more regrettable. And, finally, there will be a less complete displacement of specie from circulation if no notes of small denomination are allowed.[1]

Legislation restricting the denominations of notes dates practically from the beginning of our bank laws,[2] and agitation of the problem began quite as early.[3] It was pointed out by those who would suppress small notes that they are more liable to be unsound because they are received with less discrimination than notes of higher value, thus lending themselves more readily to the operations of the unscrupulous banker and of the counterfeiter;[4] and that losses from bad notes, in the case of small denominations, fall chiefly upon the poor.[5] The commonest argument was that the prohibition of small notes would help to keep some specie in circulation.[6] Such notes remain in circulation longer, making it easier for banks to maintain an excessive issue. They cause metallic money to leave the channels of circulation and flow into the vaults of the banks, whence, "being already collected, it is silently and suddenly withdrawn; and before the public at large can have any sufficient notice of its being gone, the banks are obliged to stop their issue, and the paper previously in circulation is withdrawn also, being returned to the banks by their debtors."[7] Small notes, since they are held largely by the poor and less informed people, increase the danger of an alarmist run upon the banks for payment.[8]

Before 1850, five or ten dollars seem to have been the minimum

---

[1] *Wealth of Nations*, book II, chap. 2 (vol. i, pp. 305–307).
[2] See Dewey, *State Banking Before the Civil War*, pp. 63–73.
[3] [Witherspoon], *Essay on Money* (1786), pp. 49, 54, for example. Niles bitterly dubbed the small notes of the times "filthy dowlass." *Register* (1825), xxix, 177.
[4] Raguet, Report of 1821, *Examiner*, ii, 341; Lord, *Principles* (1829), p. 115.
[5] Cooper, *Lectures* (1826), p. 147; Gallatin, *Considerations* (1831), p. 57; etc.
[6] [Witherspoon], *Essay on Money* (1786), p. 54. M'Cready, *Review of Trade* (1820), p. 40; Appleton, *Examination of the Banking System* (1831), p. 47.
[7] Lord, *Principles* (1829), p. 113. See Hildreth's answer in *Banks, Banking, and Paper Currencies* (1840), pp. 193, 194.
[8] *Southern Review* (Nov., 1831), viii, 25.

denominations generally favored by those who were opposed to smaller notes, so that the discussion was, after all, not exactly comparable to that which took place in England, where five pounds was usually the minimum proposed. Cooper did suggest in 1826 that the logical course would be to prohibit all denominations not higher than the largest coin being struck by the mint (twenty dollars).[1] After the middle of the century, twenty and fifty dollars apparently became the favorite minima,[2] while, as early as 1840, the editor of the Democratic Review urged the suppression of all notes under one hundred dollars.[3] It was frequently advocated that the smallest denominations be prohibited first and the minimum gradually raised until the desired level was reached. Gallatin added the suggestion (which it is interesting to compare with the law of 1864 taxing the notes of state banks out of existence) that Congress prevent the issue of undesirable denominations by imposing a prohibitive stamp duty upon them.[4] The Treasury Department, in sympathy with the hard-money sentiments of Jackson, began to discriminate against small notes in 1835, and Secretary Woodbury stated in his *Finance Report* of that year that over two thirds of the States already had highly salutary "usages or laws" in existence regulating the denominations of notes.

Hildreth devoted twenty pages of his *Banks, Banking, and Paper Currencies* to a defence of notes of smaller denominations, presenting most of the more familiar arguments in their favor. Smith's fear that the privilege of issuing trivial notes would enable men of faulty character to become bankers did not apply to the United States, he thought, because banks here had to be incorporated, or, if free, were required to furnish security for

[1] Cooper, *Lectures* (1826), p. 147. Andrew Jackson recommended that twenty dollars be the minimum in his message of 1835. Richardson, *Messages of the Presidents*, iii, 166.

[2] Middleton, *Government and Currency* (1850), p. 120; James Buchanan, Message (1857), Richardson's *Messages of the Presidents*, v, 441; John A. Dix, *Bankers' Magazine* (1859), xiii, 517.

[3] *Democratic Review* (March, 1840), vii, 202.

[4] Gallatin, Letter to Biddle (Aug. 14, 1830), *Writings*, ii, 432. Several bills to this purport were introduced in Congress during the next decade. See the *National Era* (1857), p. 196.

PRINCIPLES OF NOTE ISSUE

their notes.[1] And Smith's argument that less specie would be expelled from the country if none but large notes were authorized, was inconsistent with his other doctrine that the issue of paper money is advantageous because it displaces a costly currency with an inexpensive one.[2] It is the fears of depositors, rather than of note-holders, that tend to produce runs;[3] and of the note-holders, those having the larger denominations present their claims first, as evidenced by the greater rapidity with which large notes return from circulation.[4] Replacing the small notes in circulation with gold and silver coins would accomplish no improvement, since the banks could gain possession of that metallic money for their reserves only by contracting their loans, and the country would suffer equally from the withdrawal of a certain quantity of media of payment, whether in the form of notes or of coins.[5]

H. C. Carey disposed of the issue with accustomed ease. *Laissez faire* is a maxim as applicable in banking as elsewhere. "One-dollar notes will not be used unless the benefit derived from them exceed the cost of furnishing them, and if it do so, their use is beneficial to the whole community." [6] Colwell, consistently with his minimizing of the importance of specie, gave little weight to the argument that small notes should be prohibited to in-

---

[1] Hildreth, *Banks, Banking, and Paper Currencies* (1840), pp. 183, 184.

[2] *Ibid.*, p. 187. Smith, it should be said, also stated that commerce and industry are less secure when "suspended upon the Daedalian wings of paper money," than when they travel upon the solid ground of gold and silver. *Wealth of Nations*, book II, chap. 2 (vol. i, p. 304).

[3] Hildreth, *op. cit.*, p. 185.

[4] *Ibid.*, p. 192.

[5] *Ibid.*, p. 189. Barnard urged a similar point: "If you present a five dollar bill at the counter of a bank for coin, you do little to facilitate the transaction by having five dollars of silver already in your pocket." *Speeches* (1838), pp. 15, 26. It must be remembered, however, that the withdrawal of gold from bank reserves requires, *prima facie*, a contraction of the media of payment in proportion to the number of paper units based upon each unit of reserve, and that decreasing the relative use of fiduciary currency would lessen this tendency to magnify the influence of specie exports. Or, from Barnard's point of view, a bank would not need to contract its loans to a like extent if its debtors made repayment in larger measure with metallic money.

[6] H. C. Carey, *The Credit System*, etc. (1838), p. 117; Cp. *Letters to the President* (1857), p. 15.

crease the circulation of coins, and regarded the small-note question as unimportant.[1]

In more recent discussions no little stress has been laid on the fact that the privilege of issuing small notes, by providing an inexpensive *till money*, makes possible the extension of banking into small villages that could not support it otherwise.[2] This argument played no part in the discussion that we have reviewed. Nor is this surprising. A bank can use its own notes as till money, affording a relief to its reserve to that extent, only in meeting an *internal* drain on its *deposits*. It cannot, obviously, utilize notes in meeting the demands of note-holders; nor in meeting the demand of depositors for means of foreign remittance. But deposits were far less important, relatively, in the earlier half of the preceding century than they are to-day. The problem of an internal drain, moreover, was one to which little consideration was given before 1857.[3] Again, in order that notes may be acceptable to depositors in times of pressure, it is necessary that the banks issuing them enjoy a high degree of confidence, and this condition was not frequently present.

3. Note Issue Secured by Public Stocks

In the preceding chapter we had occasion to note a plan that received considerable attention after 1815, proposing the issue of bank notes redeemable in government stocks instead of in specie. This had not a great deal in common with the bond-secured system of issue embodied in the free banking laws of New York (1838) and other states and in the National Bank Act, although it did, like the latter, contemplate a paper currency to be given national circulation by being based upon United States

---

[1] Colwell, *Ways and Means of Payment* (1859), pp. 428, 508.

[2] E. g., Withers, *English Banking System*, pp. 43, 44.

[3] Cp. Report of the Superintendent of the Banking Department, New York (1857), *Bankers' Magazine*, xii, 622. Money markets were quite largely localized before the middle of the century and heavy demands for specie were generally induced either by adverse balances of trade, or by misgivings concerning the solvency of particular banks. The rise of New York as a financial center introduced the phenomenon, especially emphasized in 1857, of an internal drain of major magnitude.

securities.[1] We have now to deal with the discussion of government stocks as the security for a convertible note issue.

The first proposal for such a plan seems to have been that which Professor John McVickar advanced in 1827. Banks should lend, not their capital, but their credit; the capital should properly serve simply to give creditors assurance. This purpose can best be accomplished by investing the capital in permanent securities of undoubted soundness. Moreover, bank notes circulate among those who are incapable of determining the financial circumstances of the issuer, and whose interest should justly be safeguarded by the pledge of acceptable stocks. Let banking, then, be made free to all, under a general statute, upon the condition that nine-tenths of the capital be invested in government stock, and that these securities be pledged for the redemption of the bank's promissory notes, which shall not be issued in excess of the amount of stock held for this purpose.[2]

Eleazar Lord, in his *Principles of Currency and Banking*, published two years later, adopted McVickar's suggestion as alternative to the issue of paper money in limited quantities by the government itself. Note-holders would be secured by the fact that capital to the full amount of the outstanding circulation was being withheld from the hazards of commercial banking;[3] and the banks, because of the interest borne by the securities, would be able to refrain from the mischief of returning more money into circulation than had been withdrawn from it in the payment of capital.[4] Also, the undesirable elasticity of bank notes would be eliminated.[5] To prevent violation of the law, let the government, upon the deposit of the securities, turn over the proper

[1] A. M. Davis, *Origin of the National Banking System*, p. 9, regards the proposition as the first one suggestive of the National Banking System.

[2] McVickar, *Hints on Banking* (1827), reprinted in the *Financial Register* (1838), ii, 325–327. The first and second Bank of the United States, three-quarters of the capital of which was payable in government stock, and the Bank of England, whose entire capital was invested in government securities, were cited as precedents by McVickar and others.

[3] *Principles of Currency and Banking* (1829), p. 84.

[4] *Ibid.*, pp. 65–67. Cp. pp. 55–65. In reality the original capital is also returned into circulation when government stocks are bought with it.

[5] *Ibid.*, p. 54.

amount of notes, preferably uniform for all banks and officially certified.[1]

With the passage of the general banking law of New York in 1838, subsequent suggestions for a bond-secured issue lose most of their interest, and the arguments pro and con alone become significant.[2] Raguet thought that this system of note issue was, on the whole, the best.[3] It did not, however, provide any certain guaranty against excessive issue.[4] Hildreth, who had urged free banking without any government interference in his *History of Banking* (1837), modified his position three years later to the extent of sponsoring the deposit of security for notes.[5]

Barnard objected in the New York legislature to such a plan of note issue as recurring to the old land-bank fallacy of confusing ultimate security with redeemability.[6] Security, he said, in common with Charles Francis Adams, Gallatin, and others, is no guaranty against an unhealthy expansion of the currency.[7] At best, it was pointed out by one critic, it is only note issue that is limited; deposits are left free to expand indefinitely.[8] Tucker thought that the necessity of investing capital at a relatively low rate of return would deter capitalists from engaging in banking.[9] On the other hand, McVickar and Lord sought to show that the

---

[1] *Principles of Currency and Banking* (1829), p. 107.

[2] A bill was introduced in Maryland in 1831 for the establishment of free banking based upon the investment of the bank's capital in real estate, and a copy of it is said to have been before the New York legislature in 1838. The *Financial Register* (1838), ii, 400. Michigan enacted a free banking law in 1837. It called for the deposit with the government of bonds and mortgages and personal bonds as security for both notes and deposits. The law was declared unconstitutional, however. See Knox, *History of Banking*, pp. 95, 416.

[3] Raguet, *Currency and Banking* (1839), pp. 200-204.

[4] Letter to Bronson (May 11, 1838), *Financial Register*, ii, 10.

[5] Hildreth, *Banks, Banking, and Paper Currencies* (1840).

[6] Barnard, *Speeches* (1838), p. 193. Barnard was opposing the New York General Banking Bill, which made mortgages as well as stocks acceptable as security, but his criticism applied also to the latter.

[7] Adams, "Theory of Money and Banks," *Hunt's Merchants' Magazine* (1839), i, 122; Gallatin, "Suggestions" (1841), *Writings*, iii, 441; South Carolina, *Report of the Special Committee of the General Assembly* (1849), p. 13.

[8] Publius, *Remarks* (1840), p. 30.

[9] Tucker, *Theory of Money and Banks* (1839), p. 226. In 1858 Tucker wrote in favor of stock-secured notes. *Hunt's Merchants' Magazine*, xxxviii, 151.

PRINCIPLES OF NOTE ISSUE 149

profits of banking would be enhanced virtually to the extent of the interest borne by the government stock.[1] Then it was objected that in times of financial stringency, just when the security was wanted for redemption of the notes of insolvent banks, it would be likely to prove salable only at a heavy loss.[2] To this criticism the experience of New York soon gave point. Others feared that borrowing by the federal government and by the several states whose securities were made eligible would be facilitated by the creation of an artificial market for their stocks. Public extravagance would thus be fostered.[3] The New York law, it was prophesied, would tend to "raise up a clamorous horde of advocates for a perpetual State loan and national debt, to supply the demand for public stocks."[4]

A principle having a certain resemblance to that of founding bank notes upon the security of stocks and mortgages, since it also looks primarily to the ultimate security of the note-holder, is that of limiting the issue of notes to a given proportion of the bank's capital. This was popular alike in theory and in practice.[5] Three times the capital was the favored limit during the earlier years, partly in the belief, it seems probable, that this was providing for the one-third specie reserve which English bankers regarded as proper.[6] Aside from the frequent evasion of the requirement that the capital be paid in specie, such reasoning was fallacious in that there was no assurance that the specie would remain in the vaults of the bank after it began to make loans.

[1] Lord, *Principles of Currency and Banking* (1829), pp. 65–67, 89; South Carolina, *Report of 1849*, pp. 14, 15. See Sullivan, *Path to Riches* (1792), p. 36; and *Enquiry into the Tendency of Public Measures* (1794), p. 17, for criticism of the first U. S. Bank as deriving double profit. Cp. J. S. Ropes, "The Financial Crisis," *New Englander* (1857), xv, 709.

[2] Tucker, *op. cit.*, p. 229; C. F. Adams, "Theory of Money and Banks," *Hunt's Merchants' Magazine* (Aug., 1839), i, 116.

[3] C. F. Adams, *loc. cit.*, p. 120; L. McKnight, "Free Banking," *De Bow's Review* (Jan., 1853), xiii, 31, 32.

[4] "Free Banking," *Democratic Review* (1839), v, 445.

[5] See Dewey, *State Banking Before the Civil War*, pp. 53–63.

[6] This explanation is suggested by Tucker, *Theory of Money and Banks* (1839), pp. 204, 205, and H. F. Baker, "History of Banking in United States," *Bankers' Magazine* (Oct., 1856), xi, 253.

Insistence that those who control a bank bear a financial responsibility proportioned to all or certain of the bank's liabilities to the public is, of course, perfectly proper. On the other hand, it is to be admitted that some writers, in urging this policy, as well as in urging stock security and a safety fund, were more or less guilty of confusing ultimate security with redeemability on demand. For the most part, however, in view of the repeated criticism of contemporaries, it seems more logical to believe that the emphasis placed upon ultimate security was due not so much to this confusion as to inability to see how adequate provision could be made for obtaining uninterrupted convertibility. It should also be observed that both the plan of requiring a definite ratio to capital and the plan of calling for stock security were fostered in part by failure to recognize the desirability of an elastic currency.

4. Safety-Fund System

The system, adopted in New York in 1829, of requiring each bank to contribute a given percentage of its capital to a common fund for the guaranty of note circulation, calls for no extended treatment. It was hoped that, in addition to giving note-holders the added security of the fund, the plan would make it to the interest of each bank to seek to prevent bad management of the others in order that the common fund might not be depleted through insolvencies.[1] Objection was made that the scheme tended to confound prudent with careless banking, enabling unsound bankers to enjoy a volume of circulation which they would be denied on the sole basis of their own credit. The public would be lulled into a false feeling of security and the standard of banking actually lowered.[2] Also the unfairness of taxing the better banks in order to bolster the credit of weaker ones and to redeem the notes of the bankrupt was urged by critics of the system.[3] To

---

[1] Chaddock, *Safety-Fund System*, p. 260; Tucker, *Theory of Money and Banks*, p. 223; etc. Joshua Forman, who suggested this system of note issue, gave credit for the notion to a similar scheme whereby the Hong merchants of Canton who held government grants for trading with foreign countries were required to assume joint responsibility for each other's debts. See *Letter to Gov. Van Buren*, Jan. 24, 1829.

[2] W. B. Lawrence, *North American Review* (1831), xxxii, 556; Gallatin, *Considerations* (1831), p. 70.

[3] *E. g.*, Gallatin, *Considerations* (1831), p. 70.

this objection it was replied that the New York banks had no cause to complain, since bank capital was customarily taxed at a much higher rate in many states.[1] But this contention in turn was rejected on the score that contributing to the safety fund was quite different from sharing in the burden of the general expenditures of the state; in the former case it was the weaker banks that received practically all of the benefit. Certainly, since the fund was to guarantee note circulation, assessments upon the banks should be proportioned to the amount of notes outstanding, and not to capital stock.[2] Ohio, in adopting a safety-fund system in 1845, incorporated this suggestion. Finally, it was pointed out that the plan provided safety to note-holders in the case of isolated insolvencies, but that it could hardly meet the burden of wide-spread disaster. Nor was any remedy contained against that more troublesome evil, alternate inflation and deflation.[3]

These criticisms appeared while the New York bill was still under consideration, and soon became commonplace. It is to be noticed that the discussion ran almost completely in terms of bank notes. The New York law originally was worded to cover deposits as well, but this seems to have been almost inadvertent, and the statute was changed in 1842 to include only notes.[4] Little precedent for the more recent doctrine that bank deposits should be guaranteed is to be found in the discussion of the first half of the century. The principle that depositors are able to exercise their own judgment in selecting the bank in whose liabilities they place confidence, and so need no further protection by the state, seems scarcely to have been questioned.

[1] Paige Committee's Report (New York, 1829), Chaddock, *op. cit.*, p. 264.
[2] The city banks, with their circulation bearing a much smaller proportion to capital, insisted upon this. See Chaddock, *op. cit.*, p. 267; W. B. Lawrence, *North American Review* (1831), xxxii, 556.
[3] Isaac Bronson, Letter to a Member of Congress (1832), *Financial Register*, ii, 11; C. F. Adams, "Theory of Money and Banks," *Hunt's Merchants' Magazine* (Aug., 1839), i, 115.
[4] New York Assembly Document 64 (1841), iii, 16; Chaddock, *op. cit.*, p. 351.

CHAPTER XIV

PRINCIPLES OF NOTE ISSUE (*Continued*)

Legal reserve requirements. — Suffolk Bank System. — Taxing banks for regulative purposes. — Banking structure.

1. LEGAL RESERVE REQUIREMENTS

To a certain extent the old fallacy, so much in evidence during the colonial period, of confusing ultimate security with immediate redeemability, or, at least, of tending to give little attention to the latter, persisted well into the nineteenth century. Bond-secured issue, safety fund, limitation of circulation to a certain proportion to capital, received far more emphasis than specie reserve; and in some measure, at least, the cause seems to have been failure adequately to perceive the significance of reserves. As late as 1858 we find a committee of "friends of a sound currency" sponsoring a plan permitting each bank "to extend its loans and other investments to a point equal to once and a half its capital and its specie reserve," grouping the latter two as though similar in nature.[1] Against deposits a reserve of twenty per cent was at all times to be held, but no similar provision was deemed necessary for notes, since they were to be secured by a pledge of bonds.[2]

Laws requiring that a definite percentage of specie be held against note circulation were found in but few of the states before 1840,[3] nor was such legislation commonly advocated before that date.[4] A one-third ratio was often suggested, but smaller ratios were sometimes favored and even established by law.

---

[1] Opdyke [chairman], *Report on the Currency* (1858), p. 13.

[2] Opdyke, *op. cit.*, pp. 13, 15. Cp. Sullivan, *Path to Riches* (1792), p. 49; Raymond, *Elements of Political Economy* (1823), ii, 145.

[3] See Dewey, *State Banking Before the Civil War*, p. 57, for exceptions.

[4] See Report on the Currency, *American Quarterly Review* (1832), xi, 247; Barnard, *Speeches* (1838), p. 21; Webster, *Speech on the Sub-Treasury Bill* (March 12, 1838), p. 21. Also, James Buchanan, Annual Message (Dec. 1857), in Richardson's *Messages of the Presidents*, v, 438.

The desirability of tempering the rigidity of laws establishing reserve minima, in order to provide for periods of abnormal strain, received attention early in the discussion of such laws. Professor Tucker urged that a few weeks indulgence be granted whenever a drain reduced the reserve below the required ratio. The bank was to forfeit a portion of its profit in the meantime.[1] Tucker later proposed that a bank whose specie reserve became deficient "should be required to restore it by abstaining from all new loans, by calling in former loans, and by buying specie, under a daily pecuniary penalty for the delay, to be paid into the public treasury."[2] Another writer dismissed as absurd any law requiring a given reserve minimum, such as fifteen per cent. "Of what use," he asked, "is it that a bank has the gold and silver if the law forbids it to part with it? To comply with the terms of the law, the bank must have at least 30 per cent in specie, 15 per cent for use, and 15 per cent *to keep* according to law."[3] He commended the Ohio Law, which solved this difficulty by regarding demand deposits with sound banks in New York, Boston, Philadelphia, and Baltimore as equivalent to gold and silver on hand.

Others saw that imposing a minimum reserve ratio implied in fact that a larger percentage had to be maintained, but found no objection to such regulations on that account. "A legal minimum of 20 per cent will, it is believed, give a practical minimum of not less than 25 to 30 per cent," it was urged, "for no prudent bank will voluntarily occupy a position on the verge of legal death."[4] Samuel Hooper, whose *Specie in Banks* is significant for the unwonted stress it placed upon the importance of preserving an adequate reserve, also thought that no prudent banker would fail to keep sufficient reserves in excess of legal requirements to

---

[1] Tucker, *Theory of Money and Banks* (1839), p. 208. Cp. South Carolina, Report of Special Committee of the General Assembly (1849), p. 16.

[2] Tucker, "Banks or No Banks," *Hunt's Merchants' Magazine* (Feb., 1858), xxxviii, 148. See Hooper, *Specie in Banks* (1860), p. 22, for a like view.

[3] T. P. Kettell, "The Money of Commerce," *De Bow's Review* (Oct., 1848), vi, 261. Cp. J. N. C., *Southern Quarterly Review* (Sept., 1850), xviii, 129.

[4] Opdyke committee's *Report on the Currency* (1858), p. 15.

avoid infraction of the law in case of an unexpected demand for specie.[1]

After the crisis of 1857 the banks were more commonly criticized for keeping insufficient reserves than had been the case before. The tendency of surplus funds from all sections of the country to flow toward New York had already become pronounced, and it was against the New York banks in particular that most of the criticism was directed. The bank vaults of New York, Hooper observed, were the great depositories of the nation's reserves, and upon the policy of the directorates of that city the credit structure of the country depended. But the independent action of the several boards could not be relied upon.[2] "The *law* must secure the uniform ability of the banks to meet their engagements by making it imperative upon each one of them to hold the requisite amount of specie as a condition of their power to discount."[3] The Boston banks and those of other minor money centers, as well as the New York institutions, should hold such ample reserves for their several regions of the country, that balances placed in them by country banks might be confidently regarded as the equivalent of specie.[4] Edmund Dwight, who had written to the same effect in 1851, now found it opportune to repeat his views at greater length.[5]

The evil effects of paying interest upon the deposits of other banks — in particular the tendency that such a practice has to force the depository bank to expand its loans in order that costly resources may not lie idle — had been remarked upon earlier in the eighteen-fifties.[6] It was not until after the disastrous crisis of

[1] Hooper, *Specie in Banks* (1860), p. 27.

[2] The notion of a central bank, in the present-day sense of one charged with the responsibility of maintaining the reserves upon which rests the credit of the whole banking community, was almost entirely wanting. One or two writers, however, took the exceptional view that the second Bank of the United States had such a function. See below, pp. 165–167.

[3] Hooper, *Specie in Banks* (1860), pp. 43, 44. It will be recalled that Hooper believed that the passage of a minimum reserve law would bring about the keeping of surplus reserves by all prudent bankers.

[4] Hooper, *op. cit.*, p. 46.

[5] Dwight, "The Progressing Expansion," *Hunt's Merchants' Magazine* (1851), xxv, 152; "Financial Revulsion," *Ibid.*, xxxviii, 159–162.

[6] Silex, *Letters* (1853), p. 8.

1857, however, that the problem seems to have attracted much attention. The New York Clearing House Association appointed a committee to consider the matter at the beginning of 1858. The committee reported in favor of abolishing the practice of paying interest on current deposits, and especially upon those of country banks.[1] All but a few of the members of the association supported the report, but the minority could not be persuaded to discontinue paying interest.

Practically all the earlier discussion of reserves referred to their relation to circulation only. It was not until the difficulties of handling the deposits of country banks arose, and especially after the panic of 1857, that deposits received much attention in the consideration of reserve policy.[2]

2. Suffolk Bank System

The Suffolk Bank system of New England remedied one of the weakest aspects of our early banking — the poor homing power of notes. The underlying principle — that country banks should provide for the par redemption of their notes in the commercial center of the districts in which the banks were situated — promptly became popular with writers on banking, upon its adoption by the New England states. It was even suggested that there was no reason why notes should be redeemed at the place of issue if redemption were provided for at the center to which remittances had frequently to be made.[3]

Opponents of the system as adopted in New England, besides asserting the unfairness of requiring country banks to redeem their notes at two places, contended that it gave Boston, as the point of redemption, an artificial advantage, and caused her trade to prosper by reason of the arbitrary force drawing bank notes to

---

[1] *Bankers' Magazine* (April, 1858), xii (old series), 822–830. A fuller discussion is given below, in Chapter XVII.

[2] Tucker, *Theory of Money and Banks* (1839), should be excepted (see pp. 207, 208). Also the reserve laws of a few states, such as Louisiana, early required reserves of a definite ratio to notes and deposits. Dewey, *State Banking Before the Civil War*, pp. 217–224.

[3] Wilkes, "Banking and the Currency," *Hunt's Merchants' Magazine* (Aug., 1858), xxxix, 193.

her from all parts of New England.[1] In reply it was pointed out that the flow of notes toward Boston was the effect of her growth, not the cause of it; that the adoption of the system and the choice of Boston as the redeeming center were based on this very tendency of notes to be drawn into that city.[2]

As to the contention that the arrangement prevented the country banks from issuing as many notes as formerly, with the result that these outlying banks were forced to curtail their accommodations to local tradesmen, advocates of the system maintained that the reduction in country note circulation represented notes which had been issued, not by ordinary local bank loans, but "by the artifices of brokers and bank agents" at Boston.[3] One of the chief purposes of the system, several writers argued, was to make the circulation of interior banks more sensitive to changes in the state of the currency in the larger mercantile cities. With country bank notes at a discount in the cities, in the absence of provisions for redeeming them there, it was upon the city banks, whose notes were at par, that a drain for gold fell whenever an unfavorable balance of trade occurred. Meanwhile the country banks, scarcely affected by the export of gold, might continue to expand their issues, obstructing correction of the redundant currency.[4] Provision for redemption at a commercial center, it was also asserted, enabled banks to operate on a smaller reserve ratio.[5]

A nation-wide clearing system for notes, subdivided into perhaps eight or ten districts, was proposed by a number of writers. Each district was to have a clearing house of its own, with an interdistrict clearing house to complete the system.[6] Sponsors

---

[1] Smith, "The Suffolk Bank System," *Hunt's Merchants' Magazine* (March, 1851), xxiv, 319, 320.

[2] Foster, "The Suffolk Bank System," *Hunt's Merchants' Magazine* (May, 1851), xxiv, 578.

[3] Anon., *Remarks on the Banks and Currency of the New England States* (1826), p. 37.

[4] "Theory of Banking," by a Merchant of Boston, *Hunt's Merchants' Magazine* (July, 1841), v, 31; Wilkes, "Banking and the Currency," *Hunt's Merchants' Magazine* (Aug., 1858), xxxix, 194.

[5] *Bankers' Magazine* (Dec., 1850), v, 514.

[6] "Theory of Banking," *Hunt's Merchants' Magazine* (1841), v, 32–37; Wilkes, "Banking and the Currency," *Hunt's Merchants' Magazine* (1858), xxxix, 198;

of the plan claimed that a more uniform currency would result, the danger of an excessive amount of currency would be lessened, and, finally, the clearings would be economically conducted. Gallatin, however, thought the country was too large for a unified clearing and collection system.[1]

The question of par redemption of notes at points other than those at which they were issued was the subject of considerable controversy in connection with the second Bank of the United States and its branches, and in connection with the Suffolk system. Such considerations as the elimination of "shaving shops" and of wild-cat banking lent strength to the demand for par redemption at Boston, New York, and other commercial centers; and yet it was pointed out that for a country bank to redeem its notes at par in a distant city was to force it to give its notes a property which specie itself did not possess. Gallatin regarded it as improper to make "any attempt whatever to regulate exchange, to compel banks to redeem their notes at par or at a certain discount at any other place than that specified on the face of the notes, or in any way to give a uniform value in different places to bank notes, which are in their nature a local currency." It is unjust to exact of paper currency "that which gold and silver, of which it is the representative, cannot perform." [2]

3. Taxing Banks for Regulative Purposes

A fairly popular suggestion was that which would remove the motive for excessive note issue by having the government appropriate all profits above a certain percentage of the bank's capital. Raymond urged this as a substitute for government monopoly

---

Colwell, *Ways and Means of Payment* (1859), pp. 636–642. Colwell would include checks and bills of exchange in the clearings. A writer in *Hunt's Merchants' Magazine* for 1856 proposed the establishment of a national bank with many branches to serve other banks as a collection agent for checks and commercial paper. (E. Y. C., in vol. xxxiv, p. 26.)

[1] Gallatin, "Suggestions" (1841), in *Writings*, iii, 425.

[2] Idem, Letter to Flagg (Dec. 31, 1841), *Writings*, ii, 568. Cp. *Report of the Committee of Ways and Means on the Bank of the United States* (April 13, 1830), p. 13; "Bank of the United States," *American Quarterly Review* (March, 1831), ix, 226; Tucker, *Theory of Money and Banks* (1839), pp. 293–302.

of issue.[1] The committee on money and banking of the Pennsylvania legislature recommended the plan in 1821.[2] Gallatin thought not only that such a tax would make for more conservative banking, but that the profit from note issue was one in which it was peculiarly appropriate that the government participate.[3] This latter notion was of course common, although those who shared it seem to have preferred, like Raymond, to go further and have the government reserve for itself the very power of note issue.

Nathan Appleton advocated a tax levied directly upon circulation, proportioned to its authorized volume.[4] As a member of the House of Representatives he proposed such an amendment to the bill for rechartering the second Bank of the United States. This he thought, "would take away the inducement of profit, which every Bank now has, to increase its circulation to the utmost."[5] An anonymous critic pointed out the fallacy of basing a tax seeking that end upon the maximum amount of note issue authorized. Instead, the amount of circulation actually outstanding should be made the basis of the tax.[6]

More frequently, however, propositions to tax note issues for regulative purposes would impose the tax only when the notes were inconvertible. Massachusetts enacted such a tax in 1810, and the charter of the second Bank of the United States imposed a penalty of twelve per cent interest on deposits as well as notes for failure to redeem them on demand.[7] Tucker would limit the dividends of banks to six per cent whenever they suspended specie payments, and reduce the percentage still further in case of prolonged suspension.[8]

[1] Raymond, *Elements* (1823), ii, 157.
[2] Report (1821), *Examiner and Journal of Political Economy*, ii, 342.
[3] Gallatin, Letter to Biddle (Aug. 14, 1830), *Writings*, ii, 436.
[4] Appleton, *Remarks* (1841), p. 44.
[5] *Ibid.*
[6] *Remarks on Mr. Appleton's "Remarks"* (1841), pp. 42-44.
[7] Dewey, *State Banking Before the Civil War*, p. 75. The Massachusetts tax was at the rate of 24 per cent.
[8] Tucker, *Theory of Money and Banks* (1839), p. 209.

4. Banking Structure

Discussion of the question by whom banks should be governed ran mostly in terms of commonplaces. The relative merits of public and private banks was a moot question in the colonial period, but the later writers were largely of one opinion. Hamilton, while urging public participation in both the ownership and control of the first Bank of the United States, had no doubt that it was undesirable that a bank be managed wholly by the government.[1] Despite experiments by some states in government banks, — experiments that were not always happy, — the opinion of practically all writers on banking, if we except those with fanciful socialistic notions, was against banks managed by public officials. Jackson's proposal for "a national bank, founded upon the credit of the government and its revenues,"[2] was rebuked by the Committee of Ways and Means with the decisiveness of an Adam Smith. "There is no species of trade," thought the committee, "in which it would be wise for the government to embark; but of all the variety of pursuits known to human enterprise, that of lending money by the government to the citizens of the country would be fraught with the most pernicious consequences."[3] There was some suggestion of a prophetic eye in the committee's contention that every depression would bring an irresistible demand for extension of discounts, and that inflation would become the platform of every demagogue.[4]

We have noted in an early chapter the wide-spread distrust of even privately owned banks, and the fear of the sinister influence of a "monied aristocracy." Various measures for mitigating the supposed danger were proposed. Hamilton and Tucker favored rotation in electing directors.[5] Efforts to avoid concentration of share-holdings and provision for regressive voting power were

---

[1] Hamilton, Report on a National Bank (1790), *American State Papers, Finance*, i, 73, 74.

[2] First Annual Message (Dec. 8, 1829), Richardson, *Messages of the Presidents*, ii, 462.

[3] *Report of the Committee of Ways and Means* (April 13, 1830), p. 27.

[4] *Ibid.*, p. 28.

[5] Hamilton, Report on a National Bank (1790), *American State Papers, Finance*, i, 72; Tucker, *Theory of Money and Banks* (1839), p. 216.

popular.[1] Tucker and others stressed the value of publicity as a check upon abuses.[2]

As in England, the desirability of making banking the exclusive privilege of certain chartered companies was the subject of considerable controversy. It was an issue inherited from the colonial period.[3] Raymond objected to chartered banking in no uncertain terms. A "parcel of rich men," he held, combine "for no other purpose but to augment the artificial power, which money gives them, in accumulating more."[4] "I am unshaken in my opinion," wrote Thomas Cooper, "that every bank charter is unconstitutional: depriving the great majority of citizens of rights which they are entitled to be protected in exercising; and conferring exclusive privileges on another class, upon motives and pretenses often fraudulent, seldom excusable, never justifiable."[5] Professor McVickar, writing in the mood of Manchesterism at its zenith, thought that "all the evils of banking, beyond those which exist in other modes of business, flow from needless or unwise regulation."[6] Monopoly and charters, interfering with the beautiful workings of natural laws, were in his judgment the source of all the evils of banking.[7] Gouge regarded incorporation as a premium on villainy, and Hildreth asserted that the restriction of the privilege of note issue to a few corporations was a regulation "quite as wise and profound, as if the legislature should grant to a few firms in Court street and Hanover street, the exclusive right of manufacturing cotton shirts."[8] H. C. Carey found the subject fitted to illustrate his ability to formulate "laws" conveniently

---

[1] Sullivan, *Path to Riches* (1792), pp. 62–64; Dewey, *State Banking Before the Civil War*, pp. 22–33, 112–115.

[2] Tucker, *Theory*, etc. (1839), pp. 211–213. See Dewey, *op. cit.*, pp. 126–136, for legislation seeking greater publicity for banking accounts.

[3] "Objections to the Bank of Credit" (1714), *Reprints*, i, 242–248; "Letter from One in Boston" (1714), *ibid.*, i, pp. 282–285; Douglass, *Discourse* (1740), C. J. Bullock's edition, pp. 310, 353.

[4] Raymond, *Elements* (1823), ii, 121. He tempered his views fifteen years later. (See Neill, *Daniel Raymond*, p. 36.)

[5] Cooper, *Lectures* (1826), p. 157.

[6] McVickar, "Hints on Banking" (1827), *Financial Register*, ii, 321.

[7] *Ibid.*, ii, 324, 325.

[8] Hildreth, *Letter to Morton* (1840), p. 12. See also, *Democratic Review* (1837), i, 116, and (1840), vii, 199.

embodying his viewpoint. His *Credit System in France, Great Britain, and the United States* (1838) is a unique argument for a policy of complete *laissez faire* with respect to banking. Not the least remarkable feature of it is Carey's confident assertion (one year after the panic of 1837) that our own banking system was easily the best in the world, by an arithmetic law based upon relative freedom from restriction. Like Hildreth, Carey thought that "there is no more propriety or necessity for regulating who shall or who shall not issue his note, to be exchanged with those who are willing to take it, than there is for regulating who shall or who shall not grow potatoes or make shoes."[1] With the development of the idea of a bond-secured note issue, free banking upon the condition that security be offered for circulation became generally popular.

Restriction of banking privileges to corporations with exclusive charters was defended by relatively few writers. Gallatin thought that the power of note issue should be so restricted, but that the other operations of banks should be left free to all.[2] Tucker refuted the absurdities of Hildreth and Carey by observing that the interest of the community is not served when the banker manufactures his product in as large quantities as possible.[3] And the holders of bank notes are unable to exercise much choice as to the notes they will receive.[4] H. F. Baker objected to the free banking system as adopted in New York and elsewhere on the score that it "invites the inexperienced, as well as others, to enter upon a business which requires skill, experience, and talents."[5]

The defenders of free banking had to contend, in order to be logical, that multiplying the number of banks within the limits to which private capital found it profitable to do so would be advantageous to the community. At the very beginning of our national history some seem to have believed that the Bank of the

[1] Carey, *The Credit System*, etc. (1838), p. 118.
[2] Gallatin, *Considerations* (1831), p. 95; "Suggestions" (1841), *Writings*, iii, 446.
[3] Tucker, *Theory of Money and Banks* (1839), p. 244.
[4] *Ibid.*, p. 245.
[5] H. F. Baker, "Banking in the United States," *Bankers' Magazine* (July, 1854), ix, 14.

United States with its branches would suffice for the whole country and that no competitor could prosper.[1] The establishment of banks by the states soon dispelled this notion and the merits of a multiplicity of banks had to be considered. Many held, as had Smith, that the competition of numerous banks could have none but a wholesome effect. It forces each bank to keep a large reserve in order to be on its guard against possible run upon it by a rival institution, and it lessens the consequence of the failure of any one bank.[2] The danger of excessive multiplication would be sufficiently guarded against by exacting a bonus for every charter granted, thought a committee of the Virginia House of Delegates.[3] Clearings, Hildreth observed, prevent excessive expansion by any one bank; increase in the number of banks lessens the probability of their acting in concert.[4]

Dissent from the doctrine that banks should be allowed to multiply freely was expressed on the ground that larger reserves are necessary when they must be divided among many banks of issue.[5] Others feared that the "imprudent jealousy" of rival

---

[1] "On Banking Companies in the United States," *American Museum* (Sept., 1792), xii, 144. A few banks, of course, already existed at the time of the founding of the first Bank of the United States in 1791.

The question whether a system of branch banking was to be preferred to one of many independent banks came in for very little consideration. Hamilton had misgivings about the desirability of providing branches for the first Bank of the United States. Despite some advantages, he feared that the "complexity of such a plan would be apt to inspire doubts, which might deter from adventuring in it." Report on a National Bank (1790), *American State Papers, Finance*, i, 73. In 1828 Willard Phillips again turned to the question and preferred a large number of independent banks, believing that they would be more effective checks against overissue by each other — a conclusion that is hardly supported by comparison of our own banking history with that of Canada and Scotland. Phillips also prized the greater degree of local management that attends independent banking. *Manual of Political Economy* (1828), pp. 263, 264. The two Banks of the United States and some of the state banks of the South and West did, of course, have branches. See Dewey, *State Banking Before the Civil War*, pp. 136–143.

[2] Smith, *Wealth of Nations*, book II, chap. 2 (vol. i, p. 312); "On Banking Companies," etc., *American Museum* (1792), xii, 144, 145; *Suggestions on the President's Message* (1815), p. 31; etc.

[3] "Report on Banks" (1816), *Niles' Register*, ix, 159.

[4] Hildreth, *Banks, Banking, and Paper Currencies* (1840), p. 158.

[5] *American Review* (1812), iii, 286; Bollman, *Plan* (1816), p. 26.

banks would be likely to lead to runs upon their neighbors.[1] Niles, who at first had given rather little attention to banks, suddenly began to harp upon the necessity of reducing them "to a proper number." "After the evils entailed upon our country by negro slavery," he wrote, "there are none, in my opinion . . . so fatal to the freedom and prosperity of the people as the multiplication of the banking establishments." [2]

"Under any system of paper money," Gallatin wrote to the English banker, Horsley Palmer, "a single bank of issue, such as that of England was sixty years ago, such as that of France [is] now, is to me the *beau idéal*." [3] And H. F. Baker wrote in his history of American banking that, when the number of banks has been sufficiently enlarged to secure to the public the benefit of competition, "it appears to be as unwise to multiply them any farther as it would be to make any unnecessary addition to the number of our colleges." [4] Tucker, Raguet, and a number of minor writers agreed that "The increase of banks of issue when the supply of their paper is already equal to the demand, is a loss to the community, in as far as it is an increase of expenditure without any increase of utility." [5] There is a certain amount of work for banks to do, and competition is desirable, but as soon as enough banks have been established to accomplish the work and secure competition, further increase in the number of banks only adds to the expense at which the bank services will be furnished.

The question of a national bank, which played so prominent a part in our banking discussion, was largely a political issue. The underlying factors were economic, however. In some respects the problem was intimately tied up with that of the most advantageous number of banks to have. This was especially true when the establishment of a national bank enjoying a monopoly of note issue was favored.

[1] Baldwin, *Thoughts on the Study of Political Economy* (1809), p. 46.
[2] *Niles' Register* (June, 1817), xii, 263.
[3] Gallatin, Letter to Palmer (May 1, 1833), *Writings*, ii, 462.
[4] H. F. Baker, "Outline History of Banking in the United States," *Bankers' Magazine* (Oct., 1856), xi, 255.
[5] Putnam, *Tracts on . . . Political Economy* (1834), p. 9. Cp. Tucker, *Theory*, etc. (1839), pp. 217–219; Raguet, *Currency and Banking* (1839), p. 79.

The leading arguments for a national bank (passing over the claim that it would aid the fiscal operations of the government) were that it would provide a sound and uniform currency, exert a restraining influence on state banks, and reduce the cost of domestic exchange.[1]

Hildreth, who doted on applying *laissez-faire* doctrines to banking, believed free competition was the solvent of all our troubles. The supervisory influence of a national bank was hardly necessary or likely to be helpful. "You set up a National Bank to watch the other banks; but who is to watch the watcher?" he asked.[2] Tucker sought to dispose of the objection that the national bank itself might not pursue a desirable policy by urging the establishment of two or three such banks. Competition would then be furnished on this higher level of our banking hierarchy, and the power of each national bank to do evil would be diminished.[3] To this Charles Francis Adams justly objected that the ability of any one of the banks to have a beneficial influence would be proportionately lessened.[4]

"It is the right of the people," was the interesting suggestion of an obscure essayist of 1834, "under such restrictions as the wisdom of Congress may deem necessary, to furnish a sound federal currency; and the constitution confers upon the government no power to confine this privilege to a single corporation, to the exclusion of the great body of the people. We are, therefore, if possible, for abolishing all monopoly, and for substituting in the place of a *National Bank* a National System of Banking." [5] Smaller banks, with a capital of less than two million dollars, he was content to retain under state laws; but banks with capital of

[1] E. g., see Raguet, *Examiner* (1834), ii, 141; Tucker, *Theory*, etc. (1839), pp. 274–279.

[2] Hildreth, *History of Banking* (1837), p. 138. H. C. Carey also invoked the *laissez-faire* doctrine in opposing a national bank for the purpose of regulating other banks. *Past, Present, and Future* (1848), pp. 179, 180; and *Letter to the President* (Dec. 25, 1857), p. 15.

[3] Tucker, *Theory* (1839), pp. 328–330; "Banks or No Banks," *Hunt's Merchants' Magazine* (Feb., 1858), xxxviii, 155, 156.

[4] C. F. Adams, "Theory of Money and Banks," *Hunt's Merchants' Magazine* (Aug., 1839), i, 122.

[5] W. R. Collier, *Essay on the Currency* (1834), p. 8.

not less than two million dollars "ought to be freed from the trammels of State legislation, and recognized as furnishing the material for a sound federal currency."[1] He would make national banking free to all who complied with certain specified conditions, and would allow the state banks to continue to issue notes for local circulation.[2] The pamphlet contains little that is significant other than this interesting early idea of a national banking system.

Several suggestions, prompted in part by the example of the Bank of England, were made for a national bank in whose notes, themselves redeemable in specie, those of the local banks should be redeemed. Bollman outlined such a "bank of banks" at considerable length, although, characteristically, his interesting proposal had a ring of implausibility and eccentricity when developed in detail.[3] The state banks were to get the notes of the national bank by borrowing from the latter.[4]

The notion of a central bank, holding surplus lending power upon which the other banks could rely in times of difficulty, occurred to few, apparently. Three writers seem to have held that the second Bank of the United States was such an institution.[5] "Wherever national banks exist," wrote one, "to them has been confided the duty of procuring a treasure capable of sustaining nearly the entire paper circulation; and it is the only sure dependence. The country banks in England never kept more specie than in the proportion of one pound of gold to ten of paper, and the accounts of several of our state institutions exhibit similar results. Indeed, one large reserve is vastly more economical than a great number of small ones."[6]

[1] W. R. Collier, *op.cit.*, p. 9.   [2] *Ibid.*, pp. 9, 10.
[3] Bollman, *Plan* (1816), pp. 39, 40. Cp. Barker, *Private Banking* (1819), p. 18.
[4] Bollman, *Plan*, p. 39.
A national bank, with branches throughout the country, which should rediscount the commercial paper of other banks, enjoy a monopoly of note issue, and have dealings only with the government and with the local banks, was outlined in considerable detail in *Hunt's Merchants' Magazine* for 1856. See E. Y. C., "A System of National Currency," xxxiv, 20 ff.
[5] Lawrence, "Bank of the United States," *North American Review* (1831), xxxii, 558; Anon., "The Public Distress," *American Quarterly Review* (1834), xv, 525, 526; Anon., *A New Financial Project* (New York, 1837), pp. 20, 21.
[6] "The Public Distress," *American Quarterly Review* (1834), xv, 525.

The crisis of 1857 did much to bring about a sudden realization of the significance of New York as a growing financial center, and the problems of a central reserve city, if not of a central reserve bank, were now analyzed more deeply than ever before.[1] But Nathan Appleton seems to have been the only one to give much heed to the need of further centralization of control at New York. Even he did no more than to lament that the power exercised by the banks of the metropolis of giving the keynote to the whole country in the matter of expansion and contraction was subdivided among fifty-five directorates, acting independently, and no longer under the harmonizing influence of a Gallatin.[2]

About the same time appeared the noteworthy suggestion that a central bank of issue be founded at Boston, owned and controlled by all the banks of New England and New York and enjoying a monopoly of the privilege of note issue for the district. Its notes were to be receivable and payable at par by all the subscribing banks. It was to receive deposits, but, in order that it might not compete with the subscribing banks, it was to be allowed "to discount only for its stockholders, the local banks." It could thus "relieve the temporary pressures to which small banks are so liable," jealously preserving a reserve of from 33 to 50 per cent for the purpose. The author would have preferred to include the whole country in his scheme, if Congress could be prevailed upon to enact it.[3]

Some slight attention was given to the possible service of a national bank in bringing interest rates in the several sections of the country more nearly to an equality by effecting a more advantageous distribution of capital. Thus one proponent of a national bank observed that seasonal variations in the demand for money in the different parts of the country would be met by loans to each other by the branches of the national bank at the direction of the parent bank.[4] In general, however, emphasis was placed

---

[1] See Chapter XVII, below.

[2] Appleton, *Letter to Boston Daily Advertiser*, Oct. 12, 1857.

[3] J. S. Ropes, "The Financial Crisis," *New Englander* (Nov., 1857), xv, 712, 713. Some of the details given in the text have been taken from a further elaboration by the same author in *Bankers' Magazine*.

[4] John R. Hurd, *A National Bank, or No Bank* (1842), p. 40.

upon the duty of banks to care for the wants of their immediate vicinity, with little regard to the merits of an elastic flow of funds from one point to another. Charters and statutes frequently restricted the power of the banks to make loans on distant paper, and the bank commissioners of the New England states depreciated such "foreign loans" in a number of their reports.[1] The independent banking system that prevailed in most parts of the country undoubtedly contributed to this narrow conception of the scope of banking.

[1] See, in this regard, the next chapter.

PART IV

BANKING POLICY AND THE BUSINESS CYCLE

CHAPTER XV

BANKING POLICY

The importance of short loans. — The relative merits of different types of commercial paper. — The discount rate.

ACCOMMODATION loans, subject to repeated renewal, bulked large in our early banking experience. American bankers, Cooper wrote in 1826, contrary to English practice, discount accommodation loans regularly.[1] Raguet ascribed the suddenness of the crisis of 1837 to the lengthening of bank loans from the sixty-day tenor, which he believed was prevalent at the beginning of the century, to four and six months.[2]

The earliest sentiment seems to have been that banks should serve all classes alike with their loans, regardless of whether or not liquid assets result. Yet, coupled with this thesis, was a realization of the impolicy of the practice from the point of view of sound banking. Thus there was not a little opposition to early commercial banks on the ground that they are unable to extend their credit to farmers in loans for periods suitable to their purposes.[3] In order to obviate the difficulty, some wished to supplement the banks by establishing loan offices, after colonial example, and the state "property" banks in the South and Southwest were the results of efforts along this line. But others denied that advances for long periods are inconsistent with commercial banking itself. A committee of the Virginia legislature argued in 1816 that the experience of every American banker proved the contrary. Smith's dictum that a bank can advance only that part of the merchant's capital "which he would otherwise be obliged to keep by him, unemployed, and in ready money, for answering

---

[1] Cooper, *Lectures* (1826), p. 136. See also, Edward Clibborn, *American Prosperity* (1837), p. 29; Dewey, *State Banking Before the Civil War*, p. 155.

[2] Raguet, Letter to Bronson (May 11, 1838), *Financial Register*, ii, 9; *Currency and Banking* (1839), p. 96. Likewise, C. F. Adams, *Further Reflections*, etc. (1837), p. 10; Duncombe, *Free Banking* (1841), p. 53.

[3] See *supra*, Chapter IX.

occasional demands,"[1] might well be acceptable with reference to Great Britain; but the banks of this country, because of the scarcity of capital, must also make more permanent advances.[2] Nor is the making of accommodation loans, subject to repeated renewal, dangerous, for the money is commonly advanced on an endorsed note, and new signatures can be called for at each renewal, if the bank's suspicions are roused. Loans to farmers are no less proper than advances to merchants.[3] In 1839 a committee of the Indiana legislature pointed indignantly to the fact that the farmers, representing three-quarters of the state's population and wealth, received but one-quarter of the total amount of bank accommodation in the State. The committee denied that bank discounts are better suited to serve merchants than farmers, arguing that the mercantile business concerns itself largely with the importation of articles of extravagant consumption from outside the State, and, moreover, is so attractive, because of the notion that it is "a mode of getting rich without labor," that it needs little bank encouragement. The farming industry, on the other hand, "is the only one that can be uniformly relied on for profit on the capital and labor employed, and benefits to the State." If the frequency of renewals of business paper be considered, the committee thought that repayment would be found to be no more punctual than in the case of loans to farmers. "Besides, the question is not whether the farmer shall have credit from the bank, but whether he shall receive it directly from the bank itself, and in amount; or whether he and his wife and daughters shall get it through the merchant, and in the shape of merchandise."[4]

The fact that agriculture was so dominant an industry, particu-

[1] See *Wealth of Nations*, book II, chap. 2 (vol. i, p. 287).
[2] Virginia, House of Delegates, Report on Banks (1816), *Niles' Register*, ix, 160.
[3] *Ibid.*, ix, 161.
[4] Indiana, Report of the Committee on the State Bank, in U. S. House of Representatives, 26th Congress, 1st Session, Document 172, pp. 895–897. The committee's point is well taken, of course, that to the extent that traders relied upon credits due from farmers for means of paying their bank loans, the merchants' bills were themselves likely to prove frozen assets. But the real question then became whether the banks did not advance too much credit to the merchants rather than whether they advanced enough to the farmers.

larly in the West, contributed, we may well suppose, to make the development of sound banking difficult. Many of the states required that the banks lend a certain proportion of their funds to farmers for relatively long periods. Massachusetts inserted in the charter of the Union Bank of Boston (1792) the provision that "one-fifth of the whole funds of this Bank shall be always appropriated to Loans . . . wherein the Directors shall wholly and exclusively regard the Agricultural interest."[1] The loans were to be for not less than one year. This clause was repeated in most of the early bank charters granted by the state.

The importance of liquid assets was too obvious and elementary, however, to permit its neglect in theory to be very common, however long practices inconsistent with it continued to persist.[2] Bollman struck a typical note when he asserted that "the discounting of any paper, the successive renewal of which is implied, and understood, must be considered as inconsistent with sound principles of banking." Therefore, "banks in farming districts are a nuisance," he thought.[3] Cooper added similar testimony as to the necessity of liquid assets, and took exception to farm loans in particular. He doubted that farmers would usually be bene-

[1] Massachusetts, *Acts and Resolves*, 1792–1793 (1895 edition), pp. 17 ff. For further examples see Dewey, *State Banking Before the Civil War*, pp. 212–214.

[2] Nathan Appleton, who was, on the whole, a writer of sound views, regarded six months as not an excessive period for loans to run. "I do not agree with you," he wrote to a New York banker in 1857, "that the banks should confine their discounts to short paper, which, if good for the banks, is bad for the community. I have been for upwards of 40 years a director of the Boston Bank, during the greater part of which time they have confined their discounts to real business paper, which should be paid at maturity, and have not refused it even when having six months to run." *Bankers' Magazine*, xii, 407.

[3] Bollman, *Plan for an Improved System* (1816), p. 15.

Indeed, from the very beginning the importance of restricting loans to short tenors was not unappreciated by some of the bankers themselves. Upon opening for business in 1784, the Bank of New York adopted a rule to the effect that "no discount will be made for longer than thirty days, nor will any note or bill be discounted to pay a former one." How closely this extreme standard was adhered to is another matter. H. W. Domett, *A History of the Bank of New York*, p. 20.

On the other hand, we read a complaint in 1853 that the banks of New York and New England had been tending, in the two previous years, to lengthen discounts "from 6 to 8, 10 and 12 months." Silex, *Letters on Banks and Banking* (1853), p. 30. The editor of the *Democratic Review* found repeated occasion to decry excessively long terms of loan. See, for example, issue of January, 1844, p. 95.

fitted by borrowing even if special machinery were set up by the government for the purpose of making loans to them, because of the "lowness of agricultural profits, and the want of that habit of punctuality so carefully observed and exacted in mercantile transactions."[1] C. F. Adams, Gallatin, and Colwell, were other prominent writers who laid great stress on the importance of preserving an orderly stream of maturities by avoiding loans for long intervals and by refusing to make advances with the understanding that renewal would be granted.[2]

A number of writers made an exception of the investment of the bank's own capital. McVickar and Lord favored its permanent investment in government bonds and in mortgages, on the theory that a bank should utilize only its credit in commercial loans, a steady procession of maturing loans preserving the bank's assets in a liquid condition. The capital of a bank has the sole function of affording added security to creditors. This purpose is best served by withholding the capital from the risks of commercial loans, placing it instead in some high-grade investments, such as government stocks and mortgages.[3] Gallatin, Raguet, and Gouge maintained similar views.[4] Usually the Bank of England, with all its capital represented by government debt, and the two Banks of the United States, with three-quarters of their capitals paid in in that form, were referred to as examples.

Charles Francis Adams, on the other hand, contended that the necessity of keeping assets liquid applied with no less force to the employment of a bank's capital than to the use of its credit. "The first duty of the bank which emits bills of credit, is to be

[1] Cooper, *Lectures* (1826), p. 40.

[2] C. F. Adams, *Further Reflections*, etc. (1837), pp. 9, 10; Gallatin, "Suggestions" (1841), *Writings*, iii, 376; Colwell, *Ways and Means of Payment* (1859), pp. 496–500, 505.

[3] McVickar, "Hints on Banking" (1827), *Financial Register*, ii, 325–327; Lord, *Principles* (1829), pp. 57–62. Both McVickar and Lord had also some confused ideas that if a bank used but its credit in loans and discounts the needs of trade would regulate the volume of circulation, whereas if capital were also used in making commercial advances, excessive issue would result.

[4] Gallatin, *Considerations* (1831), pp. 71, 40; Raguet, *Financial Register* (May 11, 1838), ii, 7, 8; *Currency and Banking* (1839), pp. 85–88; Gouge, *Journal of Banking* (1841), p. 38; and *Hunt's Merchants' Magazine* (1843), viii, 313.

always provided with the means of instantly redeeming them when presented; hence, it is as important that the capital, which ought to furnish those means, should be frequently returned to it as that it should be profitably employed." [1]

More interesting than the discussion of the proper length of loans [2] was the consideration given to the problem of the relative merits of advances made against accommodation paper as compared with discounts of paper representing trade transactions. To a considerable degree the two problems cannot be separated. Those who insisted upon the superiority of real paper as the basis for loans were usually equally anxious that loans should be for short periods and not subject to renewal; while an analogous connection can be shown between defenders of accommodation loans and of loans of longer maturity.

Smith had urged that discounts based upon real paper cannot give rise to an unhealthy issue of bank notes,[3] and the matter still remained a moot question in England. In this country, Bollman in 1816 advanced the thesis that real loans admit of no overextension of credit,[4] and in the second quarter of the century it became a popular one. Cooper, to take a typical example, thought that the amount of bank notes in circulation would vary exactly with the wants of commerce,[5] if the policy of making none but real loans were adhered to. Accommodation loans disturbed the equilibrium, and, further, led to extravagance and bankruptcy.[6] Tucker summarized the case for real, or "business paper," as it was often called, by saying that loans of which it formed the basis were self-liquidating (to use a present-day term), encouraged industry and commerce without furnishing the means and incen-

[1] C. F. Adams, "Principles of Credit," *Hunt's Merchants' Magazine* (March, 1840), ii, 197.
[2] Call loans received an interesting analysis, but it was principally with reference to their bearing upon commercial crises and it will be treated in that connection. See the last chapter.
[3] *Wealth of Nations*, book II, chap. 2 (vol. i, p. 287).
[4] Bollman, *Plan for an Improved System* (1818), p. 15.
[5] In all but a few cases a currency varying with the needs of trade was taken to mean one varying exactly as it would if wholly metallic. See *supra*, Chapter VII.
[6] Cooper, *Lectures* (1826), pp. 133-143.

tive of overtrading, and caused the volume of media of payment to be adjusted to the requirements of the community.[1] The New York bank commissioners warned, in their report of 1840, that banks should "confine themselves strictly to paper of a business character to be paid at maturity." "It may be assumed as an undeniable axiom in the business of banking," they asserted three years later, on returning to the subject of accommodation loans of paper money, "that such issues are always excess; and that in precise proportion to their amount they derange the just relations of currency and trade."[2]

The argument for "business paper" did not go unchallenged. Mathew Carey questioned the theory that loans against real paper are liquid in the aggregate.[3] To bar accommodation loans would be to deny bank credit to a large proportion of merchants, since but a minor fraction of their business gives rise to discountable paper.[4] Gouge, in his earlier works, was inclined to doubt that accommodation loans have any more mischievous an influence than real loans,[5] although, as we shall see, he later changed his opinion. Carroll believed that accommodation paper is innocent of the evils commonly attributed to it. Loans against accommodation and real notes alike are harmful if made by a bank extending credit in excess of its capital and time deposits.[6] The Connecticut bank commissioners wrote in 1841 that the

[1] Tucker, *Theory of Money and Banks* (1839), pp. 166, 167. Note that it was not a question of the superior qualities of the acceptance as compared with the promissory note with which Tucker and his contemporaries dealt, but of loans against paper, whether buyer's or seller's, arising out of a commercial transfer of property, as compared with accommodation loans bearing no evidence that they were to be used to finance a transaction already concluded.

[2] Report (1843), U. S. House of Representatives, 29th Congress, 1st Session, Document 226, p. 274.

[3] M. Carey, *Desultory Reflections* (1810), p. 15. Carey, however, meant by "real notes" simply paper arising out of a *bona fide* transfer of goods regardless of the salability and rapidity of turnover of the latter. He used stocks and bonds as an illustration.

[4] Carey, Letter to Bronson (1816), *Essays on Banking*, p. 131.

[5] Gouge, *Short History of Paper Money* (1833), pp. 50, 51.

[6] C. H. Carroll, "Financial Heresies," *Hunt's Merchants' Magazine* (Sept., 1860), xliii, 317–319.

practice of some banks to confine their discounts exclusively to business paper, or paper that is subject to no renewal, is a great innovation, and denies to a worthy class of borrowers those facilities and advantages to which they are entitled in common with those of more various and extended business. It cannot be doubted that there is a class of borrowers of limited business whose requests for bank favors are small and infrequent, and for whom some accommodation, by way of renewal, is proper.[1]

The Massachusetts commissioners in 1839 also cautioned the banks against excessive refusal of accommodation loans.

A few writers advanced a very significant criticism of the doctrine that bank credit could have no harmful effect if issued only in response to the demands of commerce as evidenced by the offer of real paper for discount. Raguet, in a remarkable analysis of the causes of commercial crises, pointed out that a liberal loan policy, leading to rising prices, stimulates trade activity. A sellers' market results, and "purchases are made for no other reason, than that the buyers suppose they can sell the next day at a profit." Transfers of goods for speculative purpose become numerous. "Every new sale of commodities and property on credit creates new promissory notes, and these create a new demand for discounts." And so the cycle goes cumulatively on, until bank reserves become too slight and the inevitable check upon expanding credit brings disaster.[2]

C. F. Adams gave essentially the same explanation in discussing the crisis of 1837. Expanding note issues enhance prices and, therefore, profits rise. Business activity increases, and the rising prices, taken together with more frequent transfers of the same article, occasion a larger volume of real paper, the discount of which renews the process.[3] And Gouge, who later modified his original hostility toward banks and practically accepted the doctrine that no evil would result if discounting were but confined to real paper, retained sufficient of his earlier bias to protest that he would still prefer to dispense with credit banks altogether. Just as trade could not be disturbed if carried on by barter of commod-

---

[1] Connecticut, Report of Bank Commissioners (1841), in U. S. House of Representatives, 29th Congress, 1st Session, Document 226, p. 210.

[2] Raguet, "Principles of Banking," *Free Trade Advocate* (1829), ii, 7. Raguet gave a similar account in *Currency and Banking* (1839), pp. 134–137.

[3] C. F. Adams, *Reflections*, etc. (1837), pp. 9–12.

ities, so it could not become disordered if conducted by means of bank notes issued in the discount of business paper originating in completed commercial exchanges. The bank currency would, in that case, be "the exact representative of the value of those commodities." Accommodation loans, for the purchase of real estate or the payment of taxes, and like purposes, introduce disturbances.[1] Yet in one essay Gouge recognized, practically in the language of Raguet and Adams, although not so clearly, the tendency of business dealings themselves to become unwholesomely inflated.[2]

One more significant writer remains to be examined. Consistently with his general thesis that bank notes should be issued in accordance with the so-called "banking principle," their quantity being regulated simply by the requirements of business, Stephen Colwell was a staunch advocate of loans against real paper. Such loans cause the volume of bank credit to vary in harmony with that of trade itself, and are self-liquidating.[3] So completely did Colwell accept this theory, that he regarded the restraint of convertibility into specie on demand as both unnecessary and undesirable.[4] Yet he was too acute a thinker to accept the doctrine unqualifiedly. In one pregnant passage he granted that bills of exchange and promissory notes representing genuine commercial transactions may themselves be undesirably multiplied.

> In seasons of confidence, when men's notes are freely received for the commodities of trade, the first step towards the evils of undue expansion is a great issue of bills of exchange and promissory notes of merchants and dealers, who thus multiply their engagements, without immediately increasing the quantity of goods in the market; and these bills and notes being, for the convenience of the holders, converted into banknotes, an increase of circulation takes place, which is called an expansion.[5]

---

[1] Gouge, "Principles of Commercial Banking," *Journal of Banking* (1841), pp. 37, 69, 82; and "Commercial Banking," *Hunt's Merchants' Magazine* (1843), viii, 313.

[2] Idem, "Free Banking," *Journal of Banking* (1842), p. 388.

[3] *Ways and Means of Payment* (1859), pp. 450, 451.

[4] *Supra*, Chapter XII.

[5] Colwell, *op. cit.*, p. 534.

Nor did he make the point any less damaging to the principle at issue by his contention that the expansion is more properly to be described as one of individual credit than of bank credit, and that the fault lies rather with speculation than with excessive bank accommodation. He conceded much force to the objection that the "high confidence which enables the parties to make such large purchases on the strength of their own bills or notes, would not exist, but for the facility of converting them into bank paper," but rested content with the argument that the primary responsibility is that of the business man and the speculator.

That the matter of founding our banking operations upon short *real* paper is by no means settled, every reader of our recent literature realizes. The dogma that banking based upon paper representing completed commercial transactions is largely self-regulative underlies, in no small measure, the Federal Reserve Act and the regulations and policies of the Federal Reserve Board. The accepted bill of exchange has received a more complete identification with the proper type of loan than it had in the earlier discussion, but the problems at issue are essentially the same. It seems to be quite generally agreed that loans against paper resting upon particular transactions, already consummated, are more conducive to sound banking. But upon the doctrine that such advances automatically conform to the just needs of trade, the experience of recurrent business cycles has shed damaging light. We have found that its validity was gravely questioned by a few thoughtful men nearly a century ago.

In the latter-day controversy, it has already been suggested, considerable emphasis has been placed upon the mere form of commercial paper, the bill of exchange falling heir to the supposed virtues of real paper, while the promissory note has been criticized in part because of its liability to be in essence accommodation paper. In fact, the dispute has become quite specifically one concerning the desirability of substituting sellers' paper for the buyers' paper that has been prevailing in our domestic trade. Before the Civil War bills of exchange played a large part in financing our domestic trade. Abundant evidence of this is found in early bank statements from all parts of the country and in the testimony of contemporary writers on financial topics.[1] It is often difficult, however, in reading the discussion of the period, to determine whether the writer is weighing the respective advantages of the promissory note and the bill of exchange, or of accommodation paper and real paper, be the form of the real paper what it may. Terms were but loosely defined; in some cases the word "bill" seems to have been laxly used to signify commercial paper of any description.[2] Apparently, however, most of the writers were concerned chiefly with the thesis that bank discounts should be based upon paper arising out of actual commercial transactions and, while perhaps recognizing that bills of exchange are more likely to be of that nature, attached no great weight to the form of the paper as such. It seems to have been common usage to designate as accommodation paper any that is discounted with the expectation that it will be renewed if requested.[3]

As in recent years, the abuse of bills of exchange rendered it difficult to ascribe to them too readily the merits of real paper. In order to evade the usury laws, banks were prone to inform prospective borrowers that they were unable to discount notes drawn at their own counters, but had funds elsewhere that might be drawn upon. The borrower would thus be forced to pay a

[1] The reasons commonly assigned for the decline in importance of the bill of exchange since the Civil War are: first, the fluctuating value of the greenbacks, which encouraged the use of cash terms; and, second, the development of the practice of selling by means of samples, which stimulated the use of the open account (bringing with it the cash-discount policy), because the buyer was unwilling to be drawn upon before he had seen the goods and assured himself that they were of as good quality as the sample. See, for example, W. H. Steiner, *Mechanism of Commercial Credit*, pp. 114, 115, and H. L. Reed, *Development of Federal Reserve Policy*, pp. 107–109.

[2] See, for example, Report of the Bank Inspector of Vermont (1838), in U. S. House of Representatives, 25th Congress, 3d Session, Document 227, p. 53.

"Business paper" was a favorite name for real paper; the expressions "trade paper" and acceptances were rarely used.

[3] Thus the Massachusetts bank commissioners speak of business paper as "sure of payment at maturity," whereas accommodation paper derives its name from the fact that "the debtors are to be accommodated by repeated renewals and extensions." *Report*, 1839, p. 14.

fictitious exchange charge in addition to the rate of interest, and often, at maturity of the loan, was obliged to sell the bank a similar draft in order to meet the obligation. This practice was very widespread. The governor of New York complained of it in 1835; the commissioners of Massachusetts did so repeatedly from 1838 to the end of the period. The commissioners of Ohio referred to it in 1839, and those of Kentucky and Tennessee within the next few years. In 1859 the commissioners of Maine condemned this "almost universal practice of exacting illegal interest." Again, in 1854, the commissioners of Vermont found bills that were not *bona fide* being drawn mutually upon each other by two individuals as a means of evading the law that set a limit upon loans to any one borrower other than those arising from the "purchase of bills of exchange." [1]

One or two distinctive types of loans received some consideration — for the most part at the hands of the bank commissioners of the several states. Thus the Massachusetts commissioners found fault almost yearly from 1851 to 1857 with the practice of one bank borrowing from another.[2] Banks should stand upon their own resources and not upon "artificial relief" that might be withdrawn in peculiar exigencies. Investments by banks of part of their funds in commercial paper bought in New York or Boston attracted a larger amount of criticism. The Massachusetts commissioners condemned such "foreign loans" time after time, contending that paper that had to be "travelled for" was usually a poor risk. Good paper found a market at home. Moreover, banks are chartered to provide for the needs of their vicinity and not to finance the undertakings of a distant city.[3] The commissioners of Connecticut, on the other hand, saw no objection to such investments provided that they were confined to first-class, two-named business paper and that they were made with surplus resources

---

[1] Report (1854), in U. S. House of Representatives, 33d Congress, 2d Session, Document 82, p. 27. Compare the similar treatment accorded real bills by the Federal Reserve Act today.

[2] Cp. Silex, *Letters on Banks and Banking* (1853).

[3] Massachusetts Bank Commissioners, Reports, 1841, p. 11; 1842, p. 5; 1854, p. 81; etc.

remaining after local wants had been cared for.[1] Indeed, such loans represented assets that might be liquidated in times of stringency, thus affording a means of releasing funds for use in meeting the extraordinary demands of local borrowers.[2] The New Hampshire commissioners made a similar point in favor of the purchase of distant paper in 1849, and in 1852 one of them found in the investment by some of the banks of over half of their means in foreign paper "evidence only of the exuberance of our means."[3] In 1858, however, one of the commissioners objected to loans made out of the state as a device for evading the usury laws, and the following year they were regarded as evidence either of neglect of patrons at home or of the employment of an excessive amount of capital in banking.

Call loans to brokers made upon stocks as collateral were condemned by a special committee of the New York legislature on the ground that the encouragement of speculation was foreign to the purpose of banking; and in 1855 the Massachusetts commissioners argued that they were injurious to the banks themselves, since "extension upon the basis of business paper is a very different thing from distension created by speculation upon mere capital — that is, loans upon stocks, instead of discounts of promises representing something that has an intrinsic value."[4] Collateral loans were of significance primarily, however, not with respect to their basis of stocks as security, but with reference to their aspect as a secondary reserve, by virtue of being call loans, and their resultant bearing upon the problem of commercial crises.[5]

The use that might be made of a variable discount rate was but little understood. Such discussion of this matter as did occur centered around the problem of the wisdom of usury laws, with special reference to banks. Usury laws were still the order of the

[1] Connecticut Bank Commissioners, Reports, 1841, 1844, 1860.
[2] Report of Connecticut Bank Commissioners (1848), in U. S. House of Representatives, 30th Congress, 1st Session, Document 77, p. 197.
[3] Report of New Hampshire Bank Commissioners (1852), p. 37.
[4] Report of Massachusetts Bank Commissioners (1855), p. 74.
[5] See Chapter XVII.

day. Hamilton, in recommending that the first Bank of the United States be prohibited from charging more than six per cent, thought that five per cent would be a better limit if it were likely to attract an adequate subscription to the bank's capital stock. "The natural effect of low interest," he maintained, "is to increase trade and industry; because undertakings of every kind can be prosecuted with greater advantage. . . . And though laws which violently sink the legal rate of interest greatly below the market level, are not to be commended, because they are not calculated to answer their aim, yet, whatever has a tendency to effect a reduction, without violence to the natural course of things, ought to be attended to and pursued." Limitation of the rate of interest that banks might charge was an expedient in point, he thought.[1] Several proposals were made throughout the first half of the century for laws reducing the rate that banks were free to charge, founded upon mercantilistic notions regarding the relation between low interest rates and business prosperity.[2]

The desirability of giving banks a free rein in raising the discount rate was urged by Gallatin in 1830. Banks should be able to adapt their rate to the state of commerce and the money market.[3] Professor Dew shared this opinion, in a systematic treatise exposing the fallacies of usury laws.[4] "The best means, indeed, of rectifying the exchanges," wrote an unidentified contributor to the *American Quarterly Review*, "is to increase the interest of money. This tends to reduce transactions and lower prices. The fall of prices leads to the export rather than to the import of other commodities, and consequently to the return of gold and silver, till the currency is restored to its ordinary state."[5] As the law then stood in most of the states, he asserted, "when a temporary scarcity of circulating capital is occasioned by a diminished currency, all those lenders who are unwilling or afraid to

---

[1] Hamilton, Report on a National Bank, *American State Papers, Finance*, i, 76.
[2] *Suggestions on the President's Message* (1815), p. 25; *Observations on the Proposed Patriotic Bank* (1815), pp. 21, 30; Edward Kellogg, *Labor and Other Capital* (1849), pp. 252, 253.
[3] Gallatin, Letter to Biddle (1830), *Writings*, ii, 437.
[4] Dew, *Essay on Interest* (1834), especially p. 13.
[5] "The Public Distress," *American Quarterly Review* (1834), xv, 528.

demand more than the legal rate of interest, are at once withdrawn from the market." The result is a greater monetary stringency, forcing illicit interest rates still higher.[1] This is all the more regrettable because people borrow at such times, not to make profit, but to avert disaster by meeting existing debts. This writer commended the English act of 1833, which exempted the Bank of England from the usury laws with respect to its loans of less than ninety-day length.[2]

Hildreth thought that only the banks failed to evade the usury laws, being deterred by fear that they would lose their charters.[3] Inability to raise their rates compels the banks to pass abruptly from lending freely at six per cent to lending none at all, or only small amounts. Repeal of the usury laws would remedy this.

> By increasing the rate of interest whenever they found themselves beset by a multiplicity of borrowers, the banks would check the disposition to borrow in a much less violent and safer way, than by sudden and apparently capricious refusals to discount.[4]

Nathan Appleton added his protest against usury laws "so far as relates to notes of hand and bills of exchange," and cited the opinion of Norman, Tooke, and Lloyd as to the benefits England derived from the partial repeal of her usury law.[5]

The crisis of 1857 was followed by an increased number of protests against the usury laws. The New York Chamber of Commerce, which had already begun to make the matter a subject of annual petition to the legislature in 1855, now pressed the point with renewed insistence.[6] The Massachusetts bank commissioners emphasized the value of a flexible discount rate in checking speculative movements,[7] while J. S. Ropes wrote that

[1] "The Public Distress," *American Quarterly Review* (1834), xv, 528.
[2] Andreades, *History of the Bank of England*, p. 261.
[3] For evidence that the banks found abundant means of evasion see Cooper, *Lectures* (1826), p. 142; Gouge, *Short History of Paper Money* (1833), p. 31; Tucker, in *Hunt's Merchants' Magazine* (1858), xxxviii, 150; (1857), xxxvii, 575 ff.
[4] Hildreth, *Banks, Banking, and Paper Currencies* (1840), p. 168.
[5] Appleton, *Remarks* (1841), p. 47. For a curious proposal to lengthen bank loans by means of a graduated usury law, see Dwight, "The Financial Revulsion," *Hunt's Merchants' Magazine* (Feb., 1858), xxxviii, 162, 163.
[6] *Bankers' Magazine* (1858), xii, 832.
[7] Report (Oct., 1857), pp. 89, 90.

"*repeal of all usury laws,* at least so far as concerns commercial loans, would be perhaps the most effectual *single* remedy [for crises] that could be devised."[1]

Other writers took exception to the doctrine that banks should be permitted to raise their discount rates at their own discretion. In fact, for the period before 1857, it would be difficult to say whether advocates or critics of such action were the more numerous. A committee of the Rhode Island legislature, appointed in 1836 primarily to investigate usurious practices on the part of banks, defended usury laws on the ground that the demand for money reaches an extraordinary urgency at times of crises.

> The *absoluteness* of the necessity, and the *time* of the necessity, are, then, what distinguish the demand for money from all other demands, and require, certainly as it regards corporations, some degree of legislative interference. In the contract for the loan of money the parties do not meet on equal terms, the advantage being generally on the side of the lender.

Usury laws are necessary principally in times of stringency, to curb the rise of the discount rate. For this "increased rate, it ought to be remembered, adds nothing to the amount to be loaned in bank. The bank can loan what it has to loan for a lower as well as a higher sum. The pressure is the pretense, not the necessity, for the higher charge."[2]

Vethake granted the error of usury laws in general, but thought that, so long as banking remained the exclusive privilege of a few institutions, capable of combining to raise the rate of interest to exorbitant heights, entire repeal of the law against usury would be folly.[3] Henry C. Carey believed that England's modification of her usury laws with respect to the Bank of England only gave the bank inducement to bring on crises, through inflation, in order that it might reap the harvest of extreme rates.[4]

"However excellent this argument may be in the abstract,"

---

[1] J. S. Ropes, "The Financial Crisis," *New Englander,* xv, 713.

[2] Rhode Island, Report of the Committee Appointed to Visit the Banks (1836), in U. S. House of Representatives, 24th Congress, 2d Session, Document 65, pp. 54, 55.

[3] Vethake, *Principles of Political Economy* (1838), pp. 221, 222.

[4] H. C. Carey, *Principles of Social Science* (1858), ii, 393, 394. Carey would not, apparently, have offered this objection were banking in England free.

wrote a critic of Bentham's views on usury, "it will hardly apply to such a state of things as exists in the United States, where the lending of money is principally by irresponsible corporations, which have the privilege of making the money they lend." Bentham's thesis assumes "that the money lent is real money, and that the lenders are private individuals in the enjoyment of no privileges." [1]

And, finally, Tucker, commenting upon the variable discount rate of the Bank of England, doubted its efficacy in arresting a drain of specie. Requiring banks to lend at six per cent when the market rate is ten per cent enhances the likelihood of partiality in making loans. But he questioned the wisdom of permitting the banks to alter their rates freely

> until the habits of prudence and good management are more settled, and more command the public confidence. . . . The desire to increase their profits which now prompts them to excessive discounts, might then tempt them to raise the rate of interest; and the alternations from a low to a high interest, and from high to low, would give a new spring to gambling speculations with the funds of the bank, which is already sufficiently strong. Such a power, which may one day be safe and salutary would certainly be, at this time, premature and mischievous.[2]

---

[1] [Gouge?], *Journal of Banking* (1841), p. 52.
[2] Tucker, "Banks or No Banks," *Hunt's Merchants' Magazine* (Feb., 1858), xxxviii, 153.

CHAPTER XVI

THEORIES OF THE CAUSES OF CRISES AND CYCLES

Agnostic theories. — Emphasis placed upon the influence of the credit system. — Attention to the psychology of business men. — Periodicity of commercial crises. — Theory that banks cause the business cycle. — Critics of the theory that banks cause the business cycle. — Theory of the self-generating cycle. — Influence of maladjustments of production.

IN their treatment of commercial crises and business cycles our early writers were particularly stimulating. It is quite possible that a few of them had here a better understanding than any of their English contemporaries. And, certainly, in the analysis of aggravating factors in the American banking system their achievements were substantial.

The earlier writers, in America as elsewhere, regarded a commercial crisis, not as one phase of a business cycle, but as the unhappy interruption of a normal trend of business that might have continued indefinitely had it not been for the unfortunate circumstances that brought on its collapse. Their observation of the cycle centered upon its most conspicuous phase — the crisis. Accordingly, the first attempts to explain crises sought the origin of each in some particular incidents of the time. No general explanation common to all crises was offered; some writers explicitly denied that one could be formulated.[1]

A favorite explanation of crises placed the blame upon whatever tariff existed at the time. The notion that low duties cause crises by undermining domestic industry received vogue from partisanship as well as from plausibility. Henry C. Carey was,

[1] Roscher seems to be designated by more or less common consent as the outstanding exponent of this view. Denying that crises recur at regular intervals, he said: "The causes of such an economic disease are most numerous. Every circumstance which suddenly and largely increases production, or decreases consumption, or which even disturbs the ordinary course of industry, must bring with it a commercial crisis." *Ansichten der Volkswirthschaft* (1865), Bd. ii, sec. 5, p. 391. Cited in E. D. Jones, *Economic Crises*, p. 35.

of course, its best-known exponent.[1] President Monroe attributed the "pressures" of 1819–1820 to "the peculiar character of the epoch in which we live, and to the extraordinary occurrences which have signalized it."[2] Many traced the origin of the panic of 1837 to Jackson's war on the Bank, the specie circular, and similar specific events, in terms that indicated no notion that anything more might be said respecting the general nature of crises. Thus a New York bankers' convention, after enumerating in its report the conditions responsible for the distress, remarked: "Such a coincidence of extraordinary and unfortunate incidents, as produced the catastrophe, must be rare, and may never again occur."[3] Superabundant crops, poor crops, excessive taxation, and the "judgment of God," are but a few of the long list of causes advanced in explanation of our crises of before the Civil War.[4] De Bow ascribed the crisis of 1847 to the diversion of a large amount of capital from commerce into railroad investments, and thought that tariffs, inflation of bank credit, and like circumstances, showed little correlation with the occurrences of crises. "Let us alone," was the best remedy he could suggest.[5] In the opinion of Samuel Hurd Walley,

> Crises and revulsions are the necessary incidents and concomitants of a credit system; but they do not follow any known law, and cannot be subjected to any such analysis of cause and effect as will enable the most sagacious to understand and explain their mode of operation. There is no such settled and acknowledged analogy between one revulsion and another as will enable

---

[1] *The Prospect . . . at the Opening of the Year 1851*, p. 84; *Financial Crises* (1860), pp. 8 ff. Carey was a free trader, despite the sentiments of his father, until about 1843. In *Answers to the Questions*, etc. (1840), p. 55, he contended that high duties, rather than low ones, tend to produce crises. For further illustrations of the view that crises accompany low tariffs, see Ward, "Causes that Produced the Crisis of 1857," *Hunt's Merchants' Magazine* (1859), xl, 20; Taussig, *Tariff History of the United States* (6th ed.), pp. 116–122.

[2] Fourth Annual Message (Nov. 14, 1830), in Richardson's *Messages of the Presidents*, ii, 74.

[3] *Financial Register* (1838), i, 231.

[4] Cp. the three-page enumeration of the suggestions advanced to the agents of the Bureau of Labor as to the causes of industrial depressions, in the first annual report of the Commissioner of Labor, entitled *Industrial Depressions* (1886), pp. 76–78.

[5] *De Bow's Review* (Dec. 1857), xxiii, 652–659.

us to classify or systematize them. There is no recognized condition of the banks, or currency, or trade, which has existed at the happening of two or more crises, so similar as to form the basis of logical deductions for the guidance of financial pilots.[1]

His own explanation of the crisis of 1857, upon which he was commenting, lay in a long list of varied causes, and his proposals ran through the gamut of banking reforms commonly urged at the time, with suggestions in addition for a number of changes in the methods of doing business.

"In every country where credit enters extensively into the transactions of people, there must always be liabilities to what are called panics," thought Condy Raguet.[2] And Gallatin wrote: "All active, enterprising, commercial countries are necessarily subject to commercial crises. A series of prosperous years almost necessarily produces overtrading. Those revolutions will be more frequent and greater in proportion to the spirit of enterprise and to the extension or abuse of credit."[3] Walley admitted, despite his denial that the causes of different crises are sufficiently uniform to permit of generalization, that there would be little danger of crises, at least of an alarming nature, if all business were conducted by barter, or with money. It is to the introduction of the credit system that these troubles must be laid.[4]

Credit was believed to play a threefold part in producing crises. First, it enabled men to "overtrade" in periods when mutual confidence was high. Secondly, it formed a network of interrelations through which the insolvency of a few merchants embarrassed a great many others. "It is the practice of giving credit that implicates trading men so much with each other, so that one very often involves many others in his misfortunes or errors,"

---

[1] Walley, *The Financial Revulsion of 1857* (1858), p. 9. This paper was read before the American Statistical Association. Its author was a bank commissioner of Massachusetts who had previously gained prominence as a lawyer, Congressman, and financier.

[2] *Examiner and Journal of Political Economy* (1834), ii, 127.

[3] Gallatin, "Suggestions on the Banks and Currency" (1841), *Writings* (Adams's edition), iii, 385.

[4] Walley, *The Financial Revulsion of 1857* (1858), p. 8.

Willard Phillips explained in 1819.[1] Everyone depends more or less upon the ability and punctuality of his debtors for the means of meeting his own engagements, with the result that their failure may occasion his own. Distress and insolvency thus tend to spread cumulatively. Rae, also, regarded this feature of the use of credit as of prime importance.[2]

Finally, some emphasized the fact that the use of credit instruments in normal times furnishes a substitute for money, so that, when in troublous times cash payments are insisted upon in lieu of credit formerly extended, the financial stringency becomes all the more acute.[3]

Most of those who laid stress on the credit system in seeking the origin of crises made this but part of a more complete explanation. Edward Everett, however, went further. "If I mistake not," he wrote, "the distress of the year 1857 was produced by an enemy more formidable than hostile armies; by a pestilence more deadly than fever or plague; by a visitation more destructive than the frosts of Spring or the blights of Summer. I believe that it was caused by a mountain load of Debt." [4] The payment of interest upon the huge amount of indebtedness — personal, business, and public — had proved too great a strain. The remedy was simple — keep out of debt.[5]

Changes in the state of confidence in the business world were usually associated with the credit system in explaining crises. Thus we read that "a mercantile mania" followed the return of peace after the War of 1812, preparing the way for the distress of 1819.[6] Phillips described banks as "barometers to show the state of the commercial atmosphere," for "business will have its floods

---

[1] Phillips, "Review of Seybert's Statistical Annals," *North American Review* (1819), ix, 229. Cp. Mathew Carey, *Essays on Banking* (1816), p. 67.

[2] Rae, *New Principles*, etc. (1834), as edited by Mixter, under the title, *Sociological Theory of Capital* (1905), pp. 304, 305. Cp. Gouge, *Short History of Paper Money* (1833), pp. 25, 26.

[3] Gallatin, *Considerations on the Currency and Banking of the United States* (1831), pp. 34, 35; Anon., "The Public Distress," *American Quarterly Review* (1834), xv, 510–514, etc.

[4] Edward Everett, *The Mount Vernon Papers* (1859), p. 167.

[5] *Ibid.*, p. 177.

[6] John M'Cready, *Review of Trade* (1820), p. 20.

and ebbs, and the spirit of enterprise and production must necessarily be checked."[1] He had explained earlier that when "from some change, people suddenly become more cautious and distrustful of each other," the break down of the credit system results in a scarcity of money because of the unusual demand for cash payments.[2] Professor Thomas R. Dew, among others, wrote similarly of the destruction of confidence by sudden shocks, with the result that "credit no longer serves for cash."[3]

The theory so prevalent in England,[4] that crises are the reaction from recurrent "manias" of speculation, met with comparatively little favor in this country. Professor Francis Bowen almost alone gave a clear statement of it. A "fever of speculation appears at times to seize upon the whole mercantile community, producing for a while an unnatural inflation of the prices of nearly all commodities, and then, with a sudden reaction, carrying them back to a point much below their former average, and thus causing general distress, loss of confidence, and bankruptcy."[5]

More stress was placed upon the psychology of business men at the period of collapse than in the prosperity that preceded. We are told, for example, that the crisis of 1857 was at first "scouted as panic, senseless and causeless, for the full cure of which only a little confidence was needed."[6]

---

[1] Phillips, *Manual of Political Economy* (1828), p. 255.

[2] Idem, "Review of Seybert's Statistical Annals," *North American Review* (1819), ix, 228, 229.

[3] Dew, *Essay on Interest* (1834), p. 17; Gallatin, *Considerations*, etc. (1831), pp. 34, 35.

[4] See MacLeod, *Dictionary of Political Economy* (1863), pp. 105, 119, for example. John Mills, in his well known paper read before the Manchester Statistical Society in 1867, described the business cycle as a credit cycle governed by "moral causes," and asserted that "the malady of commercial crises is not, in essence, a matter of the purse but of the mind." Education of business men was his remedy. *Transactions of Manchester Statistical Society* (1867–1868), pp. 6–40.

[5] Bowen, *Principles of Political Economy* (1856), pp. 435, 436. See also, J. B. Martin, *Twenty-one Years in the Boston Stock Market* (1856), p. 9.

[6] George Dutton, "Exposition of the Crises of 1857," *Hunt's Merchants' Magazine* (1858), xxxvii, 19. See also, Walley, *The Financial Revulsion of 1857* (1858), p. 7; and Seaman, "The Panic of 1857," *Hunt's Merchants' Magazine* (Dec., 1857), xxxvii, 659. All three of these writers reject this "panic" theory of crises.

That crises recur periodically came to be believed while the century was still young — much earlier, it seems, than some present-day writers realize.[1] A writer of 1829 informs us that

> an opinion is entertained by many that every fourteen years or thereabouts, there is a sort of revolution in property — that real estate, especially, undergoes a speculative rise and fall, and that consequently wealth becomes transferred from one individual to another, by the mere operation of time. Without pretending to decide upon the fact, whether or no these fluctuations are as frequent as once in fourteen years, one thing we know to be certain, which is, that fluctuations do take place.[2]

James Buchanan, then Senator from Pennsylvania, declared in 1840 that the "cycle" (which he attributed to "periodical expansions and contractions of the currency" and to speculation) used to require from three to six years, but had now been completed in two years.[3] Amasa Walker believed that the period was seven years,[4] and Bowen, after quoting Lord Overstone's observation that the state of trade "revolves apparently in an established cycle," remarked that crises occur, both in the United States and England, "on an average, about once in every seven or eight years."[5] Another writer thought ten to fifteen years in better accord with the facts.[6] Most writers were content to assert that business is subject to more or less periodic fluctuations, without attempting to estimate the length of the period. A contributor to *Hunt's Merchants' Magazine* in May, 1848, described the country as then being convulsed by "another of those crises, which recur with apparently tidal regularity,"[7] while the Massachusetts legislature was told, even before the collapse of 1837, that "periodical revulsions occur, where banks obtain, about every three years, rising and falling within that space, with as much regularity as the billows of the ocean, and from causes as infallible in their operation."[8] One writer even ventured to de-

---

[1] See, for example, A. B. Adams, *Economics of Business Cycles*, p. 29.
[2] [Raguet?] *Free Trade Advocate* (1829), i, 303.   [3] *Niles' Register*, lvii, 422.
[4] A. Walker, *Nature and Uses of Money and Mixed Currency* (1857), p. 35.
[5] Bowen, *Principles of Political Economy* (1856), p. 435.
[6] *Hunt's Merchants' Magazine* (1850), xxii, 401.
[7] D. M. Balfour, "The Present Commercial Crisis," *Hunt's Merchants' Magazine* (May, 1848), xviii, 477.
[8] Rantoul, Speech in Massachusetts House of Representatives (March 22, 1836), p. 14.

clare it a matter of common knowledge that "revulsions in commerce have become a sort of periodical epidemic in our times, whose periods and returns can be safely affirmed by all, while the shrewd financier is tolerably aware of their precise times." [1]

Recognition of the fact that crises occur with a certain degree of regularity called for some more satisfying theory of their nature than that which referred each to the fortuitous events preceding, or that which merely indicated the bearing that sales on credit and the psychology of business men have upon the cycle.[2] From 1825 on, the fluctuating character of bank currency was most commonly regarded as the cause of variations in business prosperity. Attention began to be given also to the business cycle as a whole, as well as to its climax in the "revulsion." Thus Eleazar Lord, in 1829, after giving a description, already commonplace, of the alternating periods of rising prices, speculation, prosperity, and of falling prices and depression, added that "nothing can be more certain than that this train of disastrous results originates in an excessive issue of paper. The flexible quality of paper currency, its capacity of sudden and indefinite expansion while confidence is maintained, and of contraction when distrust or necessity requires, is the root of the difficulty." [3]

Gouge held that the remedy was to do away with banks of issue. By inflating the currency, he asserted, they raise prices above the level of other countries, inducing an unfavorable balance of trade and gold exports. As the notes are presented to

[1] J. B. Turner, "Banking," *New Englander* (1844), ii, 50. Virtually no attempt was made to apply anything like modern statistical methods to the problem of the business cycle. It was here that such writers as Jevons and John Mills made their chief contribution. As for the explanation of the causes of the cycle, it is probably just to say that these men showed less insight than some of our own writers who had preceded.

[2] As already indicated, many writers concerned themselves only with crises, without realizing that they were but one phase of a complete cycle. In some of my generalizations I have used the word "cycle" while recognizing that some of the writers referred to dealt with only part of the cycle. There is virtually no danger of ambiguity in the reader's mind, and any loss in formal precision seems more than offset by the gain of avoiding the cumbersome repetition of the phrase "cycles and crises."

[3] Lord, *Principles of Currency and Banking* (1829), p. 46.

the banks for specie to be shipped abroad, the banks are forced to call their loans, contracting the currency and precipitating a fall in prices. But "the different members of society had entered into obligations proportionate to the amount of circulating medium in the days of banking prosperity. The quantity of circulating medium is diminished, and they have not the means of discharging their debts."[1] Inability to sell their goods at the prices at which they have purchased them on credit leads to bankruptcy; the mutual dependence of merchants upon the solvency of each other causes the financial embarrassments to propagate. Finally, the reduction in the volume of bank currency reduces prices; this checks imports and stimulates exports, causing a reflux of specie into the country. The banks get renewed confidence, expand their loans, and the cycle repeats itself.[2]

"If our circulation was gold and silver," another critic of banking believed, "it would be impossible to create those ruinous fluctuations in prices that cover the land with misery and desolation, every once in five or ten years. The moment a spirit of speculation can be excited, the banks increase the flame by pouring oil upon it; the instant a reaction takes place, they add to the distress a thousand fold."[3]

"The evil from which we now suffer," wrote George Dutton in 1857, "is simply a derangement of the currency." The material wealth of the country remains undamaged. Prices depend upon the magnitude of trade in relation to the volume of currency times its velocity of circulation ($x = zy$ was his formula). The use of bank notes subjects the quantity of media of payment to the whims of corporations, upsetting the stability of the price formula and producing fluctuations in the state of business.[4] A. P. Peabody, editor of the *North American Review* and later professor in Harvard College, regarded the panic of 1857 as but the typical climax to the sequence of bank inflation, rising prices,

---

[1] Gouge, *Short History of Paper Money and Banking in the United States* (1833), p. 25.

[2] Gouge, *op. cit.*, pp. 25, 26.

[3] Theophilus Fisk, *Banking Bubble Burst* (1837), p. 25.

[4] Dutton, *The Present Crisis* (1857), pp. 4–16.

gold exports, contraction of bank credit, falling prices, and commercial crises. "We thus see, that, were all other causes inactive, our banking system alone would produce a periodical pressure, panic, and convulsion in the money market."[1] And Amasa Walker, one of the most severe critics of an elastic note issue, laid it down as an invariable rule that "the bankruptcies which take place in any community are just in proportion to the expansibility and contractibility of its currency. This is a fixed law — it must be so in the nature of things—facts show it to be so."[2] Charles H. Carroll, a most stimulating disciple of the currency school, also hit, unfortunately, upon "an absolute law by which failure becomes inevitable" where bank currency is used, and Carroll labored through a series of articles in *Hunt's Merchants' Magazine* and the *Bankers' Magazine* to lend conviction to his thesis.[3] Van Buren and Buchanan were but expressing the opinion of the majority of the contemporary students of the problem when they attributed the disastrous crises that marked their respective administrations to the operations of banks.[4]

It is interesting to note that some of those who held the alternate expansion and contraction of bank currency responsible for changes in business conditions recognized the international aspects of the matter. As early as 1820, we find Oliver Wolcott, Hamilton's successor as Secretary of the Treasury, ascribing the contemporary depression in the United States to the contraction of bank credit in England. Different countries must proceed

[1] Peabody, "The Financial Crisis," *North American Review* (1858), lxxxvi, 177, 178.

[2] A. Walker, *The Nature and Uses of Money and Mixed Currency* (1857), p. 33. This was one of the most vigorous of the American pamphlets in support of the currency principle. It gained added influence from the fact that the first four chapters had been published in *Hunt's Merchants' Magazine* in the months immediately preceding the outbreak of the panic of 1857, which now seemed to give it corroboration.

[3] "Bankruptcy in the Currency," *Hunt's Merchants' Magazine* (June, 1860), xl, 679, 680; "Congressional Movement in the Currency Question," *Hunt's Merchants' Magazine* (April, 1860), xlii, 443–447; "Organization of Debt into Currency," in *Bankers' Magazine* (Aug., 1858), xiii, 137–142; etc.

[4] Van Buren, Message to the Special Session of Congress (Sept., 1837), in Richardson, *Messages of the Presidents*, iii, 325 ff.; Buchanan, First Annual Message (Dec., 1857), *ibid.*, v, 437 ff.

pari passu in expanding or contracting their currencies, he explained. Hence sudden deflation in any major country may occasion world-wide distress.[1]

No less interesting is the observation of H. C. Carey to the effect that England enjoys an advantage with respect to crises by virtue of being a creditor nation. In all cases of change in the currency, the debtor fares worse, for it is he who is called upon to pay. "If the debtor is unable to pay, the creditor may then raise the rate of interest, as the Bank of England does, *thus profiting by the irregularity of the currency*. When that institution finds it necessary to contract in consequence of having overtraded, she does not fail, *but she compels her debtors to do so.*"[2] Carey did not tie the matter up with the foreign exchanges, however, and it would be easy to read into his idea more than he probably had in mind.[3]

Meanwhile the controversy in England between the adherents of the currency school and those of the banking school was finding its counterpart in America. On the one side were those who insisted that bank notes, unless rigidly regulated by law, introduce

[1] Wolcott, *Remarks on the Present State of Currency, Credit, Commerce, and National Industry* (1820), pp. 4–32.

[2] H. C. Carey, *Answers to the Questions*, etc. (1840), p. 42.

[3] Some years later Francis Bowen commented upon England's position as creditor to the United States in the short-time money market and seems to have been considerably mystified by it. "There is a curious feature," he observed, "in the management of trade between England and the United States, which is in marked contrast with the course of mercantile transactions between England and all other commercial nations. For some inexplicable reason the bills of exchange are all drawn one way" — on London. *Principles of Political Economy* (1856), pp. 322, 323 n. Englishmen seem to have been no less perplexed by the apparent anomaly, for Lawson, in his *History of Banking*, remarked with reference to it: "To place the trade of America on the same footing as that of all other commercial nations has long been a desideratum. Numerous appeals, in the shape of pamphlets and other publications, recommending the adoption of a course of exchange between the two countries, have brought conviction to the mind of almost every mercantile man; yet, strange to say, no step has yet been taken to effect the object; it is an evil which must ultimately work its own cure." *History of Banking* (London, 1850), pp. 51, 52, or, American edition (Boston, 1852), p. 30. The full significance of the position England enjoys, by virtue of her low discount rate, as creditor in the short-time money market, has been emphasized by J. M. Keynes in the second chapter of his *Indian Currency and Finance*.

a pernicious elasticity into the currency; on the other, those who maintained that since bank notes are issued in response to the needs of trade and are convertible on demand, they admit of no overissue. These champions of the banking system against the attacks of the currency school quite logically took exception to the doctrine that banks are the cause of the business cycle. The quantity of money is the resultant of the state of trade, they argued; to hold it responsible for business fluctuations is to confuse cause and effect. The controversy is not without its modern parallel.

Gouge, urged Professor Dew, in commenting upon the former's views on crises, has "with too much *ex parte* ingenuity referred to the operations of the banking system; thus taking the effect in many cases for the cause."[1]

It is the course of trade which produces them [crises] in the great majority of cases. They are incidental to the fluctuation of prices. . . . Bank credit may aggravate them just as private credit may, but it does not produce them. There is a certain portion of the commerce of the world that must be fluctuating — banks are requisite to carry on that portion most perfectly. Now, if hard money countries have few fluctuations, they, at the same time, have little of this commerce.[2]

Nor are countries with a purely metallic currency wholly immune from crises.[3] Yet Dew granted that the banking system, although first stimulated to increase its note issue by a speculative spirit and a rise in prices, "immediately becomes in turn a powerfully operating cause, carrying up prices still higher, and increasing the speculative mania, by the facilities it offers in the money market."[4]

The historian Richard Hildreth, one of the few to recognize clearly that variations in the volume of bank notes "are abso-

---

[1] Dew, *Essay on Interest* (1834), p. 16 n.
[2] Idem, *The Great Question of the Day* (1840), p. 4.
[3] *Ibid.*, p. 5. The financial crisis suffered by Hamburg in 1799 was frequently referred to by those who denied the guilt of banks in producing these disasters. A Congressional committee even made the exceptionable statement: "As to fluctuations in price, they were far greater in former times, when there was nothing deserving the name of commerce, no credit, and a currency entirely of gold and silver, than they now are." Committee on Ways and Means, Minority Report, March 23, 1838.
[4] *Essay on Interest* (1834), p. 16 n.

lutely necessary to keep up a due proportion between the medium of trade and the amount of trade,"[1] agreed with Dew. Price changes are caused by the conditions of supply and demand with respect to particular commodities, by catastrophes, "silly tales," and what not.[2] A bank currency simply adjusts itself to these changing conditions. Another writer, reviewing Walker's *Nature and Uses of Money and Mixed Currency*, urged that paper money "is not a measure or standard of value; neither does it influence prices any further than so much credit. It is a substitute for gold and silver, as a check, or a draft, or a bill of exchange, or a negotiable note is."[3] Walker, this critic argued, "assumes that the banks create and regulate the business of the country, when, in fact, the business exists, and the banks come in to afford facilities for transacting it."[4] Variations in the volume of bank notes are as much a consequence of conditions of commerce and industry as are changes in the magnitude of car loadings.

Willard Phillips, the author and editor, likewise denied the possibility of overissuing convertible bank notes, and then carried the attack further. Banks are first to take measures against an impending pressure.

> They serve as barometers to show the state of the commercial atmosphere. And since business will have its floods and ebbs, and the spirit of enterprise and production must necessarily be checked, for a time, the more promptly an approaching crisis can be seen and provided against, as far as practicable, the less the community will suffer.[5]

Dew seemed ready to grant that banks, if they play a passive part, on the whole, in the expansion of their credits, should be held responsible for the extent to which they permit inflation to go. "I have no doubt," he wrote, "that a well-managed banking system upon proper principles, under the influence of the laws of trade, might become the best possible check on wild speculation. . . . Because banks, by their more extended relations, and a more

---

[1] Hildreth, *Banks, Banking, and Paper Currencies* (1840), p. 157.
[2] Idem, *Letter to Marcus Morton* (1840), pp. 4 ff.
[3] George Ward, "Causes that Produced the Crisis of 1857," *Hunt's Merchants' Magazine* (Jan., 1859), xl, 20.
[4] *Ibid.*, p. 23.
[5] Phillips, *Manual of Political Economy* (1828), p. 255.

intimate knowledge of the course of exchange, are much more likely to see in advance the gathering storm, and to prepare for it by a proper system of curtailment, than isolated individuals."[1]

Henry F. Baker, an extensive writer on the history of banking in the United States, also believed that banks exert a moderating influence upon the business cycle. Overconfidence and speculation are the mainsprings of the cycle. They produce feverish activity and high profits. But an uninterrupted course of such prosperity, even if possible, would be undesirable, for, on the one hand, wage-earners and those receiving salaries suffer, while on the other, demoralizing extravagance is fostered. "Reverses, then, are the surest safeguards against approaching ruin, and banks managed by conscientious and prudent directors are the great conservatives which arrest the proclivity of financial profligacy to national destruction."[2] Similarly, Professor Bowen, having adopted the view that banks in making loans follow rather than determine the state of trade, contended that "by furnishing a steady supply to the loan-market, not enlarged in a period of speculation nor diminished in a time of pressure, their operation is like that of the balance-wheel in a machine, tending to deaden the shock of transition, and to moderate both extremes."[3] It is fluctuations in the supply of private loanable funds that cause much of the evil.

The significance of the rôle played by credit in the mutations of business prosperity was recognized by nearly all students of the problem. But whereas some asserted that changes in the volume of bank currency give the initial impulse to business activity, others maintained that the primary responsibility lies with the producers and merchants, and that banks merely meet the situation business men create. Still another group of writers, somewhat distinct from both of these, contented themselves with saying that crises originate in the abuse of credit, whether bank credit or private. Bankers stand in about the same relation to

[1] Dew, *The Great Question of the Day* (1840), p. 12.
[2] H. F. Baker, "Outline of the History of Banking in the United States, *Bankers' Magazine* (Oct., 1856), xi, 243.
[3] Bowen, *Principles of Political Economy* (1856), p. 451.

the business cycle as any other business men — it is their common "overaction" that brings on crises.[1] This position showed failure to appreciate the distinctive importance of bank notes and deposits, as compared with private instruments of credit, by virtue of their action, as a part of the currency, upon prices.

Between the views that banks cause crises and that they play an entirely passive part, there were all shades of opinion. Some of those who regarded banks as the principal cause of commercial crises, conceived of them as arbitrarily altering the volume of media of payment (and, therefore, the general level of prices) according to their own caprice. Such a notion was especially prominent in the earliest days of our banking experience, and again in the eighteen-thirties, when to damn banks or defend them became largely a matter of political faith. Not a few held that banks wilfully expand and contract the currency in their own interests; others seem to have regarded them as equally victims of their own power to do evil.

Again, there were critics who, while still attributing crises chiefly to banks, held the more moderate view that they begin to expand only when merchants and speculators have already given impulse to greater business activity. These writers differed only in degree from those who, like Dew, insisted that banks play a passive part in the period of inflation, but conceded that, after credit expansion has once received the initial impulse from prospering trade, the increased volume of bank currency in turn becomes a causal force.

At the hands of a few writers this doctrine of the mutual reaction upon each other of bank credit, trade, and prices, was so stated as to trace commercial crises primarily to the banking system, while still giving its due to the objection that banks are governed in their operations by the state of business activity. The result was a fairly complete general theory of self-generating cycles. Condy Raguet, whose writings deserve far more attention than they have received, seems to have been the first to formulate

[1] See, for example, J. S. Ropes, "Currency, Banking, and Credit," *Bankers' Magazine* (1859), xiv, 171, 176, 275.

the theory. By the operation of banks that issue notes or give deposit credit in excess of their actual capital,[1] he explained in 1829, the borrowers of the banks are brought into the market with added purchasing power. Prices rise, adding fuel to the spirit of speculation, "which never fails to be engendered by the facility of procuring the means to speculate with." Purchases are made "for no other reason than that the buyers suppose they can sell the next day at a profit." Beguiled by the apparent prosperity that attends rising prices and speculative activity, people spend more lavishly. Merchants enlarge the scale of their enterprises; manufacturers add to their plants; farmers improve their lands and buildings. All these operations give additional employment to labor. The demand of consumers for commodities becomes greater. "Every new sale of commodities and property on credit creates new promissory notes, and these create a new demand for discounts." Thus the cycle goes on, cumulatively generating its own momentum, until finally "the depreciation of the currency [*i. e.*, rise of prices] has become so great from these extraordinary issues, that timid people become alarmed, and make a run upon the banks, whilst coin is also demanded for exportation."[2] The banks are forced to call their loans and money becomes scarce. But the merchant has long since parted with the money he borrowed, in purchasing goods; the manufacturer, in building new plants; the farmer, in bettering his land; and now they find that they can realize but a fraction of their investment by selling what they have bought. Their goods are no longer salable; their credits are frozen by the similar predicament of their debtors. Widespread disaster ensues.

[1] The correct criterion of whether or not banking operations result in an increase of media of payment is, of course, issue in excess not of capital, but of cash reserve. The fallacy of thinking in terms of capital in this connection was a frequent one, and evidence of it may be found in our early laws.

[2] Raguet, *Currency and Banking* (1839), p. 136. All of this paragraph except the present quotation may also be found in "The Principles of Banking," *Free Trade Advocate* (July 4, 1829), ii, 7. The same explanation of the business cycle is virtually reproduced in *Currency and Banking* (1839), pp. 134–137. Raguet's knowledge of the nature of the business cycle makes it difficult to accept the statement that "little of value can be found in discussions [of commercial crises] published prior to 1837." E. D. Jones, *Economic Crises* (1900), p. 15.

Charles Francis Adams gave a similar explanation of the business cycle in a number of articles first published in a Boston newspaper on the eve of the crisis of 1837. Whenever the volume of bank notes begins to expand, rising prices enhance business profits and business activity increases. This in turn tends to enlarge the demand for bank credit, further raising prices. The increased activity results in some addition to the volume of production, but more largely in higher prices under the spur of keener competitive bidding. The rise in prices in its turn reacts, like the increase in the number of exchanges, upon the volume of bank currency. At last, rising prices render the balance of trade unfavorable, inducing gold exports; and contraction of bank accommodation brings an abrupt collapse.[1]

Adams made an interesting suggestion in explanation of the high profits that attend rising prices and that were admitted by all to be an essential key to the problem of heightened business activity. The "rising prices of products while on the road to the consumer furnish a profit increasing perhaps in a greater ratio than the demand for interest, and not merely supplying the means for the payment of the rate already demanded but inciting strongly to the borrowing more even at a higher rate."[2]

Vethake adopted the suggestions of Raguet and Adams regarding the origin of crises, although his statement of the doctrine is less satisfactory. He laid considerable emphasis upon the increase

---

[1] C. F. Adams, *Reflections upon the Present State of the Currency in the United States* (1837), especially pp. 9–12. Adams apparently understood less clearly than Raguet the importance of his theory. He later undertook to defend the banks against the charge of causing crises. "The course of trade," he wrote, "does not run much more smooth than that which the poet has singled out to make into a proverb. And whether credit is employed in it to a greater extent, or whether it is not, every commercial community must calculate upon it as a fact of the highest probability, that some periods will be periods of particular success, and others, again, will make themselves remembered as signally disastrous." "Principles of Credit," *Hunt's Merchants' Magazine* (March, 1840), ii, 208.

For another rather able explanation of the cycle, see Rantoul's Speech in the Massachusetts House of Representatives (March 22, 1836), p. 10.

[2] Adams, *Reflections*, etc. (1837), pp. 13, 14. This notion is of interest by reason of the emphasis since placed upon it by Professor Irving Fisher. Amasa Walker conceived of the business cycle as the accompaniment of a seven-year cycle of interest rates. *Nature and Uses of Money and Mixed Currency* (1857), pp. 35, 36.

of the velocity of circulation of money attending the period of expansion, as, indeed, several previous writers had done, but not in connection with as good a theory of the cycle as that of Vethake.[1] Gouge observed in 1833 that "Anything that excites the spirit of enterprise, has a tendency to increase the amount of Bank issues.... As the wild spirit of speculation has in most cases its origin, and in all its aliment, in Banking transactions, these various causes operate in a circle."[2] In 1842 he went into greater detail, following Raguet. A speculative demand for goods, however incited, raises prices, and at the same time "leads to the creation of a large amount of new business paper. This is discounted by the bankers, and then prices undergo an additional rise, through the additions made to the currency. This leads to a new speculative demand, which causes the creation of more business paper, and that in its turn a fresh issue of bank notes"; and thus things go on until prices are raised so high that an adverse balance of trade calls a halt.[3]

Stephen Colwell, so firm a believer in the thesis that paper money issued by banks against real commercial paper cannot become redundant that he would do away with the restraint of convertibility, gave an excellent statement of the principles explained by Raguet. He sought to reconcile this with his general system by asserting that the initial impetus to the cycle is given, not by the banks, but by speculating business men.[4]

The notion of general overproduction, or glutting of the market, in explanation of commercial crises and cycles, played little part in the American discussion. Gouge indicated that complaint was sometimes made of "all branches of trade being overdone," and he disposed of the matter rather ably. It is true, he asserted, that as contraction of the currency, by diminishing

[1] Henry Vethake, *Principles of Political Economy* (1838), p. 177.
[2] Gouge, *Short History of Paper Money*, etc. (1833), p. 64.
[3] Idem, "Free Banking," *Journal of Banking* (1842), p. 388. Gouge had started out as an intensely hostile critic of banks of issue. At this time he seemed to be vacillating between the position that notes issued against real commercial paper cannot be overissued and the doctrine which we have just studied in the text.
[4] Colwell, *Ways and Means of Payment* (1859), pp. 534, 535, 567–569.

purchasing power, spoils the market, one employer after another must release some of his workers, lending apparent plausibility to the idea that commodities in general have been produced in excess of the needs of the community. The discharge of a considerable number of employees, depriving them of their incomes, prevents their purchasing as freely as usual, thus tending to diminish production in other lines and further to increase unemployment. A progressive deterioration of the market is introduced, and with it goes like slackening of production.[1] Yet,

if the real wants of the community, and not their ability to pay, be considered, it will not, perhaps, be found that any one useful trade or profession has too many members.... But, in one sense, "all businesses" may be said to be "overdone," since all businesses are by this system rendered unprofitable.[2]

In the eighteen-fifties the notion of a general overproduction of goods was refuted by E. Peshine Smith and, with qualifications, by Francis Bowen.[3]

Hildreth emphasized, in this connection, the bearing of division of labor and its concomitant, production for a market, upon the occurrence of crises. Prices, Hildreth contended, fluctuated just as much in the eighteenth century, but people were affected less thereby because there was relatively little exchange. Most households were practically self-sustaining, buying little and producing little for sale. But with the great increase of division of labor, based upon the three broad classes of farmers, manufacturers, and merchants, people have become dependent for a livelihood, not merely on good crops and an abundant sheep-shearing, but also on a good market for the products — that is, on prices.[4]

At about the same time, Professor Dew commented upon the significance of specialization by any country in the production

---

[1] That the drop in prices (induced by deflation and by the forced liquidation of stocks made necessary by the calling of loans), in itself spoils the market, explaining the intensity of the distress, was a familiar observation.

[2] Gouge, *Short History of Paper Money*, etc. (1833), p. 27.

[3] Smith, *A Manual of Political Economy* (1853), p. 247; Bowen, *Principles of Political Economy* (1856), pp. 261–271.

[4] Hildreth, "On High and Low Prices," *Hunt's Merchants' Magazine* (Oct., 1840), iii, 305–311.

CAUSES OF CRISES AND CYCLES   205

of one or a few commodities. Crises are intense in the United States because a single commodity, cotton, constitutes a large percentage of our total exports.[1] A fall in the price of this one export seriously affects our balance of trade, and therefore disturbs the rates of foreign exchange very gravely, with the result that the country as a whole is made to suffer, instead of the depression being limited to those who are directly engaged in producing cotton. Moreover, the production of cotton is localized, being confined to one large section of the country that produces very little else. Directly or indirectly, every trade and the whole credit structure of the South are intimately connected with cotton. Distress in the cotton industry threatens the entire community with disaster.[2]

Dew seems to have had some understanding of the tendency of a particular industry to become unduly stimulated, attracting capital and labor from other lines until reaction brings a depression which spreads to all trades.[3] A similar suggestion as to the

[1] Dew wrote in 1840. The following statistics, from the report of the Secretary of the Treasury for 1843, are pertinent:

EXPORTS FOR SELECTED YEARS
(In millions of dollars)

Year	Cotton	Total Domestic goods	Total Foreign goods reëxported	All Exports
1821	20	44	21	65
1830	30	59	14	74*
1835	65	101	21	122
1836	71	107	22	129
1840	63	114	18	132

* The discrepancy between this figure and the sum of the two preceding arises in changing each to the nearest million.

[2] Dew, *The Great Question of the Day* (1840), pp. 9, 10. A drop in the price of cotton in 1836, bringing particular distress in the South, had been an important feature of the events leading to the crisis of 1837. Dew also laid emphasis, in explaining the disastrous nature of our revulsions, upon the great amount of land speculation, which is peculiarly fitted to cause crises. *Ibid.*, p. 11.

[3] Dew, *op. cit.*, pp. 7, 8, 11. Cp. Bowen, *Principles of Political Economy* (1856), p. 317.

origin of crises was made by a writer in the *Democratic Review*, who, like Dew, gave particular attention to cotton.[1] Amasa Walker, after describing the period of rising prices and business activity, followed by that of falling prices and stagnation, declared that the activity of the boom period is primarily in speculation, not production. Furthermore, agriculture does not expand as much as manufacturing, since the demand for the products of the latter increases more rapidly. There is, in truth, "more change of occupation than increase of industry."[2] And, finally, to note one other reference to the misdirection of capital as productive of crises, a writer in the *Bankers' Magazine* for 1859 observed that the "extensive absorption of capital from the floating to the fixed state [*e. g.*, railroad construction], may very easily be, and, in point of fact, has been a fruitful source of commercial embarrassments."[3]

A curious idea, found in a number of writers, was that which held, somewhat anomalously, that crises follow periods of general overconsumption. Raguet, for example, pictured the typical cycle arising from the mutual reaction upon each other of increase in the quantity of bank currency, higher prices, and enlarged volume of commercial paper, to its culmination in the crisis. At this denouement, said Raguet, — inconsistently with his preceding account, — it will be seen "that during the whole of this operation, *consumption* had been increasing, whilst *production* was diminishing — that the community was poorer in the end than when it began," and that the apparent prosperity was not unlike the affluence of the spendthrift as he runs through his estate.[4] Tucker agreed with Raguet, explaining that "by the suspension or diversion of industry from its usual employments, production is diminished, and, by creating notions of wealth

[1] "Cotton and the Currency Question," *Democratic Review* (March, 1838), i, 389, 390.
[2] A. Walker, *Nature and Uses of Money and Mixed Currency* (1857), p. 7.
[3] Crawley, "Credit, Currency, and the Precious Metals," *Bankers' Magazine* (December, 1859), xiv, 421.
[4] Raguet, "Principles of Banking," *Free Trade Advocate* (July 4, 1829), ii, 7; *Currency and Banking* (1839), p. 137.

which are fleeting and fallacious, consumption is increased."[1] A writer in *De Bow's Review* adopted the same view, and gave an inkling of its basis. It is futile, he urged, to seek in a fool-proof currency the preventive of the disasters that inevitably follow overconsumption. "The actual money of a country, or of several nations, consists only in a very small degree of either the paper circulating as money, or of specie. It is really formed of all exchangeable products. So long as any country, or section of a country, has surplus products of its industry to sell, it has money. ... All commercial revulsions resolve themselves into the same elements, and always arise from the primary fact that more has been consumed than produced."[2]

[1] Tucker, *Theory of Money and Banks Investigated* (1839), p. 40. See also the less lucid statement in the *Democratic Review* (April, 1848), xxii, 376.

[2] T. P. Kettell, "The Money of Commerce," *De Bow's Review* (Oct., 1848), vi, 247. Notice that this conception of crises as the aftermath of profligate consumption considered them only in their international (or intersectional) relations; that is, as precipitated by a drainage of specie through the foreign exchanges. It did not take into consideration crises produced by such ill-balanced investments of capital among different industries as Dew and Walker referred to.

CHAPTER XVII

SUGGESTIONS FOR MODERATING THE CYCLE

Loan policy. — Surplus reserves at New York. — Abolition of the payment of interest at New York. — The call-loan evil at New York.

ONLY Robert Hare, the chemist who occasionally, and with no little ability, made economic writing a diversion,[1] ventured to defend the cycle, questioning whether "the ultimate, or average accumulation of national wealth" was not greater in consequence of these alternating periods of activity and depression. "Such fluctuations rouse men to extraordinary exertion, and by a reaction after each subsiding wave, cause business to revive with a renovated and accumulated force. It is in consequence of the stimulus and reaction which accompany or follow great catastrophes, such as are produced by floods or fires, that after a few years, communities which have been subjected to them will appear to have made advances even greater than might have been anticipated, had no such deteriorating accident occurred."[2] Other writers, however, entertained no doubts as to the evil of the cycle, and earnestly sought measures for eliminating, or at least moderating it.

The proposal most frequently made was the obvious one — do away with the banks of circulation to which so many ascribed the instability of business conditions; or regulate their note issue so as to prevent fluctuations.[3] Gouge, Raguet, and Amasa

---

[1] See Chapter VIII.

[2] Hare, "Do Banks Increase Loanable Capital?" *Hunt's Merchants' Magazine* (June, 1852), xxvi, 705.

[3] H. C. Carey, on the other hand, thought that a *laissez-faire* policy with respect to banking, permitting everyone to engage in it without legislative restriction, was the proper specific. He maintained this thesis at length in *The Credit System in France, Great Britain, and the United States* (1838) and in numerous later writings. See also, House of Representatives, Committee of Ways and Means, Report of March 5, 1838, p. 3, and "Moral of the Crisis," *Democratic Review* (Oct., 1837), i, 116.

Walker were perhaps the most prominent of a host of writers who urged this course. But, given the facts as they were, with banks in existence and issuing notes more or less freely, what correctives were suggested?

The proper use of a variable discount rate, we have seen,[1] was understood, and then incompletely, by very few of the writers. Many urged the necessity of continuing liberal accommodations in times of panic, but did not associate this with raising the rate at which such loans were made. The burden of Mathew Carey's *Essays* of 1816 (the first noteworthy discussion of crises I have found) was that banks should pursue "a steady and systematic career."[2] The distress then prevailing among the merchants of Philadelphia he ascribed partly to the liberality of the banks in the early months of the year, but more largely to the drastic curtailment of accommodations that had followed. He repeatedly urged the banks to meet the crying needs of the business men.[3] In the introduction to the *Essays* we are told that his advice was heeded by the banks and "the very resolution to extend their discounts raised murdered Confidence from the grave, and revived her once more."[4]

The banks, in Carey's opinion, had tied up too large a portion of their funds in government securities, and when they found it necessary to contract their liabilities, had thrown the burden of the contraction too largely on commercial loans. Banks should recognize their obligations to care for the needs of merchants, and when curtailment of their advances becomes necessary, should

[1] Chapter XV.
[2] M. Carey, *Essays on Banking* (1816), p. 32.
[3] *Ibid.*, pp. 88, 133–151, etc.
[4] *Ibid.*, p. vii.

Nicholas Biddle, writing of his conduct of the Bank of the United States in 1825, said: "I then endeavored to ascertain the real state of things by separating the danger from the alarm, and having done so, on the 22d of November, the letter annexed was addressed to the Branch at New York, suggesting the propriety of increasing its loans.

"From this moment confidence revived, and the danger passed. I then thought, and still think, that this measure, the increase of the loans of the Banks, in the face of an approaching panic, could alone have averted the same consequences, which, in a few days afterwards, were operating with such fatal effect upon England." See Gouge, *Short History*, part II, p. 182.

liquidate their investments in stocks, rather than call for repayment of commercial loans.[1] William H. Crawford, the Secretary of the Treasury at the time, adopted Carey's suggestion and urged it in a letter to the president of the Bank of the United States.[2]

Emphasis continued to be put by a number of later writers upon the need of liberal discounts in times of stress, and reference was frequently made to the beneficial effects of such a policy in allaying panics in England. Nathan Appleton, a Boston business man,[3] held the New York banks chiefly responsible for the crisis of 1857, asserting that their panicky contraction had caused most of the distress.[4] Others, on the other hand, saw only the need of contracting the currency at any cost when financial pressure begins, in order to strengthen the banks and to influence specie movements by altering the balance of trade. A committee of the New York banks wrote, with reference to the crisis of 1837:

> If the share of the blame which may justly be imputed to the banks be analyzed, it will be found to consist in their not having, at an early period, duly appreciated the magnitude of the impending danger, and taken, in time, the measures necessary to guard against it; in their want of firmness — when the danger was more apparent and alarming — in yielding to the demands for increased, or continued bank facilities, instead of resolutely curtailing their loans and lessening their liabilities.[5]

When pressure arises in the money market, one writer observed, bankers must curtail their loans for perhaps two months. "If no new loans have been made during that time, the bank has then taken care of itself, as the directors are bound to see that it does, whatever may happen to themselves or others."[6] The Bank

---

[1] M. Carey, *Essays on Banking* (1816), pp. 69–73, 123–129.

[2] Crawford, Letter to William Jones (Nov. 29, 1916), in *American State Papers, Finance*, iii, 316.

[3] Appleton was one of the group that introduced the power loom in the cotton industry of America. He played a prominent part in the New England life of his time, being a member of Congress and one of the founders of Lowell, Massachusetts.

[4] Appleton, *Remarks on Currency and Banking* (third edition, 1857), pp. 59, 61. Cp. "The Banks and the Merchants," *Hunt's Merchants' Magazine* (Jan., 1858), xxxviii, 131, 132; J. S. Ropes, "The Financial Crisis," *New Englander* (Nov., 1857), xv, 704.

[5] Report of the New York delegates to the bank convention of 1837 (Dec. 15, 1837), *Financial Register*, i, 229. Albert Gallatin was one of the signers of the report.

[6] Thomas G. Cary, *Practical View of the Business of Banking* (1841), p. 5.

Commissioners of Maine in their report of 1844 warned of the dangers of an adverse balance of trade, asserting that when a considerable drain of specie results, the banks "must cease to discount," although the commissioners realized that a panic in the money market would result.[1] And Francis Bowen, after explaining the necessity of curtailing loans in a crisis, added that "the bolder policy, sometimes adopted, of increasing rather than diminishing the discounts at such a crisis, in order to lessen the distress, and thereby stop the panic, resembles the plan of crowding all sail on a ship in a storm, in the hope thereby of keeping off a lee-shore, though the increased strain thus put upon the vessel may leave her a dismantled hulk on the waters." [2]

If no great progress was made in formulating rules for a general credit policy, more satisfactory advance was achieved with regard to criticism of certain specific practices in the banking system that were peculiarly liable to aggravate crises. Especially was this true after the revulsion of 1857. Criticism was now focused, as never before, upon the banks in New York, into which the surplus reserves of the country already tended to flow. As early as 1837 the New York bank commissioners, after explaining how the Scotch banks kept their reserves on deposit in London, remarked: "Their relative situation we suppose to be very similar to that of our Western banks to New York." [3] In the eighteen-forties and fifties "Eastern deposites" seem to have been an item of considerable magnitude in the balance statements of the banks of at least several of the Western states, while the bank commissioners of the New England states were taking cognizance, from time to time, of the practice of their banks of keeping a secondary reserve on deposit at New York and Boston. The Connecticut commissioners commented upon the matter in 1841 and repeatedly thereafter, cautioning in 1848 that, "although a bank may have a large amount of what is denominated specie funds,

---

[1] U. S. House of Representatives, 29th Congress, 1st Session, Document 226, p. 36.

[2] Bowen, *Principles of Political Economy* (1856), p. 347.

[3] Report of January 27, 1837, in U. S. House of Representatives, 25th Congress, 2d Session, Document 79, p. 238.

that is, funds in the hands of banks and agents in New York and Boston, which they can draw for at sight, yet, should there be a suspension of specie payments in those cities, these specie funds would not be available as such."[1] Following the crisis of 1857 the New York superintendent of banking wrote that experience "for the first time has shown the bankers of New York that there is such a thing as suspending specie payments from an internal demand for coin." And the great lesson of the crisis he found in the demonstration that "the greatest danger to the banker, as well as to the public, lies in the large amount of his deposits, and the least in the currency he issues." Such a statement, he added, if made six months before, "would have stamped its promulgator as a tyro in banking."[2] He then pointed out the manner in which New York served as the reserve center for other parts of the country, and urged that the New York banks be required to keep a twenty per cent reserve against deposits.

Whatever demand for coin in unusual quantities may be made in this State or elsewhere, New York city must furnish it, either through the banks or citizens located within her borders. Upon no other point in this State can come a demand that can lead to a general suspension; and by a necessity that knows no law the suspension of that city is followed throughout this State and the Union.[3]

---

[1] Report, 1848, in U. S. House of Representatives, 30th Congress, 1st Session, Document 77, p. 195.

[2] Report, 1857, *Bankers' Magazine* (Dec., 1857), xii, 622.

[3] *Ibid.*, p. 632. Related to the problem presented by the holding at New York of large balances due to other banks was the practice engaged in by outside banks of investing part of their funds in commercial paper in New York City — a phenomenon that was incidental to the rise of the latter to a position of importance as financial center of the country. The bank commissioners of Massachusetts, New Hampshire, and Connecticut made frequent reference to it, beginning about 1840, usually to protest against it on the score that it implied neglect of potential borrowers at home. From the point of view of the New York money market, however, the difficulty lay in the fact that such outside funds represented but a fair-weather support, since they would probably be promptly withdrawn for use at home in times of widespread distress. The stringency in the New York money market would then be accentuated by the necessity of assuming the added burden of liquidating these assets of the outside banks. The bank commissioners of Connecticut, indeed, in their report of 1848, and the New Hampshire commissioners the following year, approved of such investments at New York on the very ground that they constituted a secondary reserve, since their liquidation in times of revulsion would fortify

Edmund Dwight, in 1851, had called attention to the distinct characteristics of the deposits of the New York banks, in so far as they consisted of balances due to interior banks. The creditor banks, Dwight observed, regarded these deposits as "specie funds," relying upon them largely for means of meeting unusual demands for specie. Hence it behooved the New York banks to keep an extra large reserve ratio, as do the central banks of Europe.[1] Dwight now reiterated his ideas after the catastrophe of 1857. Our panics, he declared, are not accidental; they are due to the inherent weaknesses of our banking system.

> The law of interest is always urging towards the last point of expansion, and that of necessity and safety hurrying them [the banks] back to contraction. The limit of expansion is not fixed by statute, nor by any rule of sound banking. The only recognized limit is *danger* — immediate and pressing *danger* — and the mode of contraction, therefore, suits the cause; it is run for life, and its motto is *sauve qui peut*.[2]

Could the New York banks be induced to keep but eight or ten millions of dollars of additional cash, much distress would be avoided. For lack of that surplus lending power the nerve-center of our financial system ceased to function when most sorely the banks for meeting the needs of their local borrowers. (Connecticut Bank Commission, Report, 1848, in U. S. House of Representatives, 30th Congress, 1st Session, Document 77, p. 179; New Hampshire Bank Commission, Report [1849], p. 15). Unfortunately the New York money market was not well organized to give a good account of itself in performing these functions as a financial center.

The Connecticut commissioners in 1844 also referred to the unwholesome effect that the accumulation, in times of ease, of outside funds in New York might have in fostering excessive speculation. (Report, 1844, U. S. House of Representatives, 29th Congress, 1st Session, Document 226, p. 234.)

A curious commentary on New York's financial position, rather fortuitously prophetic, was contained in the reflections of the New York Herald on the crisis of 1857. Each crisis, this journal observed, had resulted in strengthening New York's position as the country's financial center. "The late struggle of 1857 was in a great degree between New York and London, and has terminated to the advantage of the former city. And the time must ere long arrive, when New York, and not London, will become the financial centre, not only of the New World, but also to a great extent, of the Old World." (Quoted by D. M. Evans, in *History of the Commercial Crisis, 1851–58* (London, 1859), p. 114.

[1] Dwight, "The Progressing Expansion," *Hunt's Merchants' Magazine* (1851), xxv, 152.

[2] Idem, "The Financial Revulsion and the New York Banking System," *Hunt's Merchants' Magazine* (Feb., 1858), xxxviii, 158.

needed; the banks of New York simply "went out of business as banks of loan and discount." Dwight urged the adoption of a new customary reserve ratio and its enforcement by a board of the associated banks of the city.[1]

A special committee of the New York Clearing House gave ready support to Dwight's insistence upon more adequate reserves at the financial center.[2] Two years later the editor of the *Bankers' Magazine* renewed the agitation in an aggressive criticism of the complacent annual report of the New York banking department.[3] Samuel Hooper, a prominent Boston merchant who was a keen participant in the banking discussion of the day,[4] also urged the necessity of larger reserves at New York, and emphasized that such minor money centers as Boston should likewise keep surplus reserves in behalf of their respective districts.[5]

Hooper, Dwight, and Nathan Appleton showed some recognition of the evil of decentralized responsibility at New York.[6]

---

[1] Dwight, xxxviii, 162.   [2] *Bankers' Magazine* (April, 1858), xii, 823 ff.

[3] *Ibid.*, (March, 1860), xiv, 673–678. Despite the incisive criticism to which the whole situation at New York had been subjected since the panic of two years before, the superintendent of the New York banking department in his report of 1859 saw fit to congratulate the legislature upon the condition of the banks, adding: "While the disasters of 1857 were not a consequence of our present system of banking, yet he [the superintendent] firmly believes that that system was the fulcrum which enabled the banks of this State so speedily and successfully to resume their corporate obligations, after their suspension in 1857." He warned against meddling with the banking laws that gave such excellent results. Report, 1859, *Bankers' Magazine*, xiv, 653. It helps one to take present-day comments of a similar nature more philosophically to read that there were defenders of the New York banks after the catastrophe of 1857, who urged that, "having burned their fingers once, they are now too wise and shrewd to hazard again, at any future time, the risks of undue expansion." *Bankers' Magazine* (June, 1859), xiii, 931.

[4] Hooper, after acquiring wealth in business, served in Congress continuously from 1860 to the time of his death in 1875. He was a leading spokesman for the financial program of the administration during the Civil War. In a letter of 1869, Chief Justice Chase attributed the success of the bill establishing a national banking system to Hooper's efforts.

[5] Hooper, *Specie in Banks* (1860), p. 46.

[6] *Ibid.*, p. 43; Dwight, "The Financial Revulsion," *Hunt's Merchants' Magazine* (Feb., 1858), xxxviii, 162. For Appleton's views see *Boston Daily Advertiser*, October 12, 1857.

A measure suggestive of the use of clearing-house loan certificates (the origin of which has usually been placed in 1857, or 1860) seems to have been adopted by an association of Boston banks formed soon after the suspension of specie payments in

But the idea of a modern central bank, with the function of caring for the surplus reserves of the entire banking system, was almost wholly lacking.[1] A few writers advanced the view, which was to become prominent during the period of the National Banking System, that the independent treasury furnished a favorable agency for providing such reserve lending power. It sufficed for most of the Jacksonian critics of banking to point out that the sub-treasury system removed part of our resources from the baneful influence of the institution they opposed. The signing, "by happy coincidence, on the anniversary of the Declaration of Independence," of the bill establishing the independent treasury, was hailed, with much florid rhetoric, by "An Oration, Pronounced in Castle Garden, July 27, 1840, by Hugh Garland, of Virginia, in Celebration of the Second Declaration of Independence, or the Passage of the Independent Treasury Bill." It was left, however, for Gouge, who was for thirty years connected with the Treasury Department, to give later secretaries of the Treasury the cue for claiming a positive benefit from separation of the fiscal operations of the government from the banks. He sought to show the shortsightedness of those who regard money lying in the government's separate vaults as wasted in unproductive idleness. "In a country such as ours there ought to be somewhere a reserved fund of gold and silver, and no more appropriate place can be found for such a reservoir than the

May, 1837. The association resolved by unanimous vote that debtor members unable to settle their daily balances should give the creditor banks such security as the standing committee of the association might determine. The contemporary newspapers give no clue as to how much use was made of this provision, or concerning the report of the committee which was instructed to consider "the expediency of making arrangements forthwith for the settling of daily balances." See *Niles' Register*, iii, 195, 196.

Something of a pooling of reserves seems to have been practiced in Philadelphia twenty years earlier. In August, 1817, the banks of that city, having found it difficult to put into actual effect the resumption of specie payments for which they had voted, "agreed, instead of settling, to pay interest on the balances they owed each other, this continuing until June 20, 1818, when they were able to resume actual specie payments of the balances due." *The Philadelphia National Bank*, p. 66. And concerning the banks of the same city during the suspension of 1821, we are told: "The scheme was at this time adopted of marking checks 'good' instead of paying them." *Ibid.*, p. 97.

[1] See above, pp. 165–167.

United States Treasury," urged Gouge. Nor should the banks complain, for they themselves benefit by the system of keeping the public money in special vaults. "If in their vaults, it would lead to new inflations; if in the public depositories, more or less of it will come to their aid in times of emergency."[1] Two secretaries of the treasury in the next five years adopted Gouge's view, and Howell Cobb urged that the states adopt independent treasuries for this reason.[2] Cobb's report also shows that the doctrine that the government should alleviate depressions and their attendant unemployment by increased expenditure on public works was not unknown. His attitude toward this, however, was quite different, for he dismissed it with a homily on the limitations of the proper functions of government, written in the best vein of an Adam Smith.[3] Bowen, writing ten years after the reestablishment of the sub-treasury under Polk, criticized the system on the ground that its operations tended to disturb the money market by alternately withdrawing and restoring funds.[4]

In connection with the reserve situation at New York, the practice of paying interest on deposits, and in particular on the

[1] Gouge, "Special Report on the Public Depositories," in *Finance Report of the Secretary of the Treasury* (Dec., 1854), p. 268. Edmund Dwight had said almost as much in 1851: "The Progressing Expansion," *Hunt's Merchants' Magazine* (Aug., 1851), xxv, 149.

[2] James Guthrie, *Finance Report* (Dec., 1856), p. 32; Howell Cobb, *Finance Report* (Dec., 1857), pp. 21 ff., and *Finance Report* (Dec., 1858), p. 16. Guthrie asserted: "The independent treasury, when over-trading takes place, gradually fills its vaults, withdraws the deposits, and, pressing the banks, the merchants and the dealers, exercises that temperate and timely control, which serves to secure the fortunes of individuals, and preserve the general prosperity." Guthrie admitted, however, that it might tend to cause stringency in the money market when large surpluses of revenue were accumulating.

[3] Cobb, *Finance Report* (Dec., 1857), p. 12.

[4] Bowen, *Principles of Political Economy* (1856), pp. 364, 365. For a lengthy discussion of the early influence of the independent treasury upon the banks and the money market, see Kinley, *Independent Treasury of the United States*, pp. 69–83, 208–224. For the period since 1860, see *ibid.*, pp. 225–281, and Sprague, *History of Crises Under the National Banking System*.

The crisis of 1857 was probably aggravated by the accumulation of public funds by means of custom-house receipts in 1855, 1856, and 1857. The *Bankers' Magazine* of March, 1857, spoke of this as taking place at a "fearful rate." Later, as in 1853, the Secretary of the Treasury sought to relieve the stringency by purchasing bonds.

deposits of other banks, came in for its share of criticism after 1857. Earlier writers, referring primarily to the deposits of individuals, had favored the payment of interest, citing the benefits Scotland derived from such inducement to its people to place their money in the banks.[1] Mathew Carey had, in 1816, taken exception to a new arrangement by the banks of Philadelphia whereby they paid interest upon balances due to each other, contending that this would tend to induce each bank to contract harshly [lest it have to pay interest on adverse balances] at times when such a policy would be disastrous to the community.[2] Massachusetts enacted a law in 1837 forbidding the payment of interest by commercial banks on either time or demand deposits, except for money borrowed from the state, from savings banks, or from other commercial banks. The bank commissioners complained from time to time of violation of the statute and contended that banks "should not borrow money on time," while the payment of interest on demand deposits might tend to lure depositors to unsound banks.[3] The Connecticut commissioners thought that for the banks to borrow money by receiving deposits at interest was "to say the least of it, very questionable," as it tended to concentrate surplus capital at the points where the banks were located.[4]

But now the development of New York as the reservoir for the country's surplus reserves presented the problem in a new light. The eastern banks, after the middle of the century, were paying as much as five and six per cent for the deposits of western corre-

---

[1] Rae, *New Principles*, etc. (1834), reprint by Mixter under title, *Sociological Theory of Capital* (1905), p. 313; Tucker, *Theory of Money and Banks* (1839), pp. 219, 220, 256–258; Churchill C. Cambreling, Speech on the Removal of the Deposits, in House of Representatives, Jan. 14, 1834, pp. 18, 19. The Farmers Bank of Maryland is said to have been the first to introduce the practice of allowing interest on deposits by its action in 1804. (Bryan, *History of State Banking in Maryland*, p. 16.)

[2] M. Carey, *Letters to the Directors of the Banks of Philadelphia* (1816), Preface, p. xix.

[3] Massachusetts, Report of Bank Commissioners (Dec., 1838), pp. 19, 20.

[4] Connecticut, Report of Bank Commissioners (1854), U. S. House of Representatives, 33d Congress, 2d Session, Document 82, p. 84. A law was subsequently passed restricting the rate of interest that banks might pay on deposits to four per cent. It was repealed in 1855, but in 1862 the payment of all interest was prohibited, only to be permitted again a few years later.

spondents.[1] The superintendent of the banking department of New York, in his annual report of 1857, criticized the practice of paying interest on current deposits; and early in 1858 the New York Clearing House Association appointed a special committee to consider its discontinuance. The committee's report stated admirably the case against the paying of interest. The current deposits in the New York banks, it observed, consisted in large part of the virtual reserves of country banks. "As such deposits constitute the credit and stability of the country at large, its conservative power for sudden contingencies, they should be considered an inviolable trust, free from all risk, and consequently from direct profits."[2] But a bank, "having committed this first error of paying interest on its deposits, is therefore compelled, by the necessities of its position, to take the second false step, and expand its operations beyond all prudent bounds."[3] Furthermore, the payment of interest on deposits induces the country's reserves to flow to New York to an excessive degree. The members of the association favored the report by an overwhelming majority, but, as in later years, could not prevail upon the dissenting few to adopt the reform. After the crisis of 1857 the abolition of the practice of paying interest on current deposits became one of the stock proposals of critics of our banking system.

Still another aspect of the situation at New York attracted attention — the deceptive qualities of the call loan. Call loans, secured by stocks as collateral, seem to have become popular with the banks of New York and Boston in the eighteen-thirties, but their mischievous influence received rather little comment before the panic of 1857 had imparted its many lessons. A special committee of the New York legislature reported against such loans in 1837, but for reasons quite different from those advanced in later discussions.[4] Raguet, in enumerating various abuses

---

[1] See the report of the special bank examiner of Ohio, in *Public Documents* (1854), xviii, 356, 401, *passim*.
[2] *Bankers' Magazine* (April, 1858), xii, 824.
[3] *Ibid.*, p. 825.
[4] New York, Assembly Document 328 (1837), iv, 4 ff.

whereby banks seek to increase their earnings, included without comment the practice "adopted by many of the banks of New England, and perhaps of other places, of lending to brokers on interest, repayable on demand, a large proportion of the amount which banks in other places consider themselves bound to keep on hand, in coin, to meet possible demands."[1] The Massachusetts bank commissioners in their report of 1838 mentioned that some of the banks were making collateral loans at call "for the purpose of being prepared, at a moment's notice, to meet any contingency," and gave the practice their approval.[2] In 1855, however, they deprecated such loans, observing that "however beneficial this class of assets may be to an institution standing by itself, the current of public opinion seems to run against them as a common practice among the banks. If they become general, a sudden retrenchment of them may become general too." Such an episode they believed to have been largely responsible for the pressure in the money market of that year, and they urged the banks to substitute for this type of loan "paper so timed that it will turn up at proper intervals without surprising the public."[3] But the panic of 1857, which in its banking aspects must be grouped with those occurring under the National Banking System before 1913, marked the beginning of the latter-day agitation against call loans.

Ezra C. Seaman, the historian, writing in December of 1857, included excessive resort to call loans in a tedious recounting of the varied causes which he considered responsible for the crisis of that year.[4] The keen observer Dwight went into further detail. Resort to "the treacherous resource of 'call loans,' delusive alike to the banks and the public," he termed, "the great panic-making power. . . . Call loans with stock collaterals are put in the place of specie. The theory looks plausible as proposed by each separate bank. 'If the balances are against us we can call in our loans — get checks on other banks — and thus obtain the

[1] Raguet, *Currency and Banking* (1839), p. 309.
[2] Massachusetts, Report of the Bank Commissioners (Dec., 1838), p. 21.
[3] *Ibid.* (Dec., 1855), pp. 74, 75.
[4] Seaman, "Panic of 1857," *Hunt's Merchants' Magazine*, (Dec., 1857) xxxvii, 660.

needful coin at any moment.' But in practice it is not so. The causes which alarm one bank alarm the whole. Upon any shock to confidence, they all *call* in at once. The stock collaterals are forced upon the market at the same moment that its ability to take them is almost destroyed by the total cessation of new loans."[1] The prices of stocks collapse, while merchants are in turn adversely affected by the struggle of brokers for money to avoid sacrificing their holdings, and by the cessation of bank loans. The country banks share in the panic and the whole country becomes involved. By the operation of these call loans, millions come suddenly due, and, while they ruin fortunes, they are comparatively impotent to strengthen the banks. The calling of loans cannot increase the total of specie holdings in New York until it has had time to turn the domestic and foreign exchanges in favor of that city.[2]

The call-loan evil was referred to in the next few months by many others, including the special committee appointed by the New York Clearing House Association immediately after the crisis,[3] and a similar committee of the Boston Board of Trade.[4] The necessity of maintaining surplus reserves in the New York depository banks, of discontinuing the practice of paying interest on deposits, and of eliminating the use of call loans as a secondary reserve, were matters of commonplace knowledge after 1857. These criticisms of the specific conditions producing the crisis of that year, read in the light of what Raguet and others had to say about the more general nature of the cycle, leave the reader feeling as if he had just turned from the comments of some economist of 1908 upon the crisis of the preceding year.

[1] Dwight, "The Financial Revulsion and the New York Banking System," *Hunt's Merchants' Magazine* (Feb., 1858), xxxviii, 159.
[2] *Ibid.*, p. 160.
[3] *Bankers' Magazine* (April, 1858), xii, 826.
[4] *Ibid.* (May, 1858), xii, 253.

BIBLIOGRAPHY

BIBLIOGRAPHY

For convenience of reference I have divided my bibliography into the following parts:
1. THE ENGLISH BACKGROUND.
2. THE COLONIAL BACKGROUND.
3. THE PERIOD 1780–1860.
    (a) *Secondary Sources.*
    (b) *Primary Sources.*

1. THE ENGLISH BACKGROUND

Andreades, A. M. *History of the Bank of England.* Translated by Christabel Meredith. London, 1909.
Cannan, Edwin. *The Paper Pound of 1797–1821.* (Reprint of the Bullion Report, with a substantial introduction.) London, 1919.
Davis, A. M. *Currency and Banking in the Province of Massachusetts Bay,* part II, chapters 1–4. Cambridge, Mass., 1901.
Hollander, J. H. "Development of the Theory of Money from Adam Smith to David Ricardo," *Quarterly Journal of Economics* (1911), xxv, 429–470.
Laughlin, J. L. *The Principles of Money.* New York, 1903.
Macleod, H. D. *Dictionary of Political Economy,* vol. i. London, 1863.
———. *Theory and Practice of Banking,* 4th ed., 2 vols. London, 1883, 1886.
———. *Theory of Credit,* 2 vols. London, 1891.
M'Culloch, J. R. *A Select Collection of Scarce and Valuable Tracts and other Publications, on Paper Currency and Banking.* London, 1857.
Mill, J. S. *Principles of Political Economy,* edited by W. J. Ashley. London, 1920.
Overstone (Lord). *Tracts and other Publications on Metallic and Paper Currency.* London, 1858.
Palgrave, R. H. I. *Dictionary of Political Economy,* 3 vols. London, 1894–1899.
Pierson, N. G. *Principles of Economics.* Translated by A. A. Wotzel, pp. 454–461. London, 1902.
Silberling, N. J. *British Theories of Money and Credit, 1776–1848.* Unpublished Harvard thesis, 1919.
———. "Financial and Monetary Policy of Great Britain during the Napoleonic Wars," part II, *Quarterly Journal of Economics* xxviii, (1924), 397–439.
Smith, A. *Wealth of Nations,* edited by Edwin Cannan. London, 1904.
Tooke, T. *A Letter to Lord Grenville on the Effects Ascribed to the Resumption of Cash Payments on the Value of the Currency,* Appendix, pp. 117–127. London, 1829.
Walker, F. A. *Money.* New York, 1877.

Also, —
    Schumacher, Hermann. "Geschichte der Deutschen Bankliteratur in Neunzehnten Jahrhundert," in Schmoller's *Entwicklung der Deutschen Volkswirtschaftlehre im Neunzehnten Jahrhundert*, vol. i.

2. THE COLONIAL BACKGROUND

Davis, A. M. *Colonial Currency Reprints*, 4 vols. Boston, 1910–1911.
——. *Currency and Banking in the Province of Massachusetts Bay*, part II (Banking). New York, 1901.
Dickinson, John. *The Late Regulations Respecting the British Colonies on the Continent of America Considered*. Philadelphia, 1765.
Douglass, W. *A Discourse Concerning the Currencies of the British Plantations in America*, etc. London, 1739. Boston, 1740. Edited by C. J. Bullock. (Economic Studies of the American Economic Association, vol. ii, no. 5, pp. 265–375.)
——. *A Summary, Historical and Political . . . of the British Settlements in North America*. Boston, 1755. (See also "An Essay," 1738, in Davis's *Reprints*, no. 40.)
Francis, Tench. "Considerations on a Paper Currency" [1744?], in Pownall's *Administration of the British Colonies*, 5th ed., ii, 272–308.
Franklin, Benjamin. See p. 229.
Gould, Clarence P. *Money and Transportation in Maryland, 1720–1765*.
Hutchinson, Thomas. *History of the Colony of Massachusetts Bay*, 2d ed. London, 1765, 1768.
MacFarlane, C. W. "Pennsylvania Paper Money," *Annals of American Academy of Political and Social Science*, viii, 50–126.
Pownall, Thomas. *Administration of the British Colonies*, 5th ed., 1774.
Webbe, John. *A Discourse Concerning Paper Money*, etc. Philadelphia, 1743.
Webster, Pelatiah. See p. 235.

3. THE PERIOD 1780–1860

(a) Secondary Sources

Burton, Theodore E. *Financial Crises*. New York, 1902.
Catterall, Ralph C. H. *The Second Bank of the United States*. Chicago, 1903.
Chaddock, Robert E. *The Safety Fund Banking System in New York State: 1829–1866*. (National Monetary Commission.) Washington, 1910.
Commons, J. R., and others. "Secular Trends and Business Cycles. A Classification of Theories," *Review of Economic Statistics* (October, 1922), Prelim. vol. iv, 244–263.
Davis, Andrew McF. *The Origin of the National Banking System*. (National Monetary Commission.) Washington, 1910.
Dewey, Davis R. *Financial History of the United States*, 7th ed. New York, 1920.
——. *History of State Banking Before the Civil War*. (National Monetary Commission.) Washington, 1910.
——. *The Second Bank of the United States*. (National Monetary Commission.) Washington, 1910.

Dunbar, Charles F. "Economic Science in America, 1776–1876," *North American Review* (January, 1876), cxxii, 124–154.
———. *Economic Essays.*
Eliason, Adolph O. *The Rise of Commercial Banking Institutions in the United States.* Minneapolis, 1901.
Felt, J. B. *An Historical Account of the Massachusetts Currency,* 1839.
Furber, H. J. *Geschichte . . . zur Entwickelung der Ökonomischen Theorien in America.* Halle, 1891.
Holdsworth, John Thom. *The First Bank of the United States.* (National Monetary Commission.) Washington, 1910.
Jones, Edward D. *Economic Crises.* New York, 1900.
Knox, John J. *History of Banking in the United States.* New York, 1900.
Lalor, John L. *Cyclopaedia of Political Science, Political Economy, and of the Political History of the United States,* 3 vols. Chicago, 1882.
Leslie, T. E. C. "Political Economy in the United States," *Fortnightly Review* (1880), Old Series, xxxiv, 488–509.
McGrane, R. C. *The Panic of 1837.*
Miller, Harry E. "Earlier Theories of Crises and Cycles in the United States," *Quarterly Journal of Economics* (February 1924), xxxviii, 294–329.
Mills, John. "On Credit Cycles and the Origin of Commercial Crises," *Transactions of the Manchester Statistical Society, 1867–1868,* pp. 6–40.
"Nestor." "Thoughts on Paper Money." Reprinted in *American Museum* of 1787, pp. 38–43.
Patterson, E. M. "The Theories Advanced in Explanation of Economic Crises," *Annals of the American Academy of Political and Social Science,* 1915, pp. 133–147.
Potter, E. R., and Rider, S. S. *Some Account of the Bills of Credit, or Paper Money of Rhode Island.* R. I. Historical Tract, 1st Series, no. 8.
Seligman, Edwin R. A. "Economists," in *The Cambridge History of American Literature,* iii, 425–443. New York, 1921.
Sherwood, Sidney. *Tendencies in American Economic Thought.* Johns Hopkins University Studies in History and Political Science, 15th Series, no. 12, 1897.
Sumner, William G. *The Financier and Finances of the American Revolution.* New York, 1891.
———. *A History of American Currency.* New York, 1878.
———. *History of Banking in the United States.* New York, 1896.
Turner, John R. *The Ricardian Rent Theory in Early American Economists.* New York, 1921. (Useful for bibliographical and biographical purposes.)
United States Commissioner of Labor. *First Annual Report,* 1886. (Entitled "Industrial Depressions.")
Vernon, John W. "Banking and Currency in Rhode Island," in *The New England States* (W. T. Davis, ed.) iv, 2445–2454.
Walker, F. A. *Money in its Relation to Trade and Industry.* New York, 1879.

Biographical Dictionaries

Appleton's Cyclopaedia of American Biography. New York, 1898.
National Cyclopaedia of American Biography. New York, 1897.
Twentieth Century Biographical Dictionary of Notable Americans. Boston, 1904.

(b) *Primary Sources*

Adams, Charles Francis. *Further Reflections upon the State of the Currency in the United States.* Boston, 1837.

———. "Principles of Credit," *Hunt's Merchants' Magazine* (March, 1840), ii, 185–210.

———. *Reflections upon the Present State of the Currency in the United States.* Boston, 1837. (Anonymous review in *North American Review*, April, 1838, vol. xlvi.)

———. "The State of the Currency," *Hunt's Merchants' Magazine* (July, 1839), i, 44–50.

———. "Theory of Money and Banks," *Hunt's Merchants' Magazine* (August, 1839), i, 110–124.

American State Papers, Finance, vols. i–v. Washington, 1832.

Anon. *Bank Bills or Paper Currency, and the Banking System of Massachusetts,* etc. By a Conservative. Boston, 1856.

———. *The Banking Systems of Louisiana.* New Orleans, 1860.

———. *Bank Notes and Specie Considered as Circulating Media: with Remarks on the Effects of Discounting on Deposits.* [By S. H. Perkins?] Boston, 1856.

———. *Currency Explosions, their Cause and Cure.* New York, 1858.

———. *A Democratic View of . . . Banks on a Specie Basis Compared with those on the Basis of Paper Promises of States.* By a Citizen of New Jersey. Camden, New Jersey.

———. *An Enquiry into the Principles and Tendency of Certain Public Measures.* Philadelphia, 1794.

———. *An Essay on the Evils of the Banking System as Conducted in the United States.* Philadelphia, 1845.

———. *An Examination of Some of the Provisions [of the Safety-Fund Act].* New York, 1829.

———. *A Familiar View of the Operation and Tendency of Usury Laws.* New York, 1836.

———. *History of a Little Frenchman and his Bank Notes.* "Rags! Rags! Rags!" Philadelphia, 1815.

———. *Letters of Aegles Addressed to the Chairman of the Bank Committee.* Baltimore, 1819.

———. *Metallic Money, Its Value and Its Functions.* Philadelphia, 1841.

———. *A National Bank; Its Necessity and Most Advisable Form.* New York, 1841.

———. *National Money, or a Simple System of Finance,* etc. By a Private Citizen. Washington, 1816.

———. *A New Financial Project.* New York, 1837.

———. *A New System of Paper Money.* By a Citizen of Boston. Boston, 1837.

Anon. *Observations on the State of the Currency, with Suggestions for . . . Reducing to Uniformity the Banking System.* 1829.
——. *Origin, Provisions, and Effect of the Safety Fund Law.* New York, 1834.
——. *The Paradox Solved, or, a Financial Secret Worth Knowing.* Baltimore, 1820.
——. *Reflections Excited by the Present State of Banking Operations in the United States.* Washington, 1818.
——. [Williams, Henry?]. *Remarks on Banks and Banking and the Skeleton of a Project for a National Bank.* By a Citizen of Boston. Boston, 1840.
——. *Remarks on Money, and the Bank Paper of the United States.* Philadelphia, 1814.
——. *Remarks on New York Banking, and the Recent Disaster or Crisis.* New York, 1858.
——. *Remarks upon Mr. Appleton's "Remarks on Currency and Banking."* By a Disinterested Witness. Boston, 1841.
——. *Remarks upon the Bank of the United States.* By a Merchant. Boston, 1831.
——. *Suggestions on the President's Message* (1815?).
——. *'37 and '57. A Brief Popular Account of all the Financial Panics and Commercial Revulsions in the United States from 1690 to 1857.* New York, 1857.
——. *Thoughts on Banking and the Currency.* By a Citizen of Western New York. 1836.
——. *A Treatise on the Currency and the Exchanges,* etc. New York, 1841.
The Anti-Bank Democrat. New York, January–August, 1842 (monthly).
Appleton, Nathan. *An Examination of the Banking System of Massachusetts, in Reference to the Renewal of the Bank Charters.* Boston, 1831.
——. *Remarks on Currency and Banking.* Boston, 1841; 3d ed., 1857.
——. Sheppard, J. H. *Sketch of Hon. Nathan Appleton.*
"Aristides." *A Letter to the Secretary of the Treasury on the Commerce and Currency of the United States.* New York, 1819.
"Atticus." *Letters on the Currency, the Credit System,* etc., 1838.
Atwater, Jesse. *Considerations on the Dissolution of the United States Bank.* New Haven, 1810.
Baker, Henry F. *Banks and Banking in the United States.* Boston, 1853, 1854.
——. "History of Banking in the United States," *Bankers' Magazine* (September, 1856), ii, 321–341.
——. "Outline History of Banking in the United States," *Bankers' Magazine* (1856), ii, 241–256, 321–341, 417–430.
Baldwin, Loammi. *Thoughts on the Study of Political Economy . . . in the United States.* Cambridge, Mass., 1809.
Bancroft, George. "Examination of M'Duffie's Report," *North American Review* (1831), xxxii, 21–64.
Barker, Jacob. *Private Banking.* New York, 1819.
Barnard, Daniel. *Speeches and Reports in the Assembly of New York.* Albany, 1838.

[Barton, William.] *Observations on the Nature and Use of Paper Credit.* Philadelphia, 1781.
Barton, William. *The True Interest of the United States,* etc. Philadelphia, 1786.
[Beck, William.] *Money and Banking, or their Nature and Effects Considered.* Cincinnati, 1839.
Bilbo, W. N. *An Address on Banks and Banking.* Nashville, Tennessee, 1857.
Blodgett, Samuel, Jr. *Economica.* Washington, 1810.
Board of Currency of New York. Several reports in the *Bankers' Magazine* for 1859 and 1860.
Bollman, Eric. *Paragraphs on Banks.* Philadelphia, 1810; 2d ed., improved, 1811.
——. *Plan of an Improved System of the Money Concerns of the Union.* Philadelphia, 1816.
Bowen, Francis. *The Principles of Political Economy Applied to the Condition, the Resources and the Institutions of the American People.* Boston, 1856.
Bronson, Isaac H. See letters published in the *Financial Register* (1837–1838).
[Bronson, Isaac H.?] *Letters to the Hon. Levi Woodbury, Secretary of the Treasury of the United States.* By "Franklin." New York, 1837.
Bross, William. *Banking, its History, Commercial Importance, and Social and Moral Influence.* Chicago, 1852.
"Brutus." *Letters to George M'Duffie.* Philadelphia, 1830.
——. *Suggestions for the Organization of a National Bank.* New Orleans, 1834.
Calhoun, John C. *Works of John C. Calhoun,* edited by R. K. Crallé. New York, 1853.
Cardozo, Jacob N. (or Isaac N.). *Notes on Political Economy.* Charleston, S. C., 1826. (Reviewed by Jonathan Porter, *North American Review,* 1827, xxiv, 169–187.)
——. Review of Middleton's, "The Government and the Currency," *Southern Quarterly Review* (September, 1850), xviii, 123–132.
Carey, H. C. *Answer to the Questions: What constitutes the Currency?* etc. Philadelphia, 1840.
——. *The Credit System in France, Great Britain, and the United States.* Philadelphia, 1838.
——. *Financial Crises: Their Causes and Effects.* Philadelphia, 1864. (Originally written in 1859–1860.)
——. *Letters to the President,* etc. Philadelphia, 1858.
——. *Miscellaneous Works,* published by H. C. Baird. Philadelphia, 1862.
——. *Money.* New York, 1855.
——. *The Past, the Present, and the Future.* Philadelphia, 1848.
——. *Principles of Social Science,* 3 vols. Philadelphia, 1858–1860.
——. *Memoir of H. C. Carey.* By William Elder. 1880.
Carey, Mathew. *Debates and Proceedings of the General Assembly of Pennsylvania on . . . the Law Annulling the Charter of the Bank of North America.* Philadelphia, 1786.

Carey, Mathew. *Desultory Reflections upon the Ruinous Consequences of a Non-Renewal of the Charter of the Bank of the United States*, 3d ed. Philadelphia, 1810.
——. *Essays on Banking*. Philadelphia, 1816.
——. *Nine Letters to Adam Seybert . . . on the subject of the Renewal of the Charter of the Bank of the United States*, 2d ed., enlarged. Philadelphia, 1811.
——. *Letter to the Directors of the Banks of the City of Philadelphia*. Philadelphia, 1816.
Carroll, Charles H. Numerous articles in *Hunt's Merchants' Magazine* (1856–1860), vols. xxxv, xxxvii–xliii. Also *Bankers' Magazine* (1857–1859), Old Series, vols. xii, xiii.
Cary, Thomas G. *A Practical View of the Business of Banking*, 1845.
Chazotte, Peter S. *A New System of Banking*, etc. Philadelphia, 1815.
"Civis." *Observations on the Proposed Patriotic Bank*. Washington, 1815.
Clay, Henry. *Works of Henry Clay*, edited by Calvin Colton. New York, 1863.
Cleaveland, John. *The Banking System of the State of New York*. New York, 1857.
Clinton, George, *Essays on Banking*. Richmond, Virginia, 1829.
"Colbert." *Outline of a System of a National Currency and a Substitute for a Bank of the United States*. New York, 1834.
Collier, William R. *Essay on the Currency; in which is Proposed the Enactment by Congress of a General Bank Law*. Boston, 1834.
[Colton, Calvin.] *The Currency. Junius Tracts*, no. 2, New York, 1843.
Colwell, Stephen. *Ways and Means of Payment*. Philadelphia, 1859
[Congdon, James B.] *Defence of the Currency of Massachusetts*. Boston, 1856.
——. *A Letter to His Excellency, John Henry Clifford*, etc. Boston, 1853.
Cooper, Thomas. *Lectures on the Elements of Political Economy*. Columbia, South Carolina, 1826.
——. *A Manual of Political Economy*. Washington, 1834.
Cox, Samuel. *Elements of Banking and Currency*. Philadelphia, 1838.
Crawford, William H. Report on the Currency (February 24, 1820). *American State Papers, Finance*, iii. 494–508.
Crawley, Joseph S. Three articles in *Bankers' Magazine* for 1859.
Currency Reform Association of New York. See *Bankers' Magazine* for 1858 and 1859.
[Davies, Benjamin.] *The Bank Torpedo*, etc. New York, 1810.
Dealtry, William. *Money, its History, Evils, and Remedy*. Albany, 1858.
Dew, Thomas R. *Essay on the Interest of Money and the Policy of Laws against Usury*. Shellbanks, Virginia, 1834.
——. *The Great Question of the Day*. Washington, 1840.
——. *Lectures on the Restrictive System*. Richmond, 1829.
Duncombe, Charles. *Free Banking: An Essay on Banking, Currency, Finance, Exchanges, and Political Economy*. Cleveland, 1841.
Dutton, George. "An Exposition of the Crisis of 1857," *Hunt's Merchants' Magazine* (January, 1858), xxxviii, 19–35.

BIBLIOGRAPHY

[Dutton, George.] *The Present Crisis, or the Currency*, etc. By "Bank Crash." New York, 1857.

Dwight, Edmund. "The Financial Revulsion and the New York Banking System," *Hunt's Merchants' Magazine* (February, 1858), xxxviii, 157–163.

——. "The Progressing Expansion," *Hunt's Merchants' Magazine* (August, 1851), xxv, 147–152.

Elliot, Jonathan. The Funding System of the United States and Great Britain (1845). *U. S. Congress, Exec. Doc. No. 15, 28th Congress, 1st Session.*

Everett, Edward. "The Financial Distress of the Year 1857," *Mount Vernon Papers*. New York, 1860.

Fisk, Theophilus. *The Banking Bubble Burst; Being a History of the Enormous Legalized Frauds Practiced upon the Community by the Present American Banking System.* Charleston, South Carolina, 1837.

——. *Labor the Only True Source of Wealth; the Rottenness of the Paper Banking System Exposed.* Charleston, South Carolina, 1837.

Franklin, Benjamin. A Modest Inquiry into the Nature and Necessity of a Paper Currency (Philadelphia, 1729). *Works*, ii, 253–277.

——. Of the Paper Money of the United States of America (1784?). *Works*, ii, 421–426.

——. Principles of Trade (1774). Written in collaboration with George Whatley. *Works*, ii, 383–409.

——. Reflections on Coin (1774). *Works*, ii, 409–418.

——. Remarks and Facts relative to the American Paper Money (London, 1764). *Works*, ii, 340–354.

——. *Works of Benjamin Franklin* 10 vols., edited by Jared Sparks, Boston, 1836–1840.

——. Wetzel, W. A. Benjamin Franklin as an Economist. Johns Hopkins University Studies in History and Political Science, 13th Series, no. 9, 1895.

Franklin (Pseud.) See Isaac Bronson.

Gallatin, Albert A. A. "Bank of the United States," *American Quarterly Review* (March, 1831), ix, 246–282.

——. *Considerations on the Currency and Banking of the United States.* Philadelphia, 1831.

——. Suggestions on the Banks and Currency of the Several United States, in reference principally to the Suspension of Specie Payments (New York, 1841). *Writings*, iii, 369–484.

——. *Albert Gallatin.* By H. C. Lodge. New York, 1879.

——. *Writings of Albert Gallatin*, edited by Henry Adams. Philadelphia, 1879.

Gibbons, James S. *The Banks of New York; their Dealers, the Clearing House, and the Panic of 1857.* New York, 1858.

Gouge, William M. "Commercial Banking," *Hunt's Merchants' Magazine* (April 1843), viii, 313–321.

——. *An Inquiry into the Expediency of Dispensing with Bank Agency and Bank Paper in the Fiscal Concerns of the United States.* Philadelphia, 1837.

——. *The Journal of Banking* (July, 1841–1842). Philadelphia, 1842.

Gouge, William M. *A Short History of Paper Money and Banking in the United States*, etc. Philadelphia, 1833; 2d ed., New York, 1835. Cf. revised edition in *The Journal of Banking.*
Greene, William B. *Mutual Banking.* West Brookfield, Mass., 1850.
——. *The Radical Deficiency of the Existing Circulating Medium, and the Advantages of a Mutual Currency.* Boston, 1857.
[Hale, Nathan.] *Remarks on the Banks and Currency of the New England States.* Boston, 1826.
Hale, William H. *Useful Knowledge for the Producers of Wealth, being an Enquiry into . . . the Origin and Effects of Banking and Paper Money.* New York, 1833.
Hall, Thomas B. *Gold and the Currency. Specie Better than Small Bills.* Boston, 1855.
Hamilton, Alexander. Letter to Robert Morris (1780). *Works*, iii, 61–82.
——. Letter to Robert Morris (April 30, 1781). *Works*, iii, 82–125.
——. *The Report of the Secretary of the Treasury on the Subject of a National Bank. American State Papers, Finance*, i, 67–76.
——. *Works of Alexander Hamilton*, 8 vols., edited by H. C. Lodge. New York, 1855.
[Hanson, Alexander C.] *Remarks on the Proposed Plan of an Emission of Paper and on the Means of Effecting It.* By "Aristides." Annapolis, 1787.
Hare, Robert. *A Brief Exposition of the Injury Done . . . by the Prohibition of Bills under Five Dollars.* Philadelphia, 1841.
——. *A Brief View of the Policy and Resources of the United States.* Philadelphia, 1810.
——. "Do Banks Increase Loanable Capital?" *Hunt's Merchants' Magazine* (June, 1852), xxvi, 702–704.
——. *Proofs that Credit as Money in a Truly Free Country is to a Great Extent Preferable to Coin.* Philadelphia, 1834.
——. *Suggestions Respecting the Reformation of the Banking System.* Philadelphia, 1837.
[Henshaw, David.] *Remarks upon the Banks of the United States.* Boston, 1831.
Hildreth, Richard. *Banks, Banking, and Paper Currencies.* Boston, 1840.
——. *The History of Banks, to which is added a Demostration of the Advantages and Necessity of Free Competition in the Business of Banking.* Boston, 1837.
Hildreth, Richard. *Letter to his Excellency, Marcus Morton, on Banking and the Currency.* Boston, 1840.
Homans, J. [Isaac] Smith, ed. *The Banker's Common Place Book.* Boston, 1851.
"Homo." *National Currency.* Washington 1818.
Hooper, Samuel. *Currency or Money; its Nature and Uses, and the Effects of the Circulation of Bank-Notes for Currency.* Boston, 1855.
——. *Specie Currency. The True Interests of the People.* Boston, 1855.
——. *An Examination of the Theory and the Effects of Laws Regulating the Amount of Specie in Banks.* Boston, 1860.

Hurd, John R. *A National Bank, or No Bank; An Appeal to the Common Sense of the People,* etc. New York, 1842.
Johnson, Alexander B. *An Inquiry into the Nature of Value and of Capital and into the Operation of Government Loans, Banking Institutions, and Private Credit.* New York, 1813.
———. "A Treatise on Banking," *Bankers' Magazine* (June, 1849), iii, 733–767.
Junius Tracts. See Colton, Calvin.
"Justinian." *Remarks on the Report of the Secretary of the Treasury.* Wilmington, Delaware, 1820.
Kellogg, Edward. *The Currency: the Evil and Remedy.* By Goodwell Godek, 6th ed. New York, 1846.
———. *Labor and Other Capital.* New York, 1849.
Law, Thomas. *An Address at a Public Meeting of Washington on the Subject of a National Currency.* 1824.
———. *An Address to the Columbian Institute on a Moneyed System.* Washington, 1828.
———. *An Address to the Columbian Institute on the Question "What Ought to be the Circulating Medium of a Nation."* Washington, 1830.
Lawrence, William B. "The Bank of the United States," *North American Review* (1831), xxxii, 524–563.
Lee, Henry. *Letters to the Cotton Manufacturers of Massachusetts.* Boston, 1844.
[Logan, George.] *Letters Addressed to the Yeomanry of the United States,* etc. By an American Farmer. Philadelphia, 1793.
Lord, Eleazar. *Principles of Currency and Banking.* New York, 1829; 2d ed., 1834.
Louisiana, General Assembly. *Report of the Joint Committee on Banks and Banking.* March 4, 1857.
Lowell, John A. *Review of Mr. Hooper's Pamphlet on Specie Reserves.* Boston, 1860.
Lowndes. *Letters to Calhoun,* 1843.
———. *Plan of a Currency Agent,* etc., 1843.
[M'Cready, John.] *A Review of the Trade and Commerce of New York.* New York, 1820.
McHenry, James. *Brief Exposition of the Principles of a Bank.* Baltimore, 1795.
McKnight, Logan. "Free Banking," *De Bow's Review* (1852–1853), xii, 610–613; xiii, 127–134; xiv, 28–33, 151–157.
McVickar, John. *Hints on Banking.* New York, 1827.
———. *Outlines of Political Economy.* New York, 1825.
Malcolm, Robert. *Short Essays on a Gold Note Currency.* New York, 1858.
Massachusetts, Bank Commissioners. *Annual Reports,* 1838–1843, 1849–1850, 1851– .
Memminger, C. G. *Speech . . . in the House of Representatives of South Carolina upon the Bill and Resolutions Relating to Bank Issues and Suspensions.* Charleston South Carolina, 1858.
Mendenhall, Thomas. *An Entire New Plan for a National Currency,* etc. Philadelphia, 1834.

Middleton, Henry. *The Government and the Currency.* New York, 1850.
Morris, Gouverneur. Address to the Assembly of Pennsylvania on the Abolition of the Bank of North America, in Jared Sparks's *Life of Morris*, iii, 335–365.
Mueller, Christian G. *Observations on the Present Banking System.* Frankfort, Kentucky, 1819.
New Hampshire, Bank Commissioners. *Annual Reports*, 1844– .
Newman, Samuel P. *Elements of Political Economy.* New York, 1835.
New York Clearing House Association. *Report of the Special Committee*, March 4, 1858. *Bankers' Magazine* (April, 1858), vol. xii.
New York, Superintendent of the Banking Department. *Annual Reports.*
Opdyke, George (chairman). *A Report on the Currency.* By Friends of a Sound Currency. New York, 1858.
Paine, Thomas. *Dissertations on Government, the Affairs of the Bank, and Paper Currency.* Philadelphia, 1786.
"The Paper System." A series of eight contributions to *Niles' Weekly Register* (1818), vol. xiv.
Peabody, A. P. "The Financial Crisis," *North American Review* (January, 1858), lxxxvi, 164–191.
Phillips, Willard. *Manual of Political Economy.* Boston, 1828. See also article in *North American Review* (September, 1819), ix, 217–231.
"Publicola" [Ferris Pell?]. *Letter to Mr. Gallatin*, etc. New York, 1815.
"Publius" [Ogden, James De Peyster?]. *Remarks on the Currency of the United States.* New York, 1840.
———. *Further Remarks.* New York, 1841.
———. *The Crisis and the Remedy.* New York, 1842.
Putnam, Oliver. *Tracts on Sundry Topics of Political Economy.* Boston, 1834.
Rae, John. The New Principles of Political Economy. Boston, 1834. Reprinted by C. W. Mixter under title, *The Sociological Theory of Capital*, New York, 1905.
Rafinesque, Constantine Samuel. *Safe Banking, Including the Principles of Wealth.* Philadelphia, 1837.
Raguet, Condy. *The Examiner and Journal of Political Economy.* (August, 1833–July, 1835). Philadelphia.
———. *The Financial Register of the United States* (July, 1837–December, 1838). Philadelphia, 1838.
———. *The Free Trade Advocate and Journal of Political Economy.* Philadelphia, 1829.
———. *An Inquiry into the Causes of the Present State of the Circulating Medium of the United States.* Philadelphia, 1815.
———. *A Treatise on Currency and Banking*, 2d ed. Philadelphia, 1840.
Raymond, Daniel. *Elements of Political Economy*, 2 vols., 2d ed. Baltimore, 1823. (Apparently *Thoughts on Political Economy* was considered the first edition of this work.)
———. *Thoughts on Political Economy.* Baltimore, 1820.
———. Neill, Charles P. Daniel Raymond. Johns Hopkins University Studies in History and Political Science, 15th Series, no. 6, 1897.

Richardson, James D. *A Compilation of the Messages and Papers of the Presidents, 1789–1908*, 9 vols.
[Ronaldson, James.] *Banks and a Paper Currency: their Effects upon Society. By a Friend of the People.* Philadelphia, 1832.
Ropes, J. S. "Currency, Banking and Credit," *Bankers' Magazine* (1859), xiv, 161–176, 272–279.
———. "The Financial Crisis," *The New Englander* (1857), vol. xv.
[Scriber, Peter.] *Letter to Hon. Howell Cobb on Currency.* New York, 1857.
Seaman, Ezra C. "The Panic and Financial Crisis of 1857," *Hunt's Merchants' Magazine* (December, 1857), xxxvii, 659–668.
———. "Currency, Commerce, and Debts of the United States," *Hunt's Merchants' Magazine* (May, 1858), xxxviii, 531–551.
"Silex." *Letters on Banks and Banking.* Boston, 1853.
Simpson, Stephen. *The Working Man's Manual.* 1831.
Smith, E. Peshine. *A Manual of Political Economy.* New York, 1853.
Smith, Francis O. J. "The Currency of New England and the Suffolk Bank System," *Hunt's Merchants' Magazine* (1851), xxiv, 316–323, 439–447. Cf. discussion, *Hunt's Merchants' Magazine*, xxiv, 577–582, 707–712.
South Carolina, General Assembly. *Report of Special Committee on Bill to Define the Principles on which Joint Stock Banks Shall Be Incorporated.* Columbia, South Carolina, 1849.
———. *Report of the Special Committee (John Cunningham, Chairman) on Limiting the Denominations of Bank Notes.* Charleston, South Carolina, 1850.
Sulley, Richard. See *Hunt's Merchants' Magazine* for 1853–1858.
Sullivan, George. *Popular Explanation of the System of Circulating Medium*, etc. New York, 1839.
Sullivan, James. *Path to Riches*, etc. By a Citizen of Massachusetts. 1792.
Taylor, John. *Inquiry into the Principles and Policy of the Government of the United States.* Fredericksburg, Virginia, 1814.
Tucker, George. "Banks or No Banks," *Hunt's Merchants' Magazine* (February, 1858), xxxviii, 147–157.
———. *Theory of Money and Banks Investigated.* Boston, 1839.
United States. Committee of Ways and Means. George M'Duffie, Chairman. *Report on the Bank of the United States*, April 13, 1830.
———. Committee of Ways and Means. *Report on the Currency*, March 5, 1838. *Minority Report*, March 23, 1838.
———. Secretary of the Treasury. *Annual Reports on the State of the Finances*, 1790– .
———. Secretary of the Treasury. *Report to the House of Representatives on the Condition of the State Banks*, 1833–1863. Contains a great number of the reports of the bank commissioners of the several states.
Van Buren, Martin. *Message on the Subject of Banks, with the [Forman] Plan Suggested*, etc. New York, 1829.
Vethake, Henry. *The Principles of Political Economy.* Philadelphia, 1838.
Walker, Amasa. *The Nature and Uses of Money and Mixed Currency.* Boston, 1857.
———. Articles in *Hunt's Merchants' Magazine*, 1857–1859, vols. xxxvii, xl, xli.

Walley, Samuel H. *The Financial Revulsion of 1857. An Address before the American Statistical Association.* Boston, 1858.
Ward, George S. "Causes that Produced the Crisis of 1857 Considered," *Hunt's Merchants' Magazine* (January, 1859), xl, 19-37.
[Ware, Nathaniel A.] *Notes on Political Economy, as Applicable to the United States.* New York, 1844.
Wayland, Francis. *The Elements of Political Economy.* New York, 1837.
Webster, Daniel. *The Works of Daniel Webster*, 6 vols. Boston, 1851.
Webster, Pelatiah. *Political Essays.* Philadelphia, 1791. Essays originally published, 1776-1790.
Wilkes, George S. "Banking and the Currency," *Hunt's Merchants' Magazine* (August, 1858), xxxix, 191-197.
Wilson, James. *Considerations of the Bank of the United States* (Philadelphia, 1785). *Works of the Hon. James Wilson*, iii, 395-439, Philadelphia, 1804.
[Witherspoon, John.] *Essay on Money, as a Medium of Commerce; with Remarks on the Advantages and Disadvantages of Paper admitted into general Circulation.* By a Citizen of the United States. Philadelphia, 1786.
Wolcott, Oliver. *Remarks on the Present State of Currency, Credit, Commerce and National Industry.* New York, 1820.

Periodicals [1]

The American Museum, or Repository of Ancient and Modern Fugitive Pieces, etc. (Mathew Carey, ed.) Philadelphia, 1787-1792, 1798.
The American Quarterly Review. (Robert Walsh, ed.) Philadelphia, 1827-1837.
The American Review of History and Politics, and General Repository of Literary and State Papers. (Robert Walsh, ed.) Philadelphia, 1811-1812.
The Bankers' Magazine and Statistical Register. (Name varies at later dates.) New York, 1846- .
De Bow's Review, etc. (J. D. B. De Bow, ed.) New Orleans, 1846- .
Hunt's Merchants' Magazine and Commercial Review. (Freeman Hunt, ed.) New York, 1839- .
The New Englander. New Haven, 1843- .
Niles' Weekly Register. (Hezekiah Niles, ed.) Baltimore, 1811- .
The North American Review. Boston, 1815- .
The Southern Quarterly Review. New Orleans (later Charleston), 1842-1854.
The United States Magazine and Democratic Review. Washington, 1837- .
See also, Gouge and Raguet, above.

[1] Only those periodicals which were found to contain a number of worth-while articles on banking are mentioned.

INDEX

INDEX

Accommodation loans, 175–179.
Adams, C. F., 177, 202.
Adams, J., 20.
Appleton, N., 166, 210.
Appreciation, and interest, 37, 38.
Atwater, J., 19 n.

Baker, H. F., 199.
Balance of trade, 27, 28, 49–51, 53, 54.
Bancroft, G., 57 n., 60.
Bank charter act of 1844 (Eng.), 110, 118, 119, 141, 142.
Banking principle, 72–75, 134–138.
Bills of exchange, as media of payment, 111, 112; compared with promissory notes, 179–181.
Bollman, E., 63, 72 and n., 117, 134, 165, 175.
Bond-secured note issue, 133, 146–149.
Bowen, F., 80, 191, 199, 211, 216.
Branch banking, 162 n., 166.

Call loans, 218–220.
Cannan, E., 120.
Capital, banking and the formation of, Ch. III, 102 n.
Cardozo, J. N., 52.
Carey, H. C., 53, 54, 66 n., 111, 118, 145, 160, 185, 187, 196.
Carey, M., 21, 23, 176, 209, 217.
Carroll, C. H., 37, 53, 65, 71, 118, 119, 140, 176, 195.
Centralized banking, 165–167, 211–218.
Clearing operations, 16, 17, 156, 157, 214 n.
Colonial views, on functions of banking, 11; on inflation, 26–29; on expulsion of specie, 49; on convertibility, 125–128; on gold premium, 131 n.
Colwell, S., 16, 17, 33, 66–68, 66 n., 95, 119, 120, 135–138, 141, 178, 179, 203.
Control of banks, 159–161, 162 n., 163–166.
Convertibility of notes, 58–63, 125.
Cooper, T., 15, 24, 32, 160, 175.
Crawford, W. H., 61, 128.
Credit, and the business cycle, 189–191.

Crises, Ch's XVI, XVII; of 1857, 166, 212–220.
Currency principle, 70, 71, 110 n., 114, 139–142.

Deposits, importance of, 12 n., 13, 14, 16, 17, 109 n.; as currency, 42, 109–111; creation of, 112–120; latter-day discussion, 120–124.
Dew, T. R., 64, 111, 183, 197, 198, 204, 205.
Discount rate, 182–186, 209–211.
Douglass, W., 28, 29, 37, 38, 48.
Dunbar, C. F., 120.
Dutton, G., 194.
Dwight, E., 213, 214, 219, 220.

Elastic currency, Ch. VII.

Farmers, bank loans not available to, 92, 93.
Farmers' loans, 171–173.
Franklin, B., 27, 36 n., 40, 49, 125, 126.
Free banking, 160, 161.

Gallatin, A. A. A., 13, 35–37, 43, 44, 46, 110, 112, 115, 116, 144, 163, 183, 189.
Gouge, W. M., 19, 35, 44, 45, 72, 81, 86 and n., 96, 112, 176, 177, 193, 194, 203, 204, 215, 216.

Hamilton, A., 30, 31, 36, 43 n., 51, 95, 110, 117, 130, 159.
Hare, R., 12, 87–89, 87 n., 110, 118, 208.
Hildreth, R., 64, 74, 128, 144, 160, 164, 184, 197, 198, 204.
Hooper, S., 64, 94, 153, 154, 214 and n.

Independent treasury, 215, 216.
Interbank loans, 181, 182, 212 n.
Interest on deposits, 154, 155, 216–218.
Interest rate, banking and the, 35–37; appreciation and the, 37.

Jefferson, T., 20, 44.

Land banking, 127, 129-131.
Lending operations, 14, 15; intermediary nature of, 79-81; creation of funds loaned, 82, 83; inconsistent views, 83-87; Hare's better understanding, 87-89; present-day discussion, 90, 91; farmers not benefited, 92, 93; encourage speculation, 93-95; selection of borrowers, 95-97; length of loans, 171-174; accommodation loans, 175-179; bills *versus* notes, 179-181; interbank loans, 181, 182; call loans, 182, 218-220; relations to crises, 209-211.
Lord, E., 60, 140, 147, 174, 193.
Lowell, J. A., 64.

M'Duffie, G., Report of, 57 n.
MacLeod, H. D., 119 n., 120.
McVickar, J., 41, 147, 174.
Morris, G., 23.
Morris, R., 23, 50.

National bank, 164-167.
New York, as a financial center, Ch. XVII.
Niles' Register, 19 n., 93, 163.
Note issue, importance of, 11-14; inflationist notions, 26-35; economy of, Ch. IV; cause price fluctuations, 56, 57; convertibility and overissue, 58-63; business loans and overissue, 63-69; land as security, 127, 129-131; bond security, 133, 146-149; banking principle of, Ch. XII, 134-138; currency principle of, 139-142; prohibition of smaller denominations, 142-146; ratio to capital, 149, 150; safety-fund, 150, 151; regulation of reserves, 152-155; Suffolk Bank system, 155-157; regulative taxation, 157.
Number of banks, 161-163.

Opdyke, G., 120.
Overstone, Lord, 114.

Paine, T., 50, 80.
Peabody, A. P., 194, 195.
Periodicity of crises, 192, 193.
Phillips, C. A., 121, 122.
Phillips, W., 190, 191, 198.
Prices, influence of banking upon, Ch. VI, 102 n.
Psychology and the business cycle, 191.

Quantity theory, 28, 29, 34, 35, 51, 52, 66.

Rae, J., 15, 43, 81.
Raguet, C., 19 n., 35, 41, 42, 73 and n., 86, 96, 110, 117, 118, 132, 177, 189, 200, 201, 206.
Raymond, D., 52, 82, 83, 94, 114, 115, 140, 160.
Reserves, legal regulation of, 152-155; centralization of, 154, 155; at New York, 211-218.

Seaman, E. C., 219.
Smith, A., 33, 39, 58, 142.
Sulley, R., 89 n.
Sullivan, J., 82, 83 n., 139.

Tucker, G., 79, 153, 164, 175, 186.

Usury laws, 182-186.

Vethake, H., 185, 202, 203.

Walker, A., 44, 45, 58, 141, 142, 195.
Walley, S. H., 188-189.
Webster, D., 12.
Webster, P., 30.
Wilkes, G. S., 115.
Witherspoon, J., 51.
Wolcott, O., 196.